INTRODUCTION TO MIDDLE MISSOURI ARCHEOLOGY

INTRODUCTION TO MIDDLE MISSOURI ARCHEOLOGY

DONALD J. LEHMER

ANTHROPOLOGICAL PAPERS 1

National Park Service • U.S. Department of the Interior
Washington 1971

This publication is one of a series of studies made in connection with the various areas in the National Park System or areas in which the National Park Service has had responsibilities. It is printed at the Government Printing Office and can be purchased from the Superintendent of Documents, Government Printing Office, Washington, D.C. 20402. Price $3.75.

Library of Congress Card Catalog Number: 73–606128

FOREWORD

In 1945, the National Park Service entered into an agreement with the Smithsonian Institution, the Corps of Engineers of the Department of the Army, and the Bureau of Reclamation for the purpose of recovering prehistoric and historic materials threatened with destruction by federally constructed dams on many rivers in the United States. The administrative procedures and extensive scientific accomplishments of this monumental task during more than two decades have been set forth in numerous publications.

It is a pleasure to present, as the first volume in a new series, an evaluation of the Inter-Agency Archeological Salvage Program and a scholarly interpretation of the available archeological data obtained from the Missouri River Valley of North and South Dakota, a major aboriginal culture area of the United States which has been all but erased by the twin needs for hydroelectric power and flood control on the part of our own insatiable civilization.

Rogers C. B. Morton
Secretary of the Interior

This publication had its genesis as an administrative report submitted to the National Park Service under contract in 1965. The author went beyond a critical appraisal of the Inter-Agency Archeological Salvage Program generally, and its particular operation in the Middle Missouri Valley in the Dakotas, during the preceding 20 years; he brought together all available archeological data on the so-called Middle Missouri subarea in terms of a theoretical framework. As the work of a skilled field technician and gifted synthesizer, the report clearly merited reworking into a book that would serve both as a guide to colleagues concerned with Dr. Lehmer's field of special competence and as a prime source of information for students of American archeology on an important aboriginal culture area which had been little known beyond the Plains area itself.

George B. Hartzog, Jr.
Director National Park Service

ACKNOWLEDGMENTS

This monograph consists of a review of the work of the Inter-Agency Archeological Salvage Program in the Missouri River Valley in North and South Dakota, beginning in 1946, and a comprehensive statement of the archeology of the area, based largely on the results of that work up to 1969.

An earlier version of the monograph was issued in 1965 as an administrative report to the National Park Service at the request of John M. Corbett, Chief of the Division of Archeology, and Wilfred D. Logan, Chief, Archeological Research, Midwest Regional Office. Both men had been intimately connected with the administration of the salvage program in the Missouri Basin, and they felt that it was time to take stock of the work done so far in the Missouri Valley itself. They posed three basic questions:

1. What have we learned that justifies the time and money we have spent?
2. What has to be done to finish the job?
3. How could we do it better if we had it all to do over again?

The questions themselves are simple ones, but no one person working alone could have answered them. Many of the answers were buried in the reams of records which have accumulated in the files since the beginning of the program. Other information was only partly available because of the masses of data which must still be fully analyzed. Still other answers have been found in the memories of men who have worked with different facets of the program.

I particularly want to thank J. O. Brew, John L. Champe, John M. Corbett, Frederick Johnson, Wilfred D. Logan, the late Frank H. H. Roberts, Robert L. Stephenson, and Waldo R. Wedel for the time they spent telling me about the initial organization and the later activities of the salvage program. Warren W. Caldwell and the members of his staff at the River Basin Surveys headquarters in Lincoln, Nebr., made their records and collections available, and provided invaluable information on the archeological content of many of the unpublished excavated sites. Preston Holder, Wesley R. Hurt, Marvin F. Kivett, Carling Malouf, Carlyle S. Smith, and W. Raymond Wood were most generous in summarizing the activities of their respective organizations: University of Nebraska, University of South Dakota, Nebraska State Historical Society, University of Montana, University of Kansas, and Wood's former employer, the State Historical Society of North Dakota.

Much of the information in Part II which relates to the late cultural developments was drawn from research projects which were generously supported by the National Science Foundation and the Department of Health, Education, and Welfare. NSF Grant GS–537 underwrote a study, carried on in 1964–66, of the changes in the village cultures during the 18th and 19th centuries which resulted from the impact of the white settlement of North America. HEW funds are making possible a detailed study of the sociocultural effects of the smallpox epidemics which were such an important factor in the Middle Missouri Valley during the late 18th and the 19th centuries.

The preparation of this monograph would have been impossible without the assistance of three individuals: Clyde Mann, who made the line drawings; Wayne Nelson, who did much of the necessary photographic work; and Loretta Callahan, who typed and checked the several drafts through which the text moved toward its final form.

D.J.L.
Dana College
July 1969

CONTENTS

FIGURES

TABLES

PART ONE

INTER-AGENCY ARCHEOLOGICAL SALVAGE PROGRAM IN THE MIDDLE MISSOURI VALLEY

INTER-AGENCY ARCHEOLOGICAL SALVAGE PROGRAM

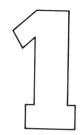

The year 1945 saw American archeology facing a major crisis. The Japanese surrender in August marked the end of World War II, and it was the signal for the United States to begin its transition back to a peacetime status. As part of that transition, the Bureau of Reclamation and the Corps of Engineers moved to activate plans for the construction of a vast reservoir system throughout the country. Well before the war ended, it was obvious that the building of the dams and the filling of the reservoirs would result in an unparalleled destruction of archeological materials (fig. 1).

ORIGINS OF THE SALVAGE PROGRAM

A few members of the profession were close enough to the Washington scene to be aware of the situation as it developed. Julian H. Steward and Frank H. H. Roberts, Jr. were both on the staff of the Smithsonian Institution. They read about the reservoir proposals in the Capital newspapers, and called on officials of the Bureau of Reclamation and Corps of Engineers to inquire about the program. The information they were given showed that the proposed developments posed a serious threat to America's archeological heritage.

Steward discussed the situation with William Duncan Strong, who was chairman of the National Research Council's Committee on Basic Needs in Archeology, and with Frederick Johnson and J. O. Brew. These four men, together with Frank Roberts, became a sort of *ad hoc* committee which was largely responsible for initiating salvage archaeology in the post-war era. Johnson and Brew aroused the concern of the Society for American Archaeology and the American Anthropological Association. With the support of Waldo G. Leland, they also enlisted the interest of the American Council of Learned Societies. All of the members of the group helped to call the attention of various Federal agencies to the salvage problem.

The National Park Service and the Smithsonian Institution were the appropriate agencies to undertake archeological

FIGURE 1 Dam building on the Middle Missouri.

salvage operations for the Federal Government. Newton B. Drury, then Director of the National Park Service, and Alexander Wetmore, former Secretary of the Smithsonian Institution, appreciated the gravity of the situation when it was brought to their attention. Members of the staffs of the two agencies began to explore the possibility of a cooperative program early in 1945. Most of the administrative personnel of the Park Service had been moved to Chicago during the war, and Associate Director Arthur E. Demaray, Herbert E. Kahler, Hillory A. Tolson, and Ronald F. Lee represented their organization while the program was being initiated. Steward and Roberts represented the Smithsonian.

A Memorandum of Understanding covering the proposed activities of the Park Service and the Smithsonian was drafted during the summer of 1945. It was signed by Director Drury on August 7, 1945, by Secretary Wetmore on September 8, and was approved by Harold L. Ickes, Secretary of the Interior, on October 9, 1945. That memorandum, together with the one which replaced it in 1961 and was amended in 1964, provided the basis for cooperation between the two agencies.

Archeologists outside the Federal service have been represented by a Committee for the Recovery of Archaeological Remains. The Committee was organized in 1945 under the joint sponsorship of the Society for American Archaeology, American Anthropological Association, and American Council of Learned Societies. Its original members were J. O. Brew, Frederick Johnson, A. V. Kidder, and William S. Webb. George F. Will and Reynold J. Ruppé subsequently served on the Committee. Its present members are: J. O. Brew, Richard D. Daugherty, Henry W. Hamilton, and Emil W. Haury. The Committee has carried on a sustained campaign to inform both archeologists and the general public of the need for archeological salvage operations. Its members have served as advisers to the administrators of the program, they have testified repeatedly before Congressional Committees, and they have been of assistance in innumerable other ways.

The memoranda of agreement between the Park Service and the Smithsonian provided for a clear division of labor between the two organizations. The National Park Service was responsible for overall planning, programing, funding, and administration of the program. The Park Service dealt directly with the non-Federal agencies engaged in salvage work. This involved encouraging universities and museums to participate in the program, drawing the contracts under which they received financial support, and integrating their work into the total research design. The Smithsonian acted in a dual capacity: as adviser to the National Park Service in the planning and programing stages, and as one of the major cooperators in carrying out the actual salvage operations in the field.

Administration and implementation of the Park Service's role in the program were carried on within the organizational framework which existed before the salvage program was begun. Initially, the program came under the direction of Ronald Lee in his capacity of Chief Historian. Lee deserves great credit for his enthusiastic support of the salvage program, especially during its formative years. Herbert Kahler succeeded Lee as Chief Historian, and continued active support of the project. John M. Corbett, appointed Archeologist in the Branch of History in 1948 and Chief Archeologist in the Division of Archeology in 1958, was given direct responsibility for Park Service participation in the salvage program. He has continued this assignment to the present, except for the period from February 1951 through September 1952, when he was in active service during the Korean War. During that time, Corbett's place was filled by John L. Cotter.

The Smithsonian Institution did a major part of the actual salvage work, and this necessitated adding new personnel and coping with a considerable administrative burden. Acting on the advice of the Committee for the Recovery of Archaeological Remains, the Smithsonian established a new department within the Bureau of American Ethnology, the River Basin Surveys. This organization was made responsible for the Smithsonian's salvage operations throughout the United States. Frank Roberts was dragooned away from his own investigations for the Bureau of American Ethnology to head the River Basin Surveys. American archeology owes him a deep debt of gratitude for sacrificing his own research interests to discharge a tedious and often vexatious assignment.

SALVAGE ARCHEOLOGY IN THE MISSOURI BASIN

It was apparent in 1946 that the drainage basin of the Missouri River would be the scene of extensive salvage operations (fig. 2). The scope of the work and the vast area of the basin necessitated localized administration for both the National Park Service and the Smithsonian Institution.

For the Park Service, administration through the headquarters of the Midwest Region in Omaha was the obvious solution. Throughout most of the history of the program, the Regional Archeologist has acted for the Park Service in the Missouri Basin. He has been responsible for planning at the regional level, for dealing with cooperating institutions, and for maintaining liaison with the Smithsonian Institution. The position was held by Jesse D. Jennings when the salvage program was first established. Jennings has been succeeded, in turn, by Gordon C. Baldwin, Paul L. Beaubien, and Wilfred D. Logan.

In 1950 the Park Service's part in the salvage program in the Missouri Basin was placed under the general supervision of the Regional Historian. Merrill J. Mattes served

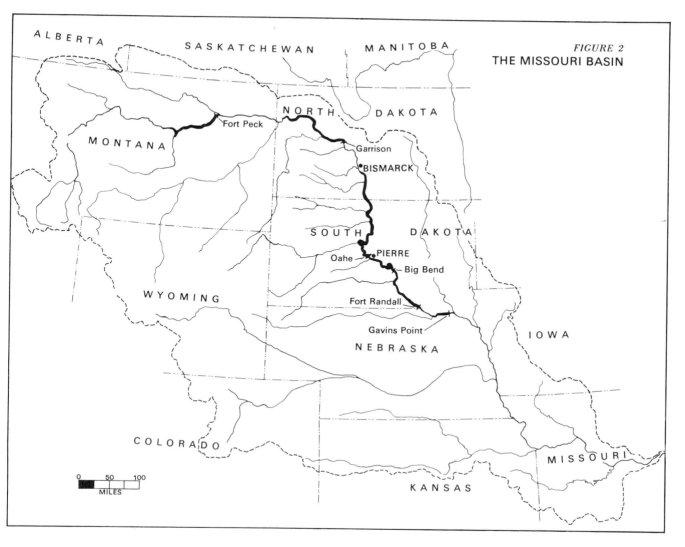

FIGURE 2
THE MISSOURI BASIN

in that capacity until 1966, and he was in immediate charge of Park Service salvage activities at various times. When the reorganization of the Park Service became effective in 1966, the responsibility for the Service's participation at the regional level was assigned to Wilfred Logan, a member of the Chief Archeologist's staff.

The amount of work anticipated in the Missouri Basin made it advisable for the Smithsonian Institution to establish some sort of regional headquarters. The Missouri Basin Project was created as a subdivision of the River Basin Surveys in 1946. The project's offices were housed initially in the Laboratory of Anthropology of the University of Nebraska at the invitation of John L. Champe, then Director of the Laboratory. By 1951 the laboratory's facilities had become so crowded that first part and then all of the operations of the Missouri Basin Project were transferred to space rented at 1517 O Street in downtown Lincoln. In 1963 headquarters of the project was shifted to 1835 P Street in Lincoln.

Waldo R. Wedel was one of the pioneers in Plains archeology, and was a logical choice as the first head of the Missouri Basin Project. He was given part-time leave of absence from his post as Associate Curator at the U.S. National Museum, and went to Lincoln in 1946 to begin laying the groundwork for the Smithsonian's salvage program in the Missouri Basin. For the next 3 years Wedel spent his summers in the West and returned to his regular duties in Washington during the winter. Paul L. Cooper served as Wedel's deputy during his absences.

Wedel found it necessary to give up the direction of the project when he was promoted to Curator of Anthropology at the U.S. National Museum, although he later headed field parties which excavated a series of key sites in South Dakota. Cooper was made Acting Field Director when Wedel resigned, and was appointed Field Director in October of 1950. Cooper continued in charge of the Smithsonian's work in the Missouri Basin until February 1952, when he asked to be relieved of his administrative duties. Ralph D. Brown was then appointed Chief of the Missouri Basin Project. Brown died in September of the same year, and was succeeded by Robert L. Stephenson. Stephenson was Chief of the Missouri

Basin Project until 1963. G. Hubert Smith served as Acting Chief while Stephenson was on academic leave from September 1954 through May 1955.

In the summer of 1963 Stephenson was transferred to Washington to take over the duties of Assistant Director of the River Basin Surveys. He was later appointed Acting Director when Frank Roberts retired from the Smithsonian. Warren W. Caldwell replaced Stephenson as Chief of the Missouri Basin Project.

In 1964 the Smithsonian merged the Bureau of American Ethnology and the Department of Anthropology of the U.S. National Museum into the new Smithsonian Office of Anthropology. Since the Smithsonian's salvage operations were by then largely confined to the Missouri Basin, the Missouri Basin Project was abolished as an administrative unit and the Lincoln office was made the headquarters of the River Basin Surveys. Caldwell was appointed Director, and served until he resigned in 1969, to join the staff of the University of Nebraska. Richard B. Johnston presided over the organization during the last months of its existence.

On June 28, 1969, the River Basin Surveys was discontinued. Its personnel, equipment, and records were incorporated into the National Park Service's newly established Midwest Archeological Center. The new administrative unit was made responsible for the archeological salvage work which had been done up to that time by the River Basin Surveys. Its program also includes comprehensive area studies, salvage operations outside the geographical boundaries of the Missouri Basin, research in Park Service areas, and the testing of new concepts in the field of archeology.

Field equipment, laboratory space, and office equipment are all essential for large-scale archeological investigations. When the Missouri Basin Project began operations, it had only the limited space which could be spared by the Laboratory of Anthropology. The early years of the project were lean ones financially, and the national economy was still plagued by a host of postwar shortages. Vehicles, excavation tools, and camping equipment were painfully accumulated, a few items at a time. So were desks, typewriters, filing cabinets, and all the other items for office and laboratory use. Many of the acquisitions were war surplus, and some of those items are still in use.

By the time the 1950 field season began, the most pressing equipment problems had been met. Since that time, available funds have allowed the accumulation of additional equipment and the replacement of worn-out items. Today there are few problems in this area.

The development of the Missouri Basin Project was, in large part, a matter of recruiting competent personnel. Staffing the project with stenographers, clerks, laboratory assistants, photographers, and illustrators has presented problems since the beginning of the work. Money spent for their salaries is money which cannot be used for fieldwork. During the first years of the project's life, when operating funds were extremely limited, it called for a considerable exercise of judgment to balance the realities of the budget against the demands of the professional staff for laboratory and clerical help.

The jobs to be filled were of a specialized nature, and it was often difficult to find people with the backgrounds necessary to handle cataloging, specimen photography, and similar chores. The grade ratings for these positions were originally relatively low, and there was a high turnover of clerical help during the early life of the Missouri Basin Project. When ratings in these categories were raised, this problem became less serious.

Professional archeologists have been directly responsible for the salvage operations. They have made the surveys which located sites within the reservoir areas. They have had charge of the excavations—organizing and supervising both the work itself and the party's field camp. They have been responsible for the analysis of the data from the fieldwork and for reporting the results of the program.

Finding and keeping qualified archeologists was a continuing problem for the administrators of the program. Salaries were never high enough to be a real attraction, and job security was always at the mercy of next year's appropriations. The archeologist working with the salvage program never enjoyed a particularly high status among his colleagues. These liabilities were inherent in the program itself, and they made it difficult to attract the best men available. They also made it difficult to keep good men.

The Missouri Basin Project also encountered problems which grew out of the academic training of the younger men who were added to the professional staff. Frank Roberts summed them up as follows:

Less important, but perennial problems, are those pertaining to personnel. At present we do not have a sufficient staff. . . . Of more concern, however, is the difficulty of obtaining properly trained people. There is not time to go into all of the ramifications of that subject, but our experience has shown that the archaeologists are not getting all that they should from the colleges and universities. While most of them recognize potsherds and projectile points, a majority of those we have had arrived with no conception of how to organize and prepare a report. That in part explains the lag in production. They have not known the fundamentals of establishing and maintaining proper field headquarters, and what is even more disconcerting is the fact that they seemingly have not been introduced to the idea that they occasionally might have to work as a member of a team, that cooperation is sometimes necessary. One young Ph. D. somewhat peevishly commented that he had always been taught that an archaeologist went off by himself and did as he damned pleased. (Roberts, 1961, p. 9)

Lack of experience of some party chiefs was partly compensated for by an excellent field manual prepared by the Missouri Basin Project. It contained instructions for routine operating procedures such as making up payrolls. It also gave helpful suggestions on almost every aspect of running a field party, from setting up latrine facilities to meeting visitors.

The first archeologists to be employed by the Missouri Basin Project joined the staff in July 1946. They were hired on a year-round basis, their summers to be spent in the field doing reconnaissance and excavation. Their winters were to be spent at the project headquarters in Lincoln, analyzing and reporting the data from the summer's fieldwork. These men, and the many others who followed them as year-round employees, were the core of the professional staff of the Missouri Basin Project. They remained with the project for periods ranging from 11 months to 15 years. Their relatively long periods of service gave them every opportunity to learn working routines and to become thoroughly familiar with the archeological problems of the area with which they were concerned.

In 1950 the Missouri Basin Project began hiring archeologists for the field season alone, without continuing their appointments into the winter months. This practice was followed during most of the succeeding years. In some cases the same men served for several seasons, in others they worked for a single summer only. These part-time professional employees have served as chiefs of either reconnaissance or excavation parties. The fact that their salaries were paid for only part of the year made it possible to stretch available funds for maximum excavations within the reservoir areas before the archeological sites there were drowned. The hiring of part-time archeologists raised a number of problems from the point of view of analyzing and reporting the data recovered. Archeologists in this category had other responsibilities during the winter. The services of the photographers, illustrators, and secretaries at the project headquarters were not readily available to them. Eventually, these drawbacks were partially avoided by writing personal services contracts for the production of site reports. A specified sum was paid when the manuscript was completed, with typing and illustrations provided by the River Basin Surveys.

In addition to the archeologists, a historian was on the Missouri Basin Project's staff from 1951 to mid-1968. A full-time paleontologist was employed from 1948 to 1953. A geologist was added during the summer of 1958 to provide expert help in connection with the excavation of a large preceramic site. A physical anthropologist was retained during the field seasons of 1956 through 1959 and from 1961 to 1963. Ray H. Mattison of the Park Service's Midwest Regional Office served as Missouri Basin Historian until his retirement in 1965. Most of Mattison's work was related directly to the salvage of historic sites.

Universities and museums also made a substantial contribution to the success of the salvage program, and the considerable expenditure of their own funds is one of the best indications of the importance of salvage archeology to the Nation's scholars. The State Historical Society of North Dakota, the Nebraska Historical Society, the University of Kansas, and the University of Nebraska took part in the program before 1950. Their work was done without Federal support, but it became obvious that the cooperating institutions could not carry the entire cost of large-scale participation in the program. Since 1950 the National Park Service has negotiated a series of contracts which have provided partial support of the non-Federal agencies.

These contracts specify the financial contributions to be made both by the Park Service and the cooperator, the site or sites to be worked, the amount of work to be done in terms of a field party of a specified size working for a stipulated number of weeks, and the archeologist who will have charge of the operations. A date for the completion of the manuscript of the final report is set, and provision is made for withholding a percentage of the Federal Government's contribution until the report has been received and approved.

The operations of the cooperating institutions have differed in a number of ways from those of the River Basin Surveys. They have been carried on with the institutions' own equipment, and the use of contract funds for equipment purchases has been proscribed. The cooperators have provided their own research facilities such as laboratories and libraries, together with the services of specialists in the allied fields of geology, biology, history, and climatology. The cooperators' supervising archeologists have usually been members of the institutions' regular staff, and the salaries for their field and the laboratory work have almost always been paid as part of the cooperators' contribution. Laboratory assistants, secretaries, draftsmen, and photographers have been drawn from the cooperators' regular staffs or from students at the universities. The cooperators have also financed the publication of a substantial number of the reports on their projects, while others have been published either in the River Basin Surveys Papers of the Bureau of American Ethnology or the Smithsonian's Publications in Salvage Archeology.

Cooperating institutions that have worked in the Missouri Valley in the Dakotas, the area with which this monograph is concerned, are:

Montana State University
1951–52.

Nebraska State Historical Society
1951–52, 1954–55.

Science Museum of St. Paul Institute
1964.

State Historical Society of North Dakota (in cooperation with the University of North Dakota in 1958 and 1959.)
1950–52, 1954–60, 1964–68.

University of Idaho
1957–58.

University of Kansas
1950–53, 1955, 1959.

University of Missouri
1969.

University of Nebraska
1960–61.

University of South Dakota
1950–61, 1963–64.

University of Wisconsin
1956.

The costs of salvage archeology in the Missouri Basin have been met partly by the Federal Government and partly by the various universities and museums which have participated in the program. The legislative basis for the original participation of Federal agencies in the program rested mainly on two acts of the Congress: the Antiquities Act of 1906 (34 Stat. 225) and the Historic Sites Act of 1935 (49 Stat. 666). The interest of Federal agencies in salvage archeology was greatly increased by the passage of the Reservoir Salvage Act of 1960 (74 Stat. 220).

The actual mechanics of Federal financing of the salvage program were arrived at gradually. A meeting was held at the offices of the Bureau of the Budget on July 27, 1945. Secretary Wetmore and Frank Roberts of the Smithsonian Institution conferred with representatives of the Bureau of the Budget, Corps of Engineers, and Bureau of Reclamation. It was the consensus that archeological salvage work was a legitimate concern of the Federal Government, that appropriations for the work could properly be requested by the construction agencies, and that the salvage work should be handled by the National Park Service and the Smithsonian Institution.

In 1946 and 1947 small sums were made available to the program by the agencies directly responsible for the reservoir construction. In November 1947 the Bureau of the Budget ruled that the construction agencies lacked the basic legislative authority to finance the program. The Bureau further stated that "unless or until new legislation on the subject is enacted, future Federal financing of archeological work on Government-owned lands and in connection with Government construction projects should be requested from Congress, pursuant to the Historic Sites Act of 1935, upon the basis of estimates submitted and justified by the Department of the Interior under our regular budgetary procedures."

As a result of this ruling, funds for salvage archeology within the Missouri Basin are appropriated to the Bureau of Reclamation in the Public Works Bill and are subsequently transferred to the National Park Service. Money for work outside the Missouri Basin goes directly to the Park Service.

Additional funds have come from such sources as contributions of the cooperating institutions, a grant made to the Smithsonian Institution by the National Science Foundation for 1961 and 1962, salaries paid by the U.S. National Museum to staff members working on the program, and payment by the Smithsonian Institution of the publication costs of the River Basin Surveys Papers of the Bureau of American Ethnology.

One fact is obvious from any audit of the salvage program. The cost of even large-scale archeological salvage is an insignificant item when it is measured against the cost of land acquisition, dam construction, power installations, transmission lines, recreation facilities, and other items in the reservoir program.

MECHANICS OF THE SALVAGE PROGRAM

Salvage work in the Missouri Basin has included investigations of archeological sites, work in historic sites such as fur trade and military posts, and the recovery of paleontological remains. While some fossil materials were found in most of the reservoir areas, they were not particularly noteworthy, and this part of the program was discontinued in 1953. Work in the historic sites along the Missouri River in North and South Dakota has been well summarized in the reports by Mattes, Mattison, G. H. Smith, and others listed in the bibliography. Archeological salvage has involved four operations: survey or reconnaissance, excavation, analysis of the data, and publication of the results.

This report is primarily concerned with the salvage archeology which has been carried out in the reservoirs on the Missouri in the Dakotas, in the section which has come to be called by archeologists the Middle Missouri Valley (fig. 21). The following discussion of the four operational aspects of the program is oriented toward that region, but many of the comments also apply to work in other parts of the Missouri Basin.

ARCHEOLOGICAL SURVEY

Archeological surveys have been as essential in planning salvage programs as engineering surveys have been fundamental to planning development of the reservoirs. In a salvage program, archeological reconnaissance has two objectives: to record the sites in a given area, and to evaluate their archeological importance.

When the salvage work began in the Missouri Valley, little was known of the archeological content of the 1,400 square miles along the mainstem which were to be inundated by the reservoirs. Maps, aerial photographs, and documentary sources provided the survey parties with initial clues to the location of sites. Information from residents of the area was also a considerable help to the reconnaissance teams. But the real survey work began when the parties actually went over the ground in vehicles and on foot.

The more arid western part of the Missouri Basin has one great advantage from a survey party's standpoint—the sparse

FIGURE 3 Field transportation—new style-old style.

grass cover. Artifacts and detritus are generally exposed on the surface of the ground, providing good indications of the contents of sites.

In the eastern part of the basin, sites frequently have more obvious surface features than those farther west. Some of them are burial mounds, often easily recognizable. Many were permanent villages, and it is usually possible to make out depressions marking houses, fortifications, and features such as graves and cache pits (figs. 4–6). In some cases, there are also prominent trash mounds in the villages. Most of the eastern sites have the disadvantage of a heavy sod cover which effectively seals in the occupational debris. Artifact samples on which to base an evaluation of the content of the site must usually be obtained through test excavations. As a result, surveys in the east have generally taken longer and been more expensive than ones made farther west.

A different kind of archeological survey, the shoreline survey, is being made now that the mainstem reservoirs are filled. Parties in boats work along the edge of the pool, looking for materials exposed in the banks cut by recent wave action. Some of these materials may be older than most of those found previously, since wave cutting may reveal sites that were too deeply buried to be seen during the surface surveys.

Nearly all of the archeological surveys in connection with the salvage program have been made by the Smithsonian Institution. Several cooperating institutions did take part in this phase of the work during the earliest years of the program, and recently several of them have conducted shoreline surveys under contract with the National Park Service.

Survey work was begun in the Middle Missouri subarea by the Smithsonian in 1947. Marvin F. Kivett worked in the Garrison Reservoir and Paul Cooper took a reconnaissance party into the Fort Randall Reservoir. Since that time, survey parties have covered almost every foot of the Missouri Valley between Gavins Point Dam and the head of Garrison Reservoir (figs. 6 and 7). In many cases, the survey parties were primarily interested in locating sites and making surface collections of artifact material. Other reconnaissance teams made test excavations to provide larger artifact samples and to determine house types.

The reconnaissance parties have recorded over 800 sites in the Middle Missouri Valley. Yet two major villages were not discovered until the summers of 1966 and 1967. The sites found have been itemized in nine reports not available for general distribution. These administrative reports served as the basis for planning the next step in the salvage program—the large-scale excavations.

A few comments on the survey work may be of value in planning future operations on the scale of those carried out in the Middle Missouri Valley. A two-man helicopter and a ground-support vehicle seem to hold considerable promise for work in open country. I am convinced that site testing in connection with survey operations can be done more efficiently with a light trenching machine rather than handtools.

The survey work in the Middle Missouri Valley might have been performed more effectively and more economically had greater attention been given to aerial photointerpretation. Good photographic coverage of the entire region is available from the Department of Agriculture and the Corps of Engineers, and numerous village sites are easily recognizable on these photographs. The River Basin Surveys used a partial set of the Department of Agriculture photographs to advantage. But more intensive study of the available aerial photographs by archeologists with some training in aerial photointerpretation would not only have provided site locations but also information on such features as village plan, fortification system, and so forth.

Relatively little use was made of the survey collections in defining archeological complexes. Cooper (1949) demonstrated that sherds collected during the surveys could provide a basis for setting up provisional pottery types. If this had been done systematically, it would almost certainly have been possible to isolate pottery assemblages representing cultural entities at the phase level. This technique had already been proven in the Southwest by Mera and the staffs of Gila Pueblo and the Museum of Northern Arizona, and its applicability to the Southeast was later demonstrated by such studies as Phillips, Ford, and Griffin's archeological survey of the

FIGURE 4 Crow Creek, an early fortified site in the Big Bend.

FIGURE 5 Nordvold, a late fortified village.

FIGURE 6 Sully, the largest earth-lodge village in the Middle Missouri.

FIGURE 7 *Field camp—no pool, no color TV.*

FIGURE 8 *Midsummer's nightmare.*

FIGURE 9 *Morning after.*

FIGURE 10 The inner man.
"Who took four pork chops?"

FIGURE 11 The inner man.
"You say your mother's looked better?"

lower Mississippi Valley. It could have been used to good advantage in the development of a more problem-oriented excavation program in the Middle Missouri subarea.

EXCAVATION PROGRAM

Site excavations require larger field parties and take far more man-hours than archeological surveys. There has been considerable variation in the size of the excavation crews and in the amount of work done at individual sites. The typical excavation party has consisted of an experienced archeologist as party chief, one or more trained field assistants, a cook, and eight to 10 laborers. In some cases, local labor has been hired, but most of the parties have been made up of student workers.

Many of the students were concentrating in anthropology at the undergraduate or graduate levels, and the educational aspect of the program has been one of its more valuable byproducts. It has offered opportunities for field experience and, in some instances, the use of field data for research papers and theses (Petsche, 1968).

The majority of the parties have established some sort of field camp (fig. 7). Frequently, tents have been the only shelters. The State Historical Society of North Dakota has used a trailer for kitchen and messhall. Permanent buildings of various kinds have been occupied when they were available, and some parties have rented houses or apartments in towns close to the sites they were working.

The weather is a matter of immediate concern to the field archeologist, both on the dig and in the field camp. This is particularly true during the summer in the Northern Plains with its high winds, violent thunderstorms, and days of excessive heat. Heavy rains invariably delay the excavations, it almost always rains when a complex feature is ready for photographing, and many a tent camp suffered from wind, rain, and hail (figs. 8 and 9).

Whatever the accommodations, the party chiefs have had to cope with the necessary camp logistics in addition to running the excavations. Food was typically bought from a mess fund to which each crew member contributed, usually at the rate of $10 a week (figs. 10 and 11). Fresh food storage was a problem which increased proportionately to the distance from the nearest town. Many camps were equipped with iceboxes or refrigerators. Supplying water for drinking, cooking, and bathing has often been a problem, and many parties have had to haul it into camp from some distance away. Latrine and bathing facilities had to be provided when field camps were set up, and a considerable amount of ingenuity was shown in this connection, especially in the construction and operation of shower baths.

Party chiefs have generally made every effort to run comfortable and well-ordered camps, and this has been an important factor in fostering efficient fieldwork. The party chiefs have also been responsible for accident prevention both in camp and on the digs. There have been accidents during the 20 years of the salvage operation, but the overall safety record has been excellent.

Excavation methods have involved adapting standard archeological techniques to the exigencies of salvage archeology. There has been a general feeling that it was justifiable to foreswear some technical nicities in the interest of obtaining maximum information under shortages of time and funds. This attitude has been expressed by limited screening and the use of heavy earth-moving machinery (Wedel, 1951). Bulldozers, road patrols, draglines, and other types of equipment have been used, and used to great advantage. The Missouri Basin was, so far as I am aware, the first archeological area in which the extensive use of heavy equipment came to be an acceptable technique. In this respect, the salvage program made a valuable contribution to archeological technology (figs. 12–17).

Specimen cleaning and cataloging are integral parts of both the archeological survey and the large-scale excavation. Many of the cooperating institutions have done at least part of this work in the field. The Smithsonian performed these tasks in the laboratory at its Lincoln headquarters.

A system of site designation was worked out in 1946, and it is now followed by practically every archeologist working in the Plains. Important sites are usually named, but every site has a trinomial designation, and recording and cataloging are done in terms of that designation. The first unit in

12

13

14

16

FIGURE 12   Excavation at a
small fortified village.

FIGURE 13   Partly
excavated circular house.

FIGURE 14   Clearing a
trading post palisade line.

FIGURE 15   Draglines move
more dirt than shovels.

FIGURE 16   Brooms get
things cleaner than shovels.

the designation is a number which indicates the State in which the site is located. The numbers were assigned to the States in alphabetical order. The second unit is a two-letter combination, written in capitals, which indicates the county where the site was found. The third unit is a number which designates the particular site within the county. Thus the trinomial designation of the Dodd Site is 39ST30. The number 39 indicates that the site is in South Dakota; ST locates it in Stanley County; and 30 is its assigned number in the county series.

Another device was the use of the term *feature*. So far as I know, it was first employed in the Plains by Duncan Strong and Albert Spaulding in 1938 and 1939. I first encountered it in 1950, and the comments made in the report on excavations at the Dodd and Phillips Ranch sites are still appropriate:

In conformance with standard River Basin Surveys usage, the term "Feature" was applied to anything which we wished to specify within the site. A house, a cache pit, a test trench, etc., were all designated as a "Feature" and distinguished by an Arabic numeral. At the beginning of the season the writer was rather dubious about this practice. At the end of the season he was completely converted to it. The use of the single term precluded the confusion which arises when something which was originally called a cache pit develops into a full-sized earth lodge. (Lehmer, 1954b, p. 6)

A series of standard forms was devised for keeping survey and excavation records. The most important ones are the Survey Form used for recording sites, the General Feature Form for recording features within a site, and the Burial Form. The survey form has a printed square on the back for indicating the location of the site within a General Land Office Survey's section; the backs of the feature and burial forms are graph paper. A Continuation Form accommodates the inevitable entries which are too long for the blank on the printed form. It is an invaluable adjunct to the primary forms, and would be helpful in many other recording systems. Standard forms were also devised for listing photographic negatives,

FIGURE 17 "Clean him up good for the picture!"

cataloged specimens, and identifications of unworked animal bone.

Number sheets prepared by the River Basin Surveys are not, strictly speaking, record forms. They are ingenious devices which have innumerable uses. They consist of 8½-by-11-inch pages which carry lists of Arabic numerals in sequence. One has the numbers 1 to 500, the other the numbers 501 to 1,000. These sheets are convenient for ticking off numbers assigned to features and the like; they are invaluable for tallying numbered items, such as specimens not stored in numerical order; and they can be utilized in other ways.

Detailed photographic records were made of every phase of the salvage operation. Black-and-white negatives and prints and color transparencies were filed under systems which include the site number for easy reference. Many of the field parties have used chartered aircraft for aerial photography in connection with both survey and excavation work.

All rim sherds and nonpottery artifacts collected by the River Basin Surveys field parties were assigned catalog numbers. Body sherds and unworked animal bone in these collections did not usually have catalog numbers inscribed on them. Once the cataloging process was completed, the specimens were boxed by sites and stored in the Lincoln headquarters until they were studied.

Excavation records were, theoretically at least, completed before the field party returned to the Lincoln headquarters. Each original sheet was given a record number in the Lincoln office, and two full-size photographic reproductions were made. A set of records for each site was then assembled. The originals were placed in the Number 1 file, which was closed to general use. The Number 2 file was kept in the River Basin Surveys headquarters for active use, and the Number 3 file was stored on the University of Nebraska campus as insurance against possible destruction of the other two.

When the file was completed for a particular site, it contained all the data pertaining to that site, except for the maps, ground plans, etc., made on large sheets of paper. Normally, a site file included an index page showing the number of sheets included in the file, survey records, a General Feature Form for each feature recorded, a Burial Form for each burial encountered, a copy of the specimen catalog, copies of the animal bone identification sheets, prints of all field photographs, and any other data relating to the investigation of the site. The site folder, field maps and drawings, black-and-white photographic prints and color transparencies, and the stored specimens provided the necessary information for writing a descriptive report of the site.

The cooperating institutions which worked in the Middle Missouri subarea used their own recording and filing systems. While there is considerable variation from one institution to another, there has been a general tendency to follow the River Basin Surveys system, often to the extent of using Smithsonian forms.

A few oversights have become apparent in the River Basin Surveys' recording system over the years. No cumulative list of all the excavated sites was kept. Site summary forms giving a concise evaluation of the content and significance of each site would have been a ready source of data for the present report and for other purposes.

Little if any attempt was made to standardize field maps and ground plans. A future undertaking of this sort might well include specifying the use of standard size sheets for mapping so that all of the field drawings not made on the feature forms could be reproduced and bound in sets like the other records.

No recording system can be better than the men who keep the records. This is the immediate responsibility of the field man, and it has been discharged competently in most cases. A few exceptions have, however, left serious gaps in the record.

SALVAGE ARCHEOLOGY IN THE MIDDLE MISSOURI

Five dams have been built on the Missouri River in the Dakotas, and salvage archeology in the Middle Missouri subarea relates directly to those dams (table 1). The southernmost is Gavins Point, just upstream from

Yankton, S. Dak. The water it impounds forms Lewis and Clark Lake, which lies on the Nebraska-South Dakota border and has a maximum length of about 25 miles. Fort Randall Dam is 44 river miles above the upper reaches of Lewis and Clark Lake. Fort Randall Reservoir extends to the foot of the third dam in the chain, Big Bend. At maximum pool elevation, the head of Big Bend Reservoir is only 5 miles downstream from Oahe Dam.

Oahe is the world's largest rolled-earth dam, and Oahe Reservoir is the longest one along the mainstem (fig. 18). It reaches 231 miles upstream from the dam, almost to Bismarck, N. Dak. The head of the Oahe pool is 86 miles downstream from Garrison Dam, the last one on the Missouri in the Dakotas. Garrison Reservoir extends upstream almost to the Montana-North Dakota line. At maximum pool level, the five reservoirs have a combined surface area of nearly 1,400 square miles, close to one-fifth the area of Lake Ontario.

The five reservoirs have drowned well over 81 percent of the 756-mile length of the Missouri River in the Dakotas. Construction of the Fort Randall and Garrison Dams was begun in 1946. Work was started on the others during the next few years. The river channel at Fort Randall was closed in 1952; after that time the waters began to be impounded in the reservoir. As one dam after another was closed, the waters in the reservoirs began to creep up, flooding more and more archeological materials with every foot of rise. Today all five reservoir pools are close to the maximum operating level. The majority of the archeological sites which will go under water have already been engulfed. There will be still more destruction during the next few years. Some sites will be affected by the construction of recreation facilities along

Table 1.—Dams and reservoirs in the Middle Missouri subarea [1]

Dam	River miles above St. Louis	Construction begun	Dam closed	Reservoir length, miles	Reservoir surface area, acres
Gavins Point	811	1952	1955	25	33,000
Fort Randall	880	1946	1952	107	102,000
Big Bend	987	1959	1963	80	55,800
Oahe	1,072	1948	1958	231	376,000
Garrison	1,389	1946	1953	178	324,000

[1] Data provided by U.S. Army Engineer Division—Missouri River, Omaha, Nebr.

FIGURE 18 Oahe Dam, looking upstream.

the shorelines. Many more will be subject to serious damage by erosion because of bank cutting along the shorelines of the new manmade lakes.

The year 1950 saw the first large-scale excavations in the Dakota reservoirs. Field parties of both the River Basin Surveys and the cooperating institutions have been in the field every season since. Some of the digs have been small ones, little more than extensive tests. Others have been large-scale operations, with big field parties working the same site for a number of seasons. By the autumn of 1969 more than 200 archeological sites had been excavated.

For the purposes of this evaluation, it was necessary to make some distinction between the small-scale site excavations and the ones which could be considered to have been large digs. Several approaches were tried—number of features recognized, number of specimens cataloged, etc. There were objections to all of them, and in the end the distinction was made on the crass but significant factor of how much the fieldwork cost. If the fieldwork at a single site or group of sites cost at least $2,500, it was counted as a major excavation. Excavation costs in this category have ranged from $2,500 to over $47,000. More than 90 major site excavations had been made under the salvage program in the Missouri Valley in the Dakotas by the end of the 1969 field season (see appendix 1).

The aboriginal sites range from preceramic occupations dating from well before the Christian era to villages occupied on the eve of the Reservation Period. They include camps, burial mounds, cemeteries, and permanent villages. Excavations have also been made in a number of fur trading posts, military establishments, etc. The results of the work are summarized in Part II of this report.

The large-scale excavations have been highly productive, and the combination of surveys and intensive excavations have provided most of our knowledge of Middle Missouri archeology. On the other hand, most of the small-scale excavations seem to have cost more than they were worth. The sherd samples generally serve to classify the site in terms of the cultural complex(es) represented. The rest of the artifact samples add little if anything to what is known from more intensive work at other sites. The data on architecture, village plan, etc., are minimal. Reporting these projects is a serious problem because there is so little to say about them. It seems likely that most of the information could have been obtained more readily and for considerably less money by machine trenching.

AERIAL PHOTOINTERPRETATION

Aerial photointerpretation played a relatively minor role during the early years of the salvage program. In the summer of 1965 the National Park Service contracted with the Itek Corporation of Alexandria, Va., for a pilot study of the application of modern techniques of aerial photography and photointerpretation to field archeology. A short section of the Missouri Valley in the Big Bend district was selected as a test area and subjected to intensive coverage. Different types of film were used, photographs were made from different altitudes, etc. The conclusions drawn by the Itek Corporation are extremely interesting, and should be of value in planning future archeological investigations. If the techniques employed had been developed during the early years of salvage work in the Middle Missouri, and if funds had been available to use them, this approach could have been useful to the operation.

At this late date, with the mainstem reservoirs at or close to maximum operating pool level, extensive new aerial photographic coverage would not seem to be justifiable. Existing photographic coverage, especially the early Department of Agriculture series, can still be used to advantage. Aerial photointerpretation can yield significant information on the size, plan, topographic situation, and fortification systems of many sites in the region.

MISSOURI BASIN CHRONOLOGY PROGRAM

Late in 1958 personnel of a number of institutions concerned with the salvage program embarked on a cooperative venture known as the Missouri Basin Chronology Program. It aimed at providing the chronological framework needed by Plains archeologists. While this program has provided a considerable amount of help, it has also brought into sharp focus a number of problems which still have to be met.

Financing and direction of the chronology program have come mainly from the Smithsonian Institution and the National Park Service. Staff members of both the Laboratory of Anthropology of the University of Nebraska and the Nebraska State Historical Society cooperated closely when the program was being organized, and numerous other individuals and institutions have made contributions at various times. The five progress reports issued by the River Basin Surveys since the inception of this program have summarized the work and presented individual specimen dates as they have become available.

The Missouri Basin Chronology Program has tried a variety of approaches. Geological-climatic dating, proportional radiation counting, and palynology have been explored, with largely inconclusive results so far. Dendrochronology and radiocarbon dating have proved to be far more useful.

Pioneer tree-ring studies by George F. Will on North Dakota materials (1946, 1948) and by Harry E. Weakly on materials from the Central Plains (H. E. Weakly, in Champe, 1946; H. E. Weakly, 1950) showed the possibility of dendrochronology in the Missouri Basin. Collection of wood specimens to serve as the basis for tree-ring studies in the Missouri Valley in South Dakota was begun by the Missouri Basin Project in 1958. During the winter of 1960–61, a master chart extending back to A.D. 1300 was compiled by Harry Weakly, then with the U.S. Department of Agriculture, Warren Caldwell, of the Missouri Basin Project staff, and Ward F. Weakly, then a student at the University of Nebraska. Ten tree-ring dates were released in Statement Number 3 of the Missouri Basin Chronology Program, published on February 1, 1962.

None of the men who had done the initial tree-ring work for the Missouri Basin Chronology Program was able to continue his efforts in this field at that time, and dendrochronology in the Missouri Basin was almost at a standstill until 1964. That year the National Park Service negotiated a contract with the Laboratory of Tree-Ring Research of the University of Arizona. Bryant Bannister, now Director of the Laboratory, was put in charge of the project. Its purpose was to verify the master chart prepared by Caldwell and the Weaklys, and to analyze the mass of wood specimens collected by the Missouri Basin Project.

Ward Weakly was engaged by the Laboratory to work with Bannister on the project. His manuscript report, submitted to the Park Service in October 1967, includes master charts for five local chronologies, a number of specimen dates, and an interpretation of the culture history of the region based on his dating.

Samples for radiocarbon dating were collected almost from the beginning of the salvage work in the Missouri Basin. A substantial series of dates from sites in the Middle Missouri subarea has been published in the MBP Chronology Program statements and in *Radiocarbon*. These dates are the main elements in the present chronological framework of Middle Missouri archeology.

PRESENTING THE RESULTS

Analysis and publication of the data from the surveys and excavations were included among the basic operations when the salvage program was initiated. Analysis has been partly a matter of considering the archeological sites in terms of their location, characteristics, and component features. It has also been a matter of sorting and classifying the specimens collected by the field parties. Some artifacts have been classified in functional terms, with the specimens being sorted according to use (or presumed use) into classes, such as hoes, arrow points, etc. Other artifacts, such as pottery vessels and sherds, have been classified according to form and decoration, and grouped into wares and types, which are broadly comparable to the biologist's genera and species.

Studies of Middle Missouri ceramic typology have been important since the inception of the salvage program. Hewes

(1949b) described a series of pottery types from some of the first salvage work in North Dakota. Cooper (1949) recognized three "categories" of pottery in his survey collections from the Oahe and Fort Randall reservoir areas, and considered them as provisionally representing three complexes within the village cultures of the region. His paper is an excellent example of the use of survey data in establishing preliminary cultural classifications. Paralleling the earlier work of Will and Hecker (1944) in North Dakota, it marked a definite advance in South Dakota archeology.

The first large-scale excavations along the Missouri River in the Dakotas were made in 1950, and the work raised a number of problems in regard to pottery classification. The materials from four sites were processed by the excavators during the winter of 1950–51. Two were villages in the Fort Randall Reservoir—Talking Crow (39BF3) and Swanson (39BR16), which had been dug respectively by Carlyle S. Smith for the University of Kansas and Wesley R. Hurt, Jr., for the University of South Dakota. The other two were the Dodd Site (39ST30) and the Phillips Ranch Site (39ST14) in the lower Oahe Reservoir, which I had excavated for the River Basin Surveys. All four sites yielded large sherd samples, and it seemed essential to develop a usable system of classification for this material.

When Hurt, Smith, and I came to grips with the problem, we knew that our materials represented a considerable range in terms of both time and cultural context. It was apparent, however, that there were relatively few attributes which could be used as the basis for a pottery classification.

We had very little data on overall vessel form. Our samples appeared to show no significant differences in such characteristics as paste, temper, wall thickness, and method of manufacture. Body sherds could be sorted into four categories on the basis of the exterior surface treatment.

The evidence suggested that all of the vessel walls had been malleated with a paddle before firing, with differences in the type of paddle used being responsible for the four surface finishes: cord roughening or cord marking, presumably the product of a cord-wrapped paddle; simple stamping,

which appeared to have resulted from the use of a grooved or thong-wrapped paddle; check stamping, a wafflelike surface apparently achieved by using a paddle grooved in two directions; and plain, which may have resulted from the use of a smooth paddle or by obliterating the imprint of a textured paddle while the clay was still plastic. Less common treatments of bodies included incisions or punctates and vertical striations in the lower rim-neck area which have been referred to as "brushed."

While these finishes were useful for sorting purposes, they were found to have limited value as cultural indicators. The most important was the contrast between cord roughening and simple stamping. Cord roughening is restricted almost entirely to the early villages in the southern part of the Middle Missouri subarea and to Woodland sites.

Rim form and decoration were the two criteria which promised finer and presumably more significant typological categorizations. Hurt, Smith, and I discussed the problem at various times, and it became apparent that we were faced with a basic difference of opinion about the relative importance of these attributes. Smith and I regarded rim form as a primary criterion and decoration as a secondary one. Hurt, on the other hand, considered rim form to be less important. A number of types which he set up for the Swanson material (Hurt, 1951a) include several different rim forms, and he continued this practice in his later reports of other pottery complexes.

In our initial studies of the Talking Crow and Dodd pottery, Smith (1951) and I adapted the concepts of named wares and types to Middle Missouri pottery. Our agreed position was expressed in these words:

The wares may be thought of as groups of types which share such fundamental characteristics as the fabric of the pottery itself, the surface finish, the general vessel form, and the basic rim form. The types themselves have all of the characteristic features of the ware, but are distinguished by the decorative treatment and sometimes minor variations in form.

(Lehmer, 1951, p. 3)

Although Smith later included both straight and S-rims in his Iona Ware (Smith and

Grange, 1958), rim form generally continues to be regarded as a highly distinctive attribute.

Subsequently, Spaulding published a report on Arzberger Site (39HU6), which was excavated before the inception of the salvage program. He subjected his pottery sample to a rigorous analysis which involved recognition of a series of attributes of the individual sherds, recording the attributes of each sherd on a punchcard, and sorting the cards to establish correlations between the attributes. It is a matter of some interest that the pottery classification which emerged from this analysis involved the recognition of two major "groups," which were distinguished by rim form. These groups are closely comparable to the wares of Smith and Lehmer. Spaulding also recognized a series of types distinguished by decorative treatment, and he subdivided his Hughes group into one named type, a subgroup with incised decoration, and another subgroup with plain rims and plain or decorated lips (Spaulding, 1956, pp. 111–167).

Deetz (1965) has made an entirely different use of Middle Missouri pottery characteristics. Like Spaulding, he recognized a series of attributes which might be present on individual sherds, and he prepared punchcards showing their occurrence on each sherd in his sample. The data on these cards were then analyzed by computer to determine associations between the various attributes. Deetz was interested in the pattern of associations as an index to possible changes in the native social organization rather than as a basis for ceramic classification.

Pottery typology has gotten badly out of hand in Middle Missouri archeology. The literature is now cluttered with more than 135 named wares and types, many of them set up on only a handful of sherds. A reordering of pottery systematics is desirable before a final synthesis can be made of the results of salvage work in the region.

Another phase of the analysis of the materials from the salvage excavations has been something of an innovation in the Plains area. The Middle Missouri villages yielded enormous amounts of unworked animal bone, and most excavators kept the complete sample of identifiable bones for laboratory study. These bone samples have given valuable information on butchering techniques, and have also provided clues to hunting patterns and economic patterns of the various village tribes (White, 1952a, 1952b, 1953a, 1953b, 1954, 1955; Lehmer, 1952b; Wood, 1962b).

Analysis of the data has gone beyond the description of the sites and the study and classification of the specimen material. It has also involved determining statistical associations between types of artifacts and features within the sites. This has been particularly important in sites which were occupied by more than one group. Analysis has also involved comparative studies of data from several sites to establish similarities and differences. In many cases, similarities between two or more sites have been close enough to indicate that a single cultural complex was represented in the different samples. Similarities between archeological complexes have also provided clues to the existence of sequences of cultural development and to interaction between different groups.

ARCHEOLOGICAL TAXONOMY

not much field work done in 1953 — federal funds curtailed

Salvage operations from 1946 through 1949 were mainly devoted to surveys and a few small-scale excavations in the reservoirs along the Missouri River. The investigations served to familiarize the men carrying out the program with the archeological resources of the region, and they provided data for working out cultural sequences in the region (cf. Wedel, 1947, 1948; Cooper, 1949; and Frank Roberts' sections in Annual Reports of the Bureau of American Ethnology). Large field parties began digging for several months at single sites in 1950, and similar operations were also carried out in 1951 and 1952 (fig. 19). Fieldwork was minimal in 1953, owing to a severe cut in federally appropriated funds.

Very little of the wealth of data gathered in 1950–52 had been published by the end of 1953, but a great deal of it had been disseminated orally among the archeologists working under the salvage program. Some of this interchange took place during visits of party chiefs to other men's excavations. There were memorable exchanges of ideas at the Hop Scotch and Silver Spur in Fort Pierre, S. Dak., gathering places for the members of the fraternity working in the southern part of the region. The most important opportunities for keeping abreast of developments were offered by the annual meetings of the Plains Conference. The conference is usually held at Thanksgiving time. Field reports are given, formal papers read, and seminars conducted. It has been common practice for participants in the conference to distribute copies of trait lists and the like for comment. There were also long and often vehement informal discussions of new ideas and problems. These exchanges of ideas and information, supplemented by a growing number of published reports on the salvage work, have been enormously important in shaping the thinking of the individuals working in the region. Many of the seasons since 1953 have seen less formal gatherings at a summer Plains Conference. These meetings took place in Pierre or Bismarck, usually in August.

The development of satisfactory taxonomic frameworks for pigeonholing the growing masses of data has been a problem throughout the life of the salvage program. Pottery classification has already been discussed.

FIGURE 19 *Specimen processing in a field lab.*

The necessity for a distinctive geographic term became apparent during the early years of the salvage program. The term "Upper Missouri" had been used for the entire run of the river north of the mouth of the Platte since the days of the St. Louis fur traders (Chittenden, 1954, pp. 768–769). The early stages of the salvage work showed that the section of the valley in North and South Dakota was extremely rich in archeological remains, and also indicated that those materials differed from the ones found in the Central Plains and in the upper reaches of the Missouri Valley. This situation seemed to call for overt recognition, and the term *Middle Missouri* was advanced to replace the older usage (Lehmer, 1954a; Stephenson, 1954). This term, which appeared in print much earlier (Will and Spinden, 1906, Map I), has won acceptance in the literature of Northern Plains archeology. It serves to distinguish the section of the Missouri Valley from the mouth of the White River in South Dakota to the North Dakota-Montana border. The term Upper Missouri is now used by archeologists to designate the section of the valley above the mouth of the Yellowstone.

Classification of archeological assemblages and the cultural complexes they represent has undergone a number of changes over the years. It seems appropriate to review the taxonomic schemes proposed for the Middle Missouri subarea at this point. During the 1950's the categories of the Midwestern Taxonomic System—especially components, foci, and aspects—were generally used, although the foci and aspects were commonly given temporal and/or spatial dimensions in addition to the strictly typological criteria called for in the original formulation of the scheme.

One of the first attempts at categorizing a series of Middle Missouri complexes was a direct outgrowth of salvage excavations in the vicinity of the Oahe Dam in 1950 and 1951. Typology and house superposition at the multicomponent Dodd Site (39ST30) and data from the nearby Phillips Ranch Site (39ST14) provided the basis for recognizing four foci. Two other assemblages were indicated by earlier work in the vicinity. Available data made it possible to arrange the foci and assemblages in a chronological sequence. The numerous trait carry-overs which were apparent from earlier to later assemblages suggested that the sequence was a developmental one which lacked any sharp breaks in the cultural continuum. This continuum was designated as the Fort Pierre Branch (Lehmer, 1952a). Today it still appears to be a valid local sequence, but sources of the changes from one stage to the next can be better understood against a much broader knowledge of Middle Missouri archeology.

During the summer of 1953 a group of archeologists connected with the salvage program formulated a more ambitious classification of the archeological materials from the southern Middle Missouri and the Central Plains. Their provisional classification was discussed at length and revised in some detail at the Plains Conference in 1953. The results were presented in two tables (Stephenson, 1954). One listed a number of components which were considered to be similar on the basis of short trait lists. In most cases the components were assigned to foci and aspects. The second table listed the foci and aspects according to geographic distribution and estimated age.

Albert Spaulding's monograph on the Arzberger Site made another important contribution to the formulation of both concepts and taxonomy in Middle Missouri archeology. His perceptive synthesis of the archeology of the Dakotas, Nebraska, Iowa, and Minnesota recognized a prehistoric Central Plains culture, represented by the Upper Republican and Nebraska aspects and the St. Helena Focus (Spaulding, 1956, pp. 67–83). He concluded that the Arzberger complex was closely related to those Central Plains manifestations, and he made a detailed analysis of possible Oneota influences on Arzberger and the Central Plains configurations. Spaulding also examined the possibility that Arzberger was ancestral to the protohistoric Lower Loup Focus of Nebraska, and stated some reservations about considering Arzberger as a direct ancestor of Lower Loup.

Spaulding recognized a second major cultural configuration in what he called the Mill Creek-Mandan Tradition. He suggested that it was rooted in the complexes represented at the Cambria and Great Oasis sites in southern Minnesota. He saw

Cambria as giving rise to the Mill Creek Complex of northwestern Iowa, while the Over Focus of southeastern South Dakota and the Missouri Valley was the result of a fusion of Cambria, Great Oasis, and Mill Creek. The Over Focus was in turn regarded as standing at the beginning of a sequence which also included the Monroe and Anderson foci (Lehmer, 1951, 1952a), Will and Hecker's (1944) Middle Mandan, and the complex indicated by Meleen's (1949b) report on the Thomas Riggs Site.

Spaulding also linked the prehistoric developments in the Middle Missouri subarea with historic village tribes. He felt that "the Over Focus seems to stand at the beginning of a cultural sequence which emerges in the historic period as the culture of the Mandan Indians," and he suggested that the Arzberger Site represented

a community with strong Upper Republican cultural affinities on the Missouri in central South Dakota [which] can hardly be interpreted as anything but an early movement of an Arikara group, quite possibly the first to advance . . . into what was to become the heart of the Arikara territory in the eighteenth century.

(Spaulding, 1956, pp. 99 and 109)

Spaulding's analysis was particularly important for the recognition of Mill Creek-Mandan as a configuration distinct from the Central Plains complexes and for the investigation of the relationships between the Plains villages and the cultures at the eastern margins of the Plains.

Two other syntheses of Plains culture history were made about the time that Spaulding was writing his Arzberger report. One of them organized the whole span of the aboriginal occupation of the Northern Plains in terms of a sequence of *time horizons*. These were predicated on the fact that the area had seen

the development of a sequence of cultural configurations which, in Kroeber's [1939] terms, might be called "culture climaxes." Within the Northern Plains, the several climaxes seem to have differed in intensity, to have centered in different parts of the area, and to have been characterized by a particular adaptation of culture to its environment. Each climax appears to have lasted over a definable period of time, usually with a minimum of overlap on its prede-

cessor or successor. Because of this, it seems possible to divide the prehistory of the area into a series of "time horizons," each horizon being a period distinguished by the dominance of a particular culture climax.

(Lehmer, 1954a, p. 139)

That paper and the synthesis presented in another article (Lehmer, 1954b, pp. 138–154) were primarily concerned with the Plains Village complex, the culture climax of the Sedentary Horizon. It was argued that all of the villages of the Northern Plains represented a single basic cultural configuration which was designed as the *Plains Village Pattern*. The main diagnostic traits of the pattern include subsistence based about equally on hunting and agriculture; semipermanent villages located close to the floodplains of the larger streams; earthlodges with enclosed entryways; undercut and straight-sided cache pits in and between the houses; grit-tempered pottery, usually having paddle-marked bodies and cord- or tool-impressed decoration; large numbers of chipped stone tools including snubnose scrapers and small, light projectile points; numerous hoes made from bison scapulae; and a wide variety of bone artifacts, including several kinds of hide-dressing tools.

As I wrote in 1954:

These traits, many of them decidedly generalized, appear as the warp of all the village cultures of the [Northern] Plains. Specific modifications of these traits, occurring in combination with other and distinctive traits, have definitely limited distributions in time and space. It is these combinations which serve to distinguish at least three broad cultural traditions within the Plains Village Pattern.

(Lehmer, 1954b, p. 140)

The three cultural traditions are the Central Plains, Middle Missouri, and Coalescent. The Central Plains and Middle Missouri Traditions correspond roughly with Spaulding's Central Plains culture and his Mill Creek-Mandan Tradition. The Coalescent Tradition is considered to have been generally later than the other two, to have been their hybrid descendant, and to have had a geographical extent which included both the Middle Missouri and much of the Central Plains subareas.

The three traditions within the Plains Village Pattern came to be generally used as integrative devices. At the same time, more specific manifestations were classified as foci and aspects. These were sometimes assigned spatial and temporal limits. A number of schemes were proposed in which new foci and aspects were related to each other in terms of developmental sequences (Hurt, 1953, 1954, 1957, 1959; and Hurt et al. 1962).

Mention should also be made of Waldo Wedel's *Prehistoric Man on the Great Plains*. Published in 1961, this comprehensive summary of Plains archeology relates the results of the salvage program up to that time to cultural developments in the Plains as a whole.

By 1965 the taxonomic situation in Middle Missouri archeology seemed to call for drastic overhauling. An adaptation of Willey and Phillips' (1962) spatial divisions and archeological unit concepts was proposed by Lehmer and Caldwell (1966). Spatial divisions included the Plains area; the Northern and Southern Plains subareas; and the Central Plains, Northwestern Plains, and Middle Missouri regions. A new spatial unit, the district, was added to those of Willey and Phillips. This was thought of as being an intermediate unit—a subdivision of a region which included two or more localities, each distinguished by its own cultural sequence.

The basic archeological units—component, subphase, and phase—were taken over directly from the Willey and Phillips system. The integrative units proposed for the Plains included technological traditions, cultural traditions, and horizons. Definitions of the last two were somewhat at variance with those proposed by Willey and Phillips.

The year 1966 also saw the publication of Gordon R. Willey's summary of North American archeology. His treatment of the Plains is not based on first-hand familiarity with the area, but it has the great advantage of a broad perspective. Following Wedel's (1961) synthesis of Plains archeology, Willey recognized five geographic subareas: Northeastern, Middle Missouri, Northwestern Plains, Central Plains, and Southern Plains. He further recognized four major periods in the occupation of the area: Paleo-Indian (to 4000 B.C.), Archaic (4000 B.C. to 0), Woodland (0 to A.D. 1000), and

Plains Village (A.D. 1000 to protohistoric and historic). He also recognized four *major cultural traditions* associated with the occupational periods in the Plains: Big Game Hunting, Plains Archaic, Woodland, and Plains Village. Smaller units within the traditions were designated as cultures or phases.

The taxonomic divisions used in the present report are modifications of ones which have already been proposed. I have followed Willey's synthesis as far as possible, both because of its intrinsic merits and because it is what is now being taught to students in most courses in North American archeology. Beyond that, I have tried to follow Willey and Phillips' (1962) spatial divisions, basic archeological units, and integrative units, with some modification of the system proposed by Lehmer and Caldwell.

SPATIAL DIVISIONS

Spatial divisions (fig. 20) include, in descending order, the Plains *area*, which is modified somewhat in the south from that shown by Wedel (1961, p. 23) and Willey (1966, p. 312). Like Wedel and Willey, I have recognized five *subareas* within the Plains. Only three of them are directly pertinent to this report—the Middle Missouri, Central Plains, and Northwestern Plains. The Middle Missouri subarea as used here includes the Missouri Valley from just below the mouth of the White River in South Dakota to just above the mouth of the Yellowstone in North Dakota. I have considerably reduced their Central Plains subarea to exclude the arid western portions, making it correspond approximately to the maximum extent of agricultural village populations in the southernmost part of South Dakota, western Iowa, northwestern Missouri, Nebraska, and Kansas north of the Arkansas drainage. There is some question as to where the southernmost part of South Dakota, including the Missouri Valley below the White River, should be assigned. Available information (Hurt, 1952; Johnston, 1967a) indicates that this section was culturally a transition zone between the Middle Missouri and Central Plains traditions, and that it was also heavily influenced by

FIGURE 20 Spatial divisions of the Plains area.

FIGURE 21 Regions of the Middle Missouri subarea.

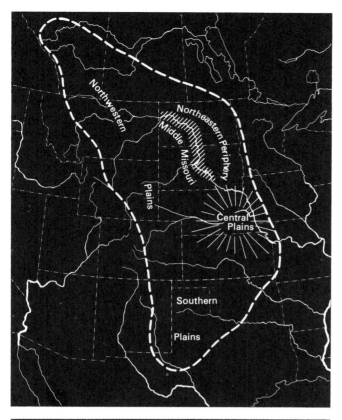

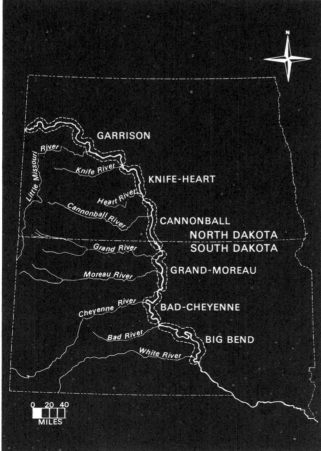

Oneota and other complexes which centered to the east. The Northwestern Plains is the subarea which runs north from the upper Arkansas drainage, between the Rockies and the Central Plains and Middle Missouri subareas, into Alberta and Saskatchewan.

All of the Plains subareas can be divided into smaller units, but I have only done this for the Middle Missouri. I have substituted the term *region* for *district* used earlier (Lehmer and Caldwell, 1966), reserving the latter concept for future use in recognizing the major subdivisions which are beginning to become apparent in the Middle Missouri regions (fig. 21). The *Big Bend region* includes the Missouri trench from below the mouth of the White River to just above the mouth of the Bad River. The *Bad-Cheyenne region* extends from the mouth of the Bad to about the old Cheyenne Indian Agency. The *Grand-Moreau region* runs upstream from there to within some 15 miles of the North Dakota-South Dakota border. The *Cannonball region* includes the Missouri Valley from the northern end of the Grand-Moreau region to just below the mouth of the Heart River. The *Knife-Heart region* reaches from below the Heart River to a short distance above the Knife River. Finally, the *Garrison region* extends upriver from above the Knife River to just beyond the mouth of the Yellowstone. Each of these regions is distinguished by a unique archeological sequence, and together they serve as integrative devices in reconstructing the culture history of the Middle Missouri subarea.

CULTURAL CATEGORIES

The broad sweep of the native cultures of the three Plains subareas with which I am concerned can readily be presented in terms of Willey's periods and of the basically equivalent time horizons proposed earlier. Here, I am using Willey's "period" in place of the older term to avoid the confusion which might well arise because of the different ways in which "horizon" has been used in recent years.

Each period represents an epoch during which there was a dominance of a particular culture climax, or major cultural tradition, in the Middle Missouri, Central Plains, and/or Northwestern Plains subareas. I have retained three of Willey's period names—Paleo-Indian, Plains Woodland, and Plains Village. I have substituted the older term Foraging for his Archaic period because the materials from the Northern Plains seem to be more closely related to the Desert cultures of the West than to the eastern Archaic. I have added an *Equestrian Period* to encompass the culture climax of the horse tribes of the 18th and 19th centuries. I have also changed the temporal boundaries of the periods in some cases (fig. 22). The hallmarks of the five periods may be indicated as follows.

PALEO-INDIAN PERIOD

The Paleo-Indian Period includes the time up to about 6000 B.C. The culture climax is expressed in the early hunting complexes of the Plains, what Willey (1966, pp. 37–51) has called the Big-Game Hunting Tradition. The geographic center in the Plains lay in the western grasslands. Representative complexes are most readily identified by distinctive projectile points. The earliest, which spread far beyond the borders of the Plains, is the Llano Complex, characterized by fluted Clovis points. The Folsom Complex, with its finely made Folsom points, is slightly later in time. Roughly the last 2,000 years of the epoch saw the

development of what appear to be localized variants distinguished by such unfluted point types as Agate Basin, Angostura, Eden, Plainview, and Scottsbluff. These complexes are often lumped together under the general term Plano culture (Krieger, *in* Jennings and Norbeck, 1964).

The Llano, Folsom, and Plano complexes differ from each other in detail, but they are linked together by a number of fundamental traits. Artifact assemblages (which include numerous knives, scrapers, and choppers), kill sites where numbers of animals were slaughtered, and the associated faunal remains combine to demonstrate that the economy rested primarily on the hunting of big game animals. The presence of occasional grinding tools in the Plano sites indicates some use of wild food plants, but I seriously doubt that this source of food was any more important then than it was to the horse tribes of historic times. The workmanship of the chipped stone artifacts, especially the projectile points, commonly exhibits a very high quality of craftsmanship. This may well reflect technological specialization made possible by a food surplus resulting from an ample game supply.

FORAGING PERIOD

The Foraging Period covers the time from roughly 6000 to 500 B.C. It is characterized

FIGURE 22 Major periods and cultural climaxes in the three Plains subareas.

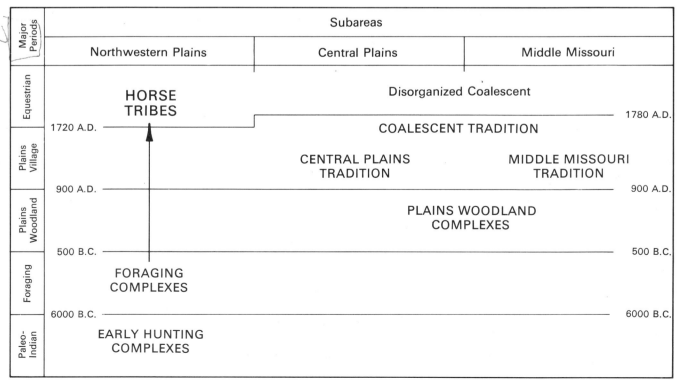

Major Periods	Subareas		
	Northwestern Plains	Central Plains	Middle Missouri
Equestrian	HORSE TRIBES (1720 A.D.)	Disorganized Coalescent — 1780 A.D.	
		COALESCENT TRADITION	
Plains Village		CENTRAL PLAINS TRADITION	MIDDLE MISSOURI TRADITION
	(900 A.D.)		900 A.D.
Plains Woodland		PLAINS WOODLAND COMPLEXES	
	(500 B.C.)		500 B.C.
Foraging	FORAGING COMPLEXES		
	(6000 B.C.)		6000 B.C.
Paleo-Indian	EARLY HUNTING COMPLEXES		

by the cultures which have been designated in the Plains as the Foraging complexes or the Plains Archaic Tradition (Willey, 1966, pp. 313–317). Most of the Foraging Period sites investigated to date have been located in the Northwestern Plains, although there are indications that the Central Plains and Middle Missouri subareas were on the peripheries of the range of the Forager groups.

A number of variations on the basic pattern seem to be distinguishable on the basis of the occurrence of projectile points such as the McKean, Duncan, and Hanna types. However, the various manifestations of the Foraging complex show a basic similarity to each other. Associated faunal remains are modern species. They have a proportionately small representation of big game animals such as bison and elk, and a high ratio of smaller forms such as deer, antelope, rabbits, and birds. The incidence of grinding slabs and mullers increases significantly over that in the Plano sites. Many Foraging sites also yield considerable quantities of heat-fractured rock which may well be a by-product of roasting vegetable foods. These contrasts with the Paleo-Indian assemblages indicate a major change in the economic orientation, characterized by a shift from a primary reliance on big game hunting to a hunting and gathering pattern like that of the older Desert cultures. Artifacts from Foraging sites are often crude, and little remains of the fine workmanship found on most of the projectile points and knives of the earlier period.

These facts combine to suggest a borderline economy. While a few sites such as Signal Butte (Strong, 1935) indicate a fair number of big game animals in limited parts of the area, the game supply seems to have been seriously depleted throughout most of the Northern Plains, This may well be a result of a period of hot-dry climatic conditions lasting from approximately 6000 to 3000 B.C.

The Foraging Period itself is dated from roughly 6000 B.C. to sometime after 500 B.C., but the basic Foraging cultures lasted down to historic times in the Northwestern Plains. Some of the Foraging people almost certainly developed into the horse tribes of the 18th century. In terms of the area as a whole, however, the Foraging cultures were greatly overshadowed by developments farther to the east during the Woodland and Plains Village periods.

PLAINS WOODLAND PERIOD

The Plains Woodland Period may possibly have begun as early as 500 B.C., but the great majority of the available dates fall after the beginning of the Christian era.

The Plains Woodland complexes, which are the culture climax for this epoch, were closely related to the Woodland cultures of eastern United States. The main geographic center includes the Middle Missouri and the Central Plains, although Woodland sites also occur much farther west. The complexes include a group of Hopewellian sites near Kansas City; the materials assigned to the Sterns Creek, Valley, and Loseke Creek foci of the Central Plains; a considerable number of Woodland sites along the Middle Missouri; and the Keith Focus of western Kansas and Nebraska and eastern Colorado.

The majority of the known sites are in or adjacent to the smaller stream valleys, and the culture itself seems to have been strongly oriented toward the exploitation of the wooded bottom lands which reproduced in miniature the forest environment of the East. Evidence of corn growing is extremely rare in sites upstream from the Kansas City area, but it seems likely that many of the Woodland peoples depended partly on cultivated crops. Associated animal bones demonstrate that hunting was important. Some bison were taken, but there is a relatively heavier representation of deer and small woodland species, especially in the Central Plains sites. The Woodland peoples were responsible for the introduction of pottery making into the Plains, and the Plains Woodland trait list also includes a wide variety of artifacts of stone, bone, and shell. Occasional shells of Pacific Coast and Gulf Coast origin indicate far-reaching trade relations.

The Plains Woodland groups also practiced elaborate rituals in connection with the disposal of the dead. The most striking evidence for this consists of mounds erected over multiple or, occasionally, individual burials. These are found in considerable numbers in the Middle Missouri subarea and in eastern Nebraska and Kansas. Multiple secondary burials in ossuaries are also common in the Central Plains.

PLAINS VILLAGE PERIOD

The Plains Village Period spans the era from roughly A.D. 900 to 1780. This was the time when the Plains Village pattern, which has already been characterized, was the dominant one in the Northern Plains. Like the preceding Plains Woodland complexes, the Plains Village cultures seem to have derived from farther east. Their geographic center lay in the Middle Missouri and Central Plains subareas, although there were minor extensions into the Northwestern Plains. Subdivisions within the basic village complex and their interaction are discussed in detail in Part II of this report.

EQUESTRIAN PERIOD

The Equestrian Period includes the time when the Northern Plains culture climax shifted westward again to the historic mounted bison hunters of the Northwestern Plains. The wealth of available historical evidence actually makes it harder to assign beginning and ending dates to this period than to the earlier ones, where centuries or even millenniums can be added or subtracted with a certain casualness. The year A.D. 1720 seems a reasonable one for the beginning of the florescence of the horse culture in the Northwestern Plains. The inception of the Equestrian Period should be placed at least 60 years later in the Middle Missouri subarea. Up to 1780 the Plains villagers continued to be a dominant enclave there; after the smallpox epidemic of 1780–82 these peoples were so reduced in number and their culture so disorganized that they took second place to the Dakota and other horse tribes. The situation was similar in the Central Plains, and the beginning of the Equestrian Period is placed at 1780 there also. It is even more difficult to assign a specific ending date to the period. I have arbitrarily chosen 1876, the year of the Sioux War and the treaties with the Arapaho, Northern Cheyenne, and Sioux.

The dominant culture of the Equestrian Period is so well known from ethnological sources that it seems unnecessary to recapitulate it here.

Categorization of the various Plains village complexes requires a more detailed nomenclature. Here I have followed Willey and Phillips as modified by Lehmer and Caldwell, but with some further modifications. The basic archeological units are *component*, *subphase*, and *phase*, as defined by Willey and Phillips (1962, pp. 21–24). Willey and Phillips added two "integrative units," *horizon* and *tradition*. Willey later organized his synthesis in terms of units which he called "major cultural traditions" (1966, pp. 4–5). One of them is the Plains Village Tradition, which corresponds to what had earlier been designated as the Plains Village Pattern (Lehmer, 1954b, pp. 139–140; Wedel, 1961, p. 168). This basic complex has major subdivisions which must be recognized in any satisfactory taxonomic scheme. The concepts and the terminology of Central Plains, Middle Missouri, and Coalescent Traditions are now so firmly embedded in the literature that I have continued to use them here. It should be clearly understood, however, that these traditions are of a lesser order of magnitude than Willey's major cultural traditions.

In adapting the Willey and Phillips system to the Northern Plains, Caldwell and I redefined horizons as temporal divisions which crosscut traditions, with the implication that horizons were sequent cultural stages. While such divisions can certainly be recognized within the village cultures of the Middle Missouri subarea, they are less apparent in other subareas. Richard S. Krause has argued that divisions of this order of magnitude within the Central Plains Tradition appear to be roughly contemporaneous regional variations of the basic Central Plains configuration rather than sequent stages (*in* Wood, 1969, pp. 94–96). This situation seems also to hold, at least in part, for what were formerly called the Initial and Extended Horizons of the Middle Missouri Tradition.

Under these circumstances, I am substituting a new category, *variant*, for the Lehmer and Caldwell concept of horizon. A variant may be defined as *a unique and reasonably uniform expression of a cultural tradition which has a greater order of magnitude than a phase, and which is distinguished from other variants of the same tradition by its geographic distribution, age, and/or cultural content.*

To sum up: the classificatory system used here for the Plains villages recognizes three traditions—Central Plains, Middle Missouri, and Coalescent. The Central Plains Tradition is mainly outside the scope of this

Table 2.—Cultural traditions and variants in the Middle Missouri subarea

Major Cultural Tradition (Pattern)	Tradition	Variant	Dates
Plains Village	Coalescent	Disorganized	1780–1862
		Post-Contact	1675–1780
		Extended	1550–1675
		Initial	1400–1550
	Middle Missouri	Terminal	1550–1675
		Extended	1100–1550
		Initial	900–1400

report and no attempt will be made to deal with its subdivisions. Variants are recognized for the Middle Missouri Tradition and the Coalescent Tradition in the Middle Missouri subarea. The names proposed earlier for the horizons are retained for the variants in order to minimize confusion in terminology (table 2).

Analysis of the data from the operations of the salvage program in the Middle Missouri is far from complete. Much of the definition of taxonomic units at the level of phase and subphase remains to be done. It is possible, however, to assign the great majority of the known village components to a variant of one of the cultural traditions. These assignments have been made on the basis of geographic distribution, age, and such traits as settlement pattern, fortification systems, basic house type, certain pottery characteristics, and the presence or absence of some diagnostic artifact types.

MIDDLE MISSOURI ARCHEOLOGY 1902–69

The 22 years between the inception of the salvage program and the writing of this report witnessed an explosive growth in archeological research in the Middle Missouri subarea. Each one of the dozens of excavated sites contributed something to the picture, and major excavations at key spots filled in blank sections of the canvas (fig. 23). While some details are still locked up in unstudied materials and the few surviving unexcavated sites, the data now available represent an enormous increase in our knowledge of the past. But in order to evaluate the results of the salvage work properly, they must be considered against the background of earlier investigations.

MIDDLE MISSOURI ARCHEOLOGY BEFORE 1946

When salvage archeology began in the Middle Missouri, only parts of the subarea were known archeologically. A few pioneer investigations had provided some indications of the cultural complexes and the archeolgical content of sites in one or the other of the Dakotas.

Archeological investigations in North Dakota began just after the turn of the century. The first serious effort of which I am aware consisted of mapping the more prominent village sites in the Missouri Valley near Bismarck. Most of this work was done by E. R. Steinbrueck and A. B. Stout between 1902 and 1909. Some of their maps have been published by Bowers (1965); others are preserved in the files of the State Historical Society of North Dakota in Bismarck. Despite some inaccuracies in detail, these maps are an invaluable record of village plans and various features, many of which were later obliterated.

An even more remarkable pioneering effort in North Dakota was the work of two Harvard undergraduates, George F. Will and Herbert J. Spinden. In the summer of 1905, Will and Spinden and two classmates carried on excavations at the Double Ditch Site (32BL8), north of Bismarck, under the paternal sponsorship of Roland B. Dixon and Frederic W. Putnam. The results of their work were published the following year

FIGURE 23   Rising waters surround the excavated Red Horse Hawk Site.

along with extensive notes on Mandan ethnography culled from historical sources (Will and Spinden, 1906). They recognized the fact that the Mandan had lived in a group of villages near the mouth of the Heart River during the first half of the 18th century, and had later moved upstream to the vicinity of the Knife River after smallpox had wiped out a large part of the population and left them easy victims of Sioux raids.

George Will continued to be active in North Dakota archeology, and Herbert Spinden rejoined him to do survey work for short periods in 1911 and 1919 (Will, 1924, pp. 291–292). Will's report of 1924 is mainly a catalog of sites in the Missouri Valley in North Dakota, but it also represents an advance in the interpretation of the data gathered:

An impression gradually grew up that there were two rather distinct types of sites in the region, distinct enough in fact so that nearly every site could be referred readily to one or the other group. The center for one type seems to be below the Heart River, with the Huff site as perhaps the best representative. The second type is found at and above the mouth of the Heart River altogether, although the lower sites seem to overlap. A basis of racial difference seems hardly practicable as sites of both types can, with little question, be attributed to the Mandan. A reasonable conclusion therefore seems to be that the two types must represent a difference in time and culture between two periods of occupation by the same tribe.

(Will, 1924, p. 341)

A short paper by O. G. Libby (1908) containing detailed information on village plans asserted that it is possible to distinguish between Mandan and Hidatsa sites on the basis of the presence of plazas in the former.

Charles De Land's (1906) report on the Arikara—a blend of archeological and historical facts, traditions, and fantasies—is mainly a historical curiosity today, but it does represent one of the earliest attempts to deal with South Dakota archeology.

In 1923, M. W. Stirling, of the U.S. National Museum, conducted excavations at several burial sites along the Missouri River near Mobridge, in north-central South Dakota (Stirling, 1924; Hrdlička, 1927; Wedel, 1955). W. H. Over was active in the State during the 1920's and 1930's, often assisted by Elmer E. Meleen. Unfortunately, little of their work found its way into print, and the two most important papers (Meleen, 1938; Over and Meleen, 1941) dealt with materials to the east of the Missouri Valley. Mention should also be made of David Bushnell's studies (1922, 1927) which, like Will and Spiden's monograph, tapped ethnohistorical resources pertaining to the region.

The earliest reports on work in the Middle Missouri subarea were largely factual, and showed little concern with synthesizing the available data. This situation changed considerably during the 1930's. William Duncan Strong excavated in the vicinity of Mobridge in 1932 and at several sites in North and South Dakota in 1938. He also sponsored an excavation party, directed by Albert C. Spaulding, which worked in South Dakota in 1939. Strong's summary (1940) is a landmark in the growth of the understanding of Middle Missouri archeology. He recognized three periods or stages—Historic, Protohistoric, and Prehistoric. Prehistoric materials in the Missouri Valley were equated with the Upper Republican culture in Nebraska. This was done on the basis of Spaulding's work at the Arzberger Site (39HU6) near Pierre. Protohistoric and historic sites in the valley were identified with the Arikara, Mandan, Hidatsa, and Cheyenne.

In 1944 George Will and Thad C. Hecker coauthored a monograph which included a synthesis of the archeology of the Missouri Valley in North Dakota. Surveys and limited excavations carried on over a number of years indicated that the early North Dakota villages had a distinctive house type—a long-rectangular lodge. These structures contrasted sharply with both the squarish Upper Republican houses found in the Central Plains and the circular earthlodges of the historic village tribes. Using pottery and architecture as diagnostic traits, Will and Hecker set up a sequence of three stages for North Dakota village culture: Archaic Mandan, Middle Mandan, and Late Heart River.

Alfred W. Bowers presented still another synthesis of Middle Missouri archeology in his doctoral dissertation submitted at the University of Chicago in 1948. The dissertation, based both on archeological fieldwork which Bowers had done for the Logan Museum of Beloit College from 1929 through 1931 and on his ethnological studies among the Mandan and Hidatsa, has never been published and hence has had a limited effect on colleagues working in this subarea.

Thus, when work began under the salvage program, there was at least a skeleton outline of the archeology of the Middle Missouri. The complexes which dated from the period of direct and indirect contact were better known than the earlier ones. Strong's essay suggested that the late complexes were partly rooted in an Upper Republican-like ancestral form represented at the Arzberger Site. Will and Hecker's Mandan sequence, in contrast, derived from a less familiar base which was distinguished in part by the long-rectangular house form.

SALVAGE ARCHEOLOGY 1946–53

The first fieldwork conducted in the Missouri Valley in South and North Dakota under the Inter-Agency Archeological Salvage Program consisted of surveys and limited excavations in Fort Randall, Oahe, and Garrison Reservoirs. By 1950 enough data had been collected to permit the planning of an excavation program, and funds were available for intensive work. Major site investigations were begun that year by both the River Basin Surveys and cooperating institutions. But in 1953 the Federal appropriations for salvage archeology were seriously reduced. The River Basin Surveys staff was drastically cut and not much fieldwork was done. Excavations made up to that time, however, provided the basis for building a fairly coherent reconstruction of some of the more important developments in the history of the native cultures of the Middle Missouri.

Work in 1950–53 centered in four separate sections of the valley—the lower end of Garrison Reservoir, Oahe Reservoir between the dam site and the Cheyenne River, the section of Fort Randall Reservoir near the mouth of the White River, and the lowermost reaches of Fort Randall Reservoir.

Pertinent data for the major sites excavated are presented in appendix 1.

Nearly all of the sites dug in Garrison were late, and they were concentrated in the downstream end of the reservoir. Their importance lay in their contribution to the knowledge of the final stages of the native culture sequence. Rock Village (32ME15) and Night Walker's Butte (32ML39) both date after A.D. 1780. Star Village (32ME16) is documented as having been occupied by the Arikara in 1862. Site 32ML2 consisted of two trading posts, Fort Berthold I and II, and Like-a-Fishhook Village, established in 1845 by remnants of the Hidatsa and Mandan, who were later joined by the few remaining Arikara.

The only early manifestations encountered in Garrison Reservoir were a preceramic component at Rock Village, which yielded no diagnostic artifacts, and Grandmother's Lodge (32ME59), a Middle Missouri Tradition house located far upstream from other sites representing this complex.

The Scalp Creek (39GR1), Ellis Creek (39GR2), Oldham (39CH7), and Hitchell (39CH45) sites are all situated below the section included here in the Middle Missouri subarea. The work at these sites (Hurt, 1952; Johnston, 1967a) demonstrated the presence of Woodland components and also of village components which seem to have drawn their traits from the Central Plains and the Middle Missouri, and from northwestern Iowa and southwestern Minnesota.

The section of the Missouri Valley between the mouths of the White and Cheyenne Rivers, the heart of the Big Bend and Bad-Cheyenne regions, was a critical zone of culture growth and culture contact. The work done there through 1953 served to establish the regional cultural sequence, and it yielded a considerable amount of detailed information on most of the complexes involved.

Excavations at the multicomponent Dodd Site (39ST30) provided information on the culture sequence which was invaluable before radiocarbon dates were available. Work in the early components at Dodd and at the Swanson Site (39BR16) also produced the first information on the Initial Variant of the Middle Missouri Tradition in the Missouri Valley. This complex had previously been known only from sites in southeastern

South Dakota (Meleen, 1938; Over and Meleen, 1941). The Dinehart (39LM33) and King (39LM55) sites were also related to Initial Middle Missouri.

Hurt's excavations at the Thomas Riggs Site (39HU1) and Wedel's first season at the Cheyenne River Site (39ST1) greatly expanded knowledge of the Extended Middle Missouri Variant. The Talking Crow Site (39BF3) had an early component which represented Initial Coalescent (C. S. Smith, 1951; 1960). The Black Widow Site (39ST3), a poorly defined component at the Cheyenne River Site, and the Spain Site (39LM301) were the only representatives of Extended Coalescent excavated under the salvage program through 1953.

Post-Contact Coalescent components topped the list in terms of numbers excavated. They included the Oacoma sites (39LM26 and 39LM27) and the late Talking Crow component near Chamberlain. A second cluster of excavated sites lay between Pierre and the Cheyenne River. It was made up of the late component at the Cheyenne River Site, Buffalo Pasture (39ST6), late Dodd, Phillips Ranch (39ST14), Indian Creek Site (39ST15), and Spotted Bear (39HU26). These early salvage excavations, together with the pre-salvage investigations, made it possible to recognize a number of archeological complexes in the Pierre region and to arrange them in chronological order (Lehmer, 1952a). They correspond to what are now known as the Initial and Extended Middle Missouri and the Extended and Post-Contact Coalescent Variants. The Initial Coalescent complex was also recognized, although there was some question as to just how it related to the cultural continuum which extended from Initial Middle Missouri to Post-Contact Coalescent.

Extra-regional relationships of some variants were apparent. Hurt (1951a, pp. 15–16) identified the village component at the Swanson Site (Initial Middle Missouri Variant) with the Over Focus, which had been set up on the basis of Over and Meleen's earlier work in southeastern South Dakota. He also recognized a relationship between the Thomas Riggs Site (Extended Middle Missouri Variant) and the early village components in the Bismarck region which had been described by Will and Hecker, and lumped them into what he called "the Northern Complex" (Hurt, 1953, pp. 60–61). Similarities between the Arzberger Site (Initial Coalescent Variant) and the Central Plains Tradition had already been pointed out by Strong (1940, pp. 382–383). It was also possible to see similarities between Post-Contact Coalescent components in the Middle Missouri and Central Plains (Lehmer, 1954b, pp. 147–154).

SALVAGE ARCHEOLOGY 1954–69

Salvage work was revived, on a large scale, in 1954. From that year through 1966 the River Basin Surveys and cooperating institutions put out as many as 10 excavation parties a season in the mainstem reservoirs. One or two small parties were also assigned to making test excavations and intensive surveys during 1954, 1956–59, and 1964. In 1967 and 1968 the scale of the program was reduced to two or three parties each year.

In addition to the work under the salvage program, the University of Kansas conducted excavations in the burial grounds of the Leavenworth (39CO9) and Larson (39WW2) sites under the direction of William M. Bass, III. These investigations were financed by grants from the National Science Foundation and the National Geographic Society.

By the end of the 1968 field season, major salvage excavations had been made in 96 sites in the Missouri Valley in the Dakotas. The sites worked after 1953 added enormous amounts of new data which are summarized, region by region, below. The regional sequences are shown in figure 24.

GARRISON REGION

The only major salvage excavations after 1953 in this region were an additional season's work at Like-a-Fishhook Village and Fort Berthold, and one season at a fur trading establishment, Kipp's Post (32MN1).

The work demonstrates that the Garrison region was mainly an area of hunting camps and other temporary settlements, with very few permanent villages. The regional sequence appears to include an occupation

FIGURE 24 Regional cultural sequences in the Middle Missouri subarea.

38

GARRISON	KNIFE-HEART	CANNONBALL	GRAND-MOREAU	BAD-CHEYENNE	BIG BEND
Disorganized Coalescent	Disorganized Coalescent		Disorganized Coalescent		
	Post-Contact Coalescent		Post-Contact Coalescent	Post-Contact Coalescent	Post-Contact Coalescent
	Terminal Middle Missouri	Terminal Middle Missouri	Extended Coalescent	Extended Coalescent	Extended Coalescent
Extended Middle Missouri			Extended Middle Missouri	Extended Middle Missouri	Initial Coalescent
				/////////	
	Extended Middle Missouri	Extended Middle Missouri		Extended Middle Missouri	Modified Initial Middle Missouri
				Initial Middle Missouri	Initial Middle Missouri
Woodland	Woodland	Woodland	Woodland	Woodland	Woodland
(Foraging)					Foraging

during the Foraging Period which is evidenced by the preceramic component at Rock Village. A very small part of the sample from Night Walker's Butte suggests a Woodland component there. Grandmother's Lodge (32ME59) represents a very limited occupation by Middle Missouri Tradition peoples. The rest of the Indian sites where major excavations were made are villages dating after the smallpox epidemic of 1837. As manifestations of the Disorganized Coalescent Variant, they indicate that the lower Garrison region was a refuge area for the village tribes during the last years of their long history.

KNIFE-HEART REGION

Since this region does not lie within a reservoir area, it was not investigated under the salvage program. Available data from other sources, however, provide some information on the regional sequence. Test excavations made in 1969 at a butte-top site some 7 miles north of Stanton demonstrated the presence of a Woodland occupation area there. There seems to have been a progression from Extended Middle Missouri to a very intensive Post-Contact Coalescent occupation during the 18th century. Almost all the villages in the southern half of the region were abandoned shortly after 1780. The Disorganized Coalescent sites are concentrated in the northern section and include the Mandan and Hidatsa villages in the vicinity of the Knife River, which were occupied during the first half of the 19th century.

CANNONBALL REGION

Some preliminary investigations had been made in the Cannonball region in 1947 by Gordon W. Hewes (1949a), under the auspices of the State Historical Society of North Dakota and the University of North Dakota. Intensive investigations were carried on there between 1955 and 1960, and again from 1964 through 1968. The work at the Boundary Mounds (32SI1) and limited investigations of the Schmidt (32MO20), Tschida (32MO207), and Alkire (32SI200) mounds defined the earliest element in the regional sequence (Neuman, 1961a; Henning, 1965). This was an expression of the Plains Woodland complex. The mounds were low, dome-shaped earthen structures covering pits which often contained several human skeletons.

After 1933 a number of early village sites were worked in the Cannonball region. Havens (32EM1), Fire Heart Creek (32SI2), Paul Brave (32SI4), Ben Standing Soldier (32SI7), and South Cannonball (32SI19) can all be classified as Extended Middle Missouri. They were unfortified, apparently represent a fair span of time, and show some range in size and settlement pattern. Fire Heart Creek and Paul Brave consist of small scattered clusters of houses. Havens, Ben Standing Soldier, and South Cannonball are fairly large and compact villages.

Three large villages enclosed within fortification ditches were also excavated—Tony Glas (32EM3), Shermer (32EM10), and Huff (32MO11). These sites may be classified as Terminal Middle Missouri and appear to represent the final stage of the village tribes' intensive occupation of the region.

The Demery Site (39CO1) and the upper component at Fire Heart Creek revealed two minority elements in the archeological picture. Demery, located in the southernmost part of the region, proved to be the northernmost Extended Coalescent village discovered to date. The same complex also appears to have been present in a prehistoric component at the Fort Manuel trading post (39CO5), downstream from Demery. The late component at Fire Heart Creek was a hunting camp which was apparently occupied by the Arikara around A.D. 1800. It is almost the only Post-Contact Coalescent manifestation known in this region.

Salvage work in the Cannonball region amplified and confirmed the culture sequence which had been suggested earlier by Will and Hecker (1944). The earliest element known to date is a Woodland occupation represented by a number of burial mounds and occasional finds of Woodland potsherds. This was followed by a very intensive occupation representing the Extended Middle Missouri Variant, which was in turn succeeded by a Terminal Middle Missouri occupation. Extended Coalescent and Post-Contact Coalescent sites are almost completely absent from the Cannonball region.

GRAND-MOREAU REGION
The first major excavations in the Grand-Moreau region were undertaken in 1954. Salvage work went on there through the summer of 1966, with 1956, 1962, and 1963 being particularly active seasons. This region, and especially the section around the mouth of the Grand River, was extremely rich in archeological remains.

Excavations were made in a number of Woodland sites. Swift Bird (39DW233),

Grover Hand (39DW240), and Arpan (39DW252) were burial mounds. Stelzer (39DW242) appears to have been one of the very few Woodland habitation areas discovered in the Middle Missouri Valley. Sites representing the Middle Missouri Tradition are rare in the Grand-Moreau region. Calamity Village (39DW231) is the only one which has been intensively investigated to date. It proved to have a well-developed fortification system, but the houses appear to have been much less substantial than those found elsewhere in similar contexts.

Investigations have shown that there was a very intensive Extended Coalescent occupation of the region and that the sites of this variant fall into several groups. Potts (39CO19), Molstad (39DW234), and Hosterman (39PO7) were villages with a small and compact fortified nucleus of houses surrounded by a fairly extensive scattering of other houses. The evidence suggests that these and comparable sites are early and may well represent the first movement of Extended Coalescent peoples into the region.

Work at the Spiry Site (39WW10) and in the early component at Swan Creek (39WW7) produced no clear evidence of fortification. These components may represent a middle-period Extended Coalescent occupation. The Payne Site (39WW302), with an enclosing palisade but no fortification ditch, seems to have been anomalous.

The Davis Site (39CO14), which was worked intensively, and the unexcavated site (39WW8) across the Missouri from Molstad represent still another settlement pattern within the Extended Coalescent Variant. Here the majority of the houses making up the village were crowded together within an area bounded by a fortification ditch which formed an irregular rectangle. While the Davis collections have not yet been studied in detail, a preliminary examination suggests that the complex was transitional between the Extended and Post-Contact Coalescent Variants.

The Post-Contact Coalescent sites in the Grand-Moreau region were also investigated intensively. The late component at the Swan Creek Site provided the data for the first recognition of what was called the Le Beau Focus (Hurt, 1957). Subsequent work indicated that the late component at Anton Rygh (39CA4) and the Bamble

(39CA6), Red Horse Hawk (39CO34), Four Bear (39DW2), Rosa (39PO3), Larson (39WW2), and Spiry-Eklo (39WW3) sites all represent essentially the same cultural configuration as the late Swan Creek component. The work at these sites served to isolate and characterize one expression of the Post-Contact Variant of the Coalescent Tradition. Two seasons' digging at the Leavenworth Site (39CO9), a historically documented Arikara village occupied from about 1797 to 1832, provided considerable data on a Disorganized Coalescent occupation.

The cultural sequence in the Grand-Moreau region contrasts sharply with those established farther upstream. The earliest Grand-Moreau element was again a Woodland occupation. The region has only minimal indications of an Extended Middle Missouri occupation, and no Terminal Middle Missouri sites are known. The first major occupation by the village tribes is represented by a large number of Extended Coalescent sites which show considerable variation in form and content. This was followed by an intensive Post-Contact Coalescent occupation prior to the closing years of the 18th century. The historic Arikara towns seem to have been the last occupation of the region by the village tribes. They were finally abandoned in 1832.

BAD-CHEYENNE REGION

The Bad-Cheyenne region (lower Oahe Reservoir) embraces part of the area of the most complex archeological developments in the Missouri Valley. The cultural sequence in this region was established before 1953, and it was confirmed and amplified by later work. Two sites, Fay Tolton (39ST11) and Breeden (39ST16), provided a considerable amount of additional data on the Initial Middle Missouri Variant there. Further excavations at the Cheyenne River Site (39ST1) provided more information on an Extended Middle Missouri component, and a site (39ST203) on Black Widow Ridge included another Extended Middle Missouri component. There are no indications of a Terminal Middle Missouri occupation in this region.

Initial Coalescent components have never been clearly demonstrated to exist in the Bad-Cheyenne region, although Brown (1966a) felt that tests at the Gillette Site

(39ST23) suggested the possibility of an Initial Coalescent occupation. Definition of the Extended Coalescent occupation rests largely on work done since 1953. The No Heart Creek Site (39AR2) was the only single-component Extended Coalescent village intensively excavated in the Bad-Cheyenne region. Extended Coalescent components were found during other major excavations on the right bank at Cheyenne River Site, Black Widow (39ST3), H. P. Thomas (39ST12), Breeden (39ST16), Fort Bennett (39ST26), and Leavitt (39ST215). On the left bank, part of the occupation of the Sully Site (39SL4), the largest village found in the Middle Missouri subarea, appears to date from Extended Coalescent times. Testing and surface collecting at a considerable number of other sites on both banks clearly demonstrated a heavy Extended Coalescent occupation of the Bad-Cheyenne region.

Work done before 1953 had provided a substantial amount of information on the Post-Contact Coalescent occupation of the region. This was supplemented by later excavations at Cheyenne River Site, H. P. Thomas, Black Widow Ridge (39ST25, 39ST50, and 39ST203), and Sully. In addition to the work in the late villages, extensive excavations were made in the cemetery at the Sully Site. These provided a wealth of data on burial customs, together with material for anthropometric studies. Additional materials of this sort were supplied by the excavation of the cemetery component at the Leavitt Site.

The Bad-Cheyenne regional sequence is somewhat more complex than those described previously. Following a suggested Woodland occupation, there was a fairly heavy occupation by Initial Middle Missouri groups that seems to have been entirely confined to the right bank of the Missouri. A considerable number of Extended Middle Missouri sites have been found, and the available dates suggest that they may have overlapped somewhat in the closing years of the Initial Middle Missouri occupance. There is no definite evidence of an Initial Coalescent occupation of the Bad-Cheyenne region, but many Extended Coalescent sites are present. The large number of Post-Contact Coalescent villages which have been recorded demonstrates a heavy occupation during the early years of the contact period. Historical sources show that the village tribes abandoned the region to the Dakota in 1795.

BIG BEND REGION

Excavations at the Medicine Crow Site (39BF2) revealed a Foraging Period component. Similar materials were found underlying earthen mounds at four sites nearby—Truman (39BF224), Sitting Crow (39BF225), Side Hill (39BF233), and McBride (39BF270) (Neuman, 1964a). This concentration of preceramic materials in a limited area in the immediate vicinity of the Big Bend Dam is the best evidence to date for occupation of the Middle Missouri during the Foraging Period.

Investigations also showed that there was a very heavy concentration of Woodland components in the Big Bend region. The mound sites mentioned above were originally excavated for Woodland materials. Neuman (1964a, p. 174) reported some 90 mounds between the lower end of the Big Bend and the mouth of Crow Creek, a distance of a little over 16 miles. A Woodland component was also recognized at the La Roche Village (39ST9) (Hoffman, 1968, p. 77).

During the period from 1954 through 1967 large-scale excavations were made in a number of Initial Middle Missouri villages in the Big Bend region. They included work at the Jiggs Thompson (39LM208), Langdeau (39LM209), and Pretty Head (39LM232) sites, and in the Initial Middle Missouri components at Crow Creek (39BF4 and 39BF11), Pretty Bull (39BF12), Stricker (39LM1), and Cattle Oiler (39ST224). With the exception of La Roche, where there was a Woodland component, these Initial Middle Missouri manifestations were the earliest ones found in the multicomponent sites. As a result, they provided information on relative chronology as well as a great deal of data regarding the Initial Middle Missouri Variant.

Four sites located near each other on the right bank of the Missouri in the upper part of the Big Bend region were excavated from 1964 through 1966. Sommers (39ST56), Ketchen (39ST223), the late component at Cattle Oiler (39ST224), and Durkin (39ST238) all seem to represent a late and previously unrecognized modification of the basic Initial Middle Missouri complex. Results of the work at these sites threw a considerable amount of new light on the cultural developments in the region.

The Hickey Brothers Site (39LM4) proved to be the only known example of an Extended Middle Missouri village in the Big Bend region. Investigations there showed that, as at Calamity Village, the settlement had an elaborate fortification system, but that the houses were flimsy structures rather than the substantial ones usually found in such sites.

An Initial Coalescent occupation of the Big Bend region had been demonstrated by Spaulding's work at Arzberger in 1939 and by the work at Talking Crow (39BF3) early in the salvage operations. Excavations at the Crow Creek (39BF4 and 39BF11) and Medicine Creek (39LM2) sites isolated Initial Coalescent components which overlay Initial Middle Missouri occupations. Black Partizan (39LM218) proved to have an Initial Coalescent component underlying one representing the Extended Coalescent Variant.

The Clarkstown Site (39LM47) was the only single-component Extended Coalescent village excavated in the Big Bend region after 1953. Stricker, Black Partizan, and La Roche had Extended Coalescent components overlying the remains of earlier occupations. The single-component Two Teeth Site (39BF204) proved to be late on the basis of the presence of a few items of European origin. The cultural complex at that site seems to have been more or less transitional between Extended and Post-Contact Coalescent Variants.

Only four major excavations were made in Post-Contact Coalescent components in the Big Bend region after 1953. Fort George Village (39ST17) and the late component at Chapelle Creek (39HU60) showed trait complexes which closely resembled those of the late Post-Contact Coalescent sites on the right bank in the Bad-Cheyenne region. The late components at the Medicine Crow and Pretty Bull sites were more like the late component at Talking Crow.

The Big Bend country has the longest and most complex regional sequence found in the Middle Missouri Valley. There is evidence of an occupation during the For-

FIGURE 25 Building foundation at Fort Sully.

FIGURE 26 Remains of a building at Fort Sully.

FIGURE 27 *Foundation and porch of commanding officer's quarters at Fort Stevenson.*

FIGURE 28 *Brick floor of commissary storehouse at Fort Stevenson.*

aging Period, and the region was heavily settled by Plains Woodland groups. Initial Middle Missouri sites occur in large numbers along both banks of the Missouri, but indications of an Extended Middle Missouri occupation are minimal. This is the one region in the Middle Missouri Valley where an Initial Coalescent occupation is well established. Extended Coalescent and Post-Contact Coalescent sites also occur in considerable numbers. There are indications that the latter may have been abandoned about the middle of the 19th century.

OVERVIEW

The work in the Dakotas under the Inter-Agency Archeological Salvage Program began in 1946 when Waldo Wedel, then Director of the Missouri Basin Project, made a brief reconnaissance along the mainstem. During the years which followed, the survey teams and excavation parties of the River Basin Surveys and cooperating institutions unlocked the region's archeology. Reconnaissance and excavation techniques were adapted to the varied archeological situations and to the exigencies of the salvage program. The inherent complexities of the individual sites were coped with one by one. As more and more data were collected, the typological categories of houses and artifacts were recognized, and descriptive terminologies were gradually evolved for them. Functional interpretations of many of the artifacts were made, largely on the basis of the enthnographic literature. It also became possible to recognize a number of cultural complexes, and to reconstruct their histories and patterns of interaction.

Numerous forts and trading posts representing the earlier European occupation of the Missouri Valley were also investigated under the salvage program (figs. 25–28). Major excavations of this sort are listed in appendix 1.

The essential aim of the salvage program was the collection and preservation of information and specimens which would have been irretrievably lost had the work not been done. These salvaged data provide the main basis for the reconstruction of the culture history of the Middle Missouri subarea as a whole which is presented in Part II.

PART TWO   MIDDLE MISSOURI ARCHEOLOGY AS OF 1969

MIDDLE MISSOURI ENVIRONMENT

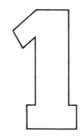

The Northern Plains have been aptly characterized as a land of sun, wind, and grass. The climate and native vegetation, along with the physiography and native animal life, provided the environmental stage on which the drama of the human occupation of the area was played out.

PHYSIOGRAPHY

Today the valley of the Missouri River in the Dakotas is an almost continuous chain of manmade lakes. But before those lakes were created, the valley was a world of its own, providing a habitat which contrasted sharply with the surrounding uplands of the Missouri Plateau.

The Missouri Valley is a comparatively recent geological phenomenon. Like so many physiographic features of the Dakotas, it is a product of the Pleistocene glaciations. Before the advance southward of the great continental ice sheets, the drainage pattern of the Northern Plains was vastly different from the present one. A continental divide appears to have run from northeastern to southwestern South Dakota, crossing the present Missouri Valley between the Bad and the Cheyenne rivers. There is evidence that the streams from the Cheyenne north flowed to the northeast, emptying into Hudson Bay via the Red River of the North. From the Bad southward, the drainage led to the southeast, running diagonally across Iowa and eventually into the Mississippi (Flint, 1957, fig. 10–2). The advance of the Pleistocene glaciers blocked both the northern and southern drainage systems. The result was the development of a large glacier-margin river which persists today as the middle reaches of the Missouri. Flint (1957, pp. 168–169) points out several anomalous features of the Middle Missouri Valley, including the fact that it flows at right angles to the regional slope and that it has no major tributaries running into it from the east. He then goes on to reconstruct the process of valley formation which took place.

One of the ice sheets before the last one, which invaded South Dakota from the northeast, reached its maximum extent along the site of the present Missouri River and blocked the former east-flowing streams. . . . Each ponded stream rose and spilled over the lowest part of the interfluve that

FIGURE 29   The Missouri River trench.

separated it from the major valley southeast of it. Most of the low points occurred between the heads of opposed minor tributaries. The overflow rapidly trenched the bedrock, an erodible shale. In effect the water flowed up one former tributary and down another opposed tributary. When the glacier margin retreated it failed to uncover the former east-draining valleys until after the temporary trenches across the interfluves had become so deep that the diverted waters were unable to return to their former routes. The floors of the ancient valleys, filled with drift, were left standing somewhat above the profile of the new river, the present Missouri.

The date of the diversion is not known with certainty, but it is probable that this event occurred at the Illinoian maximum.
(Flint, 1957, p. 169)

This geologic history is clearly reflected in the character of the valley itself (fig. 29). During Recent times the Missouri River flowed through the Dakotas at the bottom of a deeply incised trench which the river had carved for itself. The depths below the adjoining high ground range from minimums of slightly over 200 feet to maximums in excess of 400 feet. Widths at the bottom of the trench showed a greater range, varying from as little as one-half mile to as much as 4 miles. Most of the narrow sections of the valley undoubtedly represent interfluve cutting initiated during the glacial maximum; most of the wider sections appear to be examples of more mature channels developed by preglacial streams.

The variable nature of the valley is also reflected in the physiographic zones within the trench itself. The trench margins are steep and heavily eroded. These "breaks" are an ever-present feature except where they are interrupted by the valleys of the major tributaries (fig. 30). In a few sections the breaks drop down almost to the borders of the river channel, with nothing in the way of intervening terraces or flood plain. Generally, however, there are two other physiographic zones within the Missouri trench.

One consists of a discontinuous system of fairly level terraces. They blend into the lower borders of the breaks at the sides of the valley, and are commonly mantled there with outwash from the breaks. The edges of

FIGURE 30 *The Missouri River "breaks."*

FIGURE 31 *The Missouri River terrace and flood plain.*

FIGURE 32 *The Missouri River flood plain.*

the terraces toward the river drop sharply down to the flood plain or channel (fig. 31). I am not aware of any detailed study of the terrace system throughout this whole section of the valley. While it is possible that the terraces reflect an episode in the geologic history of the present valley, it also seems likely that many of them are the old floors of different preglacial valleys which are now incorporated into the valley of the Missouri.

The final physiographic unit within the trench includes the flood plain, usually lying 10 to 30 feet below the adjoining terrace edge, and the islands and sandbars in the channel itself (fig. 32). The flood plain zone is sometimes as much as 2 miles wide, and there is considerable evidence that the river channel has repeatedly meandered back and forth across it.

There are striking differences between the sections of the Missouri Plateau to the north and east of the Missouri trench and those to the south and west. These seem to have been of considerable importance in dictating land utilization outside the valley by the Indian populations.

The sections of the Missouri Plateau to the east and north of the river clearly exhibit marks of the Pleistocene glaciations. They have little vertical relief because of abrading of the hills and the filling of the old valleys with glacial drift. The area is often described as "level," but it is certainly not flat. Instead it is generally a region of very low rounded hills surrounding shallow basins which usually contain ponds, swamps, or meadows. Major relief features are very sizable moraines. The eastern margin of the plateau drops down along a sloping escarpment into the Central Lowlands.

The country west and south of the Missouri shows only limited effects of glaciation. The land surface, especially near the Missouri trench, is rugged and uneven with some large badland areas. The topography reflects intensive erosion by the large tributary drainage systems on this side of the Missouri.

The patterns of modern land use differ significantly from one side of the river to the other. These differences, closely related to the topographic characteristics of the glaciated and unglaciated sections of the Missouri Plateau, are reflected in the population distribution along the river. Today there is a significantly heavier concentration on the left (nominally the east) bank. The large towns along the river—Bismarck, Mobridge, Pierre, and Chamberlain—are all east of the Missouri. The only one west of the river is Bismarck's twin city, Mandan. The population densities of the North and South Dakota counties bordering the Missouri upstream from the White River are also significant. The 10 counties to the south and west have an average density of only 3.8 people per square mile. The population density in the 13 counties across the Missouri is more than twice as great, averaging 8.3 individuals per square mile.

While there are no comparable figures for the archeological manifestations, available data indicate that the prewhite population distribution was the reverse of the one found today. Over 60 percent of the nearly 400 village components which can be assigned to a cultural variant are located on the right bank of the Missouri.

The modern population figures reflect differences in land utilization. The part of the Dakotas east of the Missouri is preponderantly well-populated farm country— a land of tractors, combines, plowed fields, and bib-overalls. The area of the two States west of the Missouri is preponderantly thinly populated ranch country and Indian reservations—a land of horse trailers, grazing lands, and blue denims.

The economy of the prewhite villages duplicated, in a very general way, the modern economies of the area. The native subsistence pattern depended partly on horticulture and partly on hunting big game (especially bison), which was broadly comparable to modern ranching. The native agricultural activities seem to have been restricted to the bottom lands along the Missouri. The best hunting ranges lay west of the river, which would have favored the right bank for village localities. Another factor which favored the right bank, at least during historic times, was the existence of a pattern of intertribal trade which involved the village tribes, the mounted bison hunters of the Northwestern Plains, and the migratory groups who lived east and north of the river. Right-bank villages were better situated for intercepting trading parties coming in from the west, and there is a possibility that an equivalent factor operated in prehistoric times.

CLIMATE

The climate is not likely to make a resort area of the Middle Missouri. Summers have day after day of crushing heat, winters have weeks of subzero cold. Snowstorms and summer rainstorms are often violent. The wind seems to blow most of the time, parching the land in the summer and driving the powdery snows in blinding flurries. But anyone who can survive these hardships finds that there is good weather too. There are spring days when the whole countryside comes gloriously alive after its winter hibernation. There are crisp weeks in autumn when the air provides a sparkling clarity to the colors and contours of the land. In winter there are days of brilliant sunshine which give a cameo quality to the black and white snowscapes. The native village farmers must likewise have seen and felt these daily and seasonal changes in the weather, but it was the year-to-year exigencies of the climate which regulated their lives.

Moisture is a matter of supreme importance to agricultural peoples. Most precipitation in this area is in the form of rainfall, and most of this comes in the spring and summer, with May, June, and July being the wettest months. Total average annual precipitation decreases upstream along the Missouri, from over 18 inches near the mouth of the White River to just over 15 inches in the vicinity of the mouth of the Knife River and a scant 14 inches at the mouth of the Yellowstone River.

Averages do not tell the whole story of precipitation, however. The annual rainfall varies enormously from year to year throughout the Dakotas. For example, the mean annual precipitation for the two States is 17.93 inches. The mean precipitation rose to 23.95 inches in 1915 and dropped to 9.88 inches in 1936. There must have been comparable wet and dry years in the past, and they would certainly have affected the farming and the pasturage for the large game animals in the area.

Length of the growing season is another important factor to a farming population. The average period between the last killing frost in the spring and the first one in autumn is consistently higher within the Missouri trench than on the adjacent portions of the Missouri Plateau. Like the annual rainfall, it decreases upstream from averages of 150 days per year at Chamberlain and 161 at Pierre, S. Dak., to 133 at Washburn and at Williston, N. Dak. This decrease closely parallels the decrease in mean July temperature, which drops from 76.0° F. at Pierre to 69.4° F. at Williston.

The foregoing suggests that the climatic conditions for native agriculture were least favorable in the northern sections of the Middle Missouri Valley. This does not, however, seem to have been the case. Certainly the enormous trash mounds and heavy layers of sheet refuse found in many sites in the Knife-Heart region indicate a greater geographic stability than that of the communities farther downstream. There are also good indications that the northern villages were, on the average, appreciably larger than those in South Dakota. Both facts argue for a more productive agriculture in the north, and it seems likely that this relates to climatic factors.

The key to the situation may lie in the fact that the Knife-Heart region has a more favorable effective precipitation. This is well illustrated by maps showing the ratio of annual precipitation to potential evapotranspiration (cf. Bryson and Wendland, 1967, fig. 77). Most of the Missouri Valley between the White and Cannonball Rivers falls in a zone with values between −25 and −35, whereas the Knife-Heart region lies in the more favorable −20 to −25 zone. The effects seem to be reflected in the more lush vegetation found in the northern area today. Similar conditions appear to have existed at the beginning of the 19th century, since Tabeau (Abel, 1939, p. 69) speaks of tree growth being heavier in the vicinity of the Mandan villages than at the Arikara towns in northern South Dakota.

FLORA AND FAUNA

The native plant and animal populations of the region were of enormous importance to the Middle Missouri village tribes and their predecessors. The vegetation cover can be described briefly in terms of the four physiographic zones which, for the most part, run parallel to the course of the Missouri. The Missouri Plateau on both sides of the trench is short-grass plains. The breaks at the edges of the trench are grassland, with some stunted trees (including hardwoods such as oak) along the many gullies. Below the breaks the terraces are grass covered and almost devoid of trees. Finally, the river flood plain, except for small enclosed tall-grass areas, has a heavy growth of trees—mainly cottonwoods or willows, with a scattering of junipers.

Each of these vegetation zones offered a different resource potential to the native populations. The grasslands of the Missouri Plateau were hunting grounds, especially the sections to the south and west of the river. Some game must also have been taken in the breaks and on the terraces. The terraces were also used for horse pasturage during Post-Contact times. The fact that the terraces were high enough to be above the level of all but the worst floods made them the preferred location for permanent settlements.

The flood plain and the larger islands were vital to the argicultural aspects of the villagers' life. It was here that the fields were laid out and the crops grown (cf., Wilson, 1917, p. 9). The heavy stands of trees furnished shelter and firewood for the winter villages which nestled in the timbered sections of the flood plain. The trees also provided building materials for earth lodges, palisades, and other features of both summer and winter villages.

The Missouri River was itself an important factor in the villagers' environment. I know of no evidence of the historic bull boat from archeological sites, but it seems likely that this ingenious craft has considerable antiquity in the region. Numerous bone fishhooks and occasional fish bones attest to the importance of fish in the diet of the prehistoric as well as the historic groups. It seems reasonable that driftwood salvaged from the river was a major source of firewood in precontact as well as in historic times. It also seems likely that the postcontact practice of recovering drowned buffalo carcasses for use as food is a fairly ancient one.

The grasslands and the timbered flood plains were also important for a host of minority plant species used during historic times. Many of them undoubtedly were also used much earlier. The prairie turnip (*Psoralea esculenta*), chokecherry, and buffalo berry are commonly mentioned in the ethnographic accounts. The list of usable plants is much longer. Gilmore (1919), in one of the pioneer studies of American ethnobotany, inventories well over 150 species with notes on their use by the native populations. While Gilmore was primarily concerned with the Pawnee, Omaha, Ponca, and Teton Dakota, he also includes some notes on the upriver groups. Many of his other remarks can undoubtedly be applied to the village tribes of the Dakotas.

The enormous quantities of animal bone found in the village sites in the Middle Missouri subarea are evidence of the richness and variety of the native fauna and of its importance to the native economy. The large bison herds which occupied the region, especially west of the river, were by far the prime faunal resource. Their importance to the historic Plains tribes as a source of food and hides, bone, and sinew for making artifacts can hardly be overemphasized. The archeological data demonstrate a comparable importance during precontact times since bison often makes up over 90 percent of the total identifiable animal bone found in the excavated villages. Antelope, deer, dog, and elk were next in importance on the basis of bone samples recovered. Other mammals, represented by occasional bones, include badger, beaver, bobcat, coyote, fox, gopher, ground squirrel, porcupine, prairie dog, jackrabbit, cottontail, squirrel, skunk, vole, and wolf.

The Middle Missouri Valley is rich in birdlife, and it is also one of the major flyways for migratory waterfowl. In view of this, bird bone is surprisingly rare in the village sites. Varieties represented include the bittern, crow, eagle, goose, grouse, grackle, hawk, heron, magpie, owl, passenger pigeon, prairie chicken, raven, whistling swan, and whooping crane. Duck bones are extremely rare, although they have been reported from the Huff Site (Wood, 1967, p. 100).

Catfish bones are reported from a fair number of village sites, and garpike remains occur rarely (Lehmer and Jones, 1968, p. 102). Frog and turtle remains are found with some regularity, and various kinds of fresh-water mussel shells have been recovered from almost every excavated village site in the Middle Missouri subarea.

CHRONOLOGY
IN MIDDLE
MISSOURI
ARCHEOLOGY

Assignment of absolute dates to the Middle Missouri archeological complexes is difficult at this time. There are three sources for such dates: written records, tree-ring studies, and radiocarbon determinations. The written records do not reach beyond 1700, and thus cover only the final stages of the region's culture history. Dendrochronology is still in its infancy in the area despite the fact that George Will's investigations in this field were begun more than 30 years ago.

Ward Weakly, in his manuscript report, "Tree-ring Dating and Archaeology in South Dakota," sets forth three local chronologies which he believes can be used to date archeological specimens. One is applicable to the vicinity of the Big Bend of the Missouri, another to a small area around the mouth of Chapelle Creek, and the third to the area of the Little Bend opposite the mouth of the Cheyenne River.

The first chronology "is 332 years in length extending from A.D. 1963 back to A.D. 1631. With the inclusion of archaeologically derived materials, it extends back to A.D. 1531 or a total of 432 years." The Chapelle Creek chronology "is 270 years in length extending from A.D. 1963 back to A.D. 1693. With the addition of archaeologically derived materials, this chronology is 362 years in length extending back to A.D. 1601. On a tentative basis, specimens from other archaeological sites extend the chronology back to A.D. 1288 or a total of 675 years. The latter extension is of such a tentative nature that the portion from A.D. 1601 to A.D. 1288 is not included in the chronology presented here, and the dating in this time range can only be used with caution." The Little Bend chronology is described as "313 years in length extending from A.D. 1959 back to A.D. 1646. With the inclusion of archaeologically derived specimens the Little Bend chronology is 380 years long going back to A.D. 1579. In addition, material from other sites that is tentatively dated pushes this chronology back to A.D. 1288 or 671 years. This latter portion is not included . . . because of its tentative nature" (Weakly, MS., pp. 30, 41, and 45). Thus the three charts are judged to be reliable back to A.D. 1531, 1601, and 1579, respectively; the ranges of the second and third chronologies, back to A.D. 1288, are char-

FIGURE 33 Upper- and lower-level house floors, Cheyenne River Site.

acterized as tentative, and dates falling within those ranges must be used with caution. It should also be noted that an outer ring date of A.D. 1385 was the earliest one established in these charts.

The three regional chronologies were used to obtain tentative dates for 107 wood specimens from archeological contexts. Only three of these dates are regarded as being close to cutting dates. The great majority of the specimens lack the outer rings and there is no way of determining the year in which the trees were cut. The most that can be said for them is that they cannot be younger than the tentative dates assigned to them.

Some radiocarbon dates have been obtained so far from archeological sites in the Middle Missouri, but these also present problems. It is often difficult to assess the significance of a particular radiocarbon date. The practitioners of the esoteric art of carbon-14 dating have repeatedly pointed out the numerous variables which affect their results, and most of them emphasize the fact that no single run can be counted on to reflect the true age of the sample. The situation is readily apparent in the results of dating runs on different samples from three specimens taken from the Cheyenne River Site (39ST1) (fig. 33).

A sample (I–581) from a piece of charcoal from the early component at the site was dated by Isotopes Inc., at A.D. 1175 $\pm$125. Two other samples from the same piece of charcoal were dated at A.D. 920$\pm$60 (SI–12) and 1160$\pm$60 (SI–117) by the Division of Radiation and Organisms of the Smithsonian Institution. In another case, a sample (M–840) from a specimen was dated at A.D. 1300$\pm$200 by the Radiocarbon Laboratory of the University of Michigan. Two other samples (SI–17 and SI–118) from the same specimen were each dated at A.D. 1080$\pm$60 by the Smithsonian laboratory. Two samples from a third specimen were dated at A.D. 1600$\pm$85 (I–582) and 1150$\pm$60 (SI–116). These instances provide concrete examples of the fallibility of a single radiocarbon date.

Other and more general considerations have been raised during the past few years by a number of workers in the field of radiocarbon dating. One has to do with a changed value for the half-life of carbon-14. Al-though published dates continued to be calculated from the traditional half-life base of 5568$\pm$30 years, more recent studies suggest a more accurate value of 5730$\pm$30 years (Stuiver and Suess, 1966, p. 536). This means that the published radiocarbon ages are all roughly 2.9 percent lower than the true radiocarbon ages. This can be corrected by multiplying the published radiocarbon age (before present) by 1.03. The radiocarbon date is then obtained by subtracting the product from the standard A.D. 1950 base.

A more important reservation concerns the amount of carbon-14 present in the atmosphere in the past. This was originally assumed to have been constant. Today there is a growing body of data which seems to indicate that this level has varied from time to time. If this were the case, there would be differences between radiocarbon ages and true ages of samples studied; in extreme cases the differences may be in excess of 100 years. The situation has been presented recently in some detail by Minze Stuiver and Hans E. Suess (1966), together with data on the actual divergences for the last 950 years.

The data given in Stuiver and Suess' Table I were used to plot a detailed version of their chart showing the relationships between conventional radiocarbon years and calendar years. This chart was then used to convert conventional radiocarbon ages and dates to calendar ages and dates for archeological samples from the Middle Missouri. It should be noted that the conversions have a general tendency to raise the dates earlier than A.D. 1225, to make little change in ones between 1225 and 1400, and to lower most of those later than 1400. The converted dates thus tend to compress the time span of the various archeological complexes recognized in the subarea.

Estimated time ranges for the archeological horizons in the Middle Missouri are indicated in figure 34 and are discussed in some detail in following sections of this report.

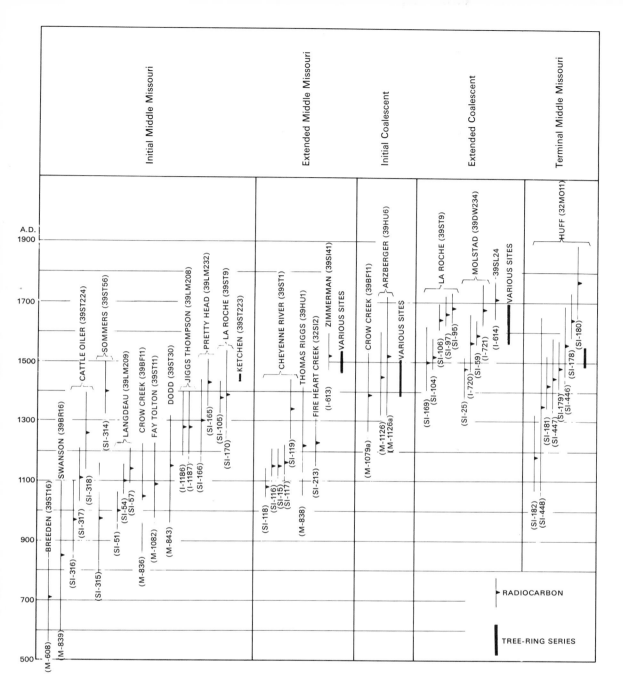

FIGURE 34   Date ranges
for the cultural variants.

PRE-VILLAGE
CULTURES
OF THE
MIDDLE
MISSOURI

Archeological investigations in the Middle Missouri subarea concentrated on sites of relatively late groups who lived in fixed villages and depended mainly on farming and hunting for their subsistence. Some evidence has been found, however, which pertains to earlier peoples on the mainstem.

To the best of my knowledge, a single Plainview point from the deepest excavations at the Medicine Crow Site (fig. 35) is the only indication of an occupation which may date from the Paleo-Indian Period (Neuman, 1964a, p. 180). The apparent absence of Paleo-Indian remains is not too surprising in light of the geological history of the region. During the peaks of the Wisconsin glacial advances, the river seems to have flowed along or near the southwestern margins of the ice sheets. There was a great deal of valley cutting during the final glacial recession, and this would have destroyed whatever evidence there might have been of human occupancy of the Missouri River Valley during early postglacial times.

A number of sites in the vicinity of the Big Bend of the Missouri in South Dakota have yielded McKean and Duncan points and other specimens which indicate an occupation during the Foraging Period (Neuman, 1964a). Reports on these sites have yet to be published. Radiocarbon dates from them range from 2450±250 B.C. to 525±150 B.C. (Missouri Basin Chronology Program, Statement No. 4, Samples I–560 and I–447).

The 1952 excavations at Rock Village (32ME15) in North Dakota encountered a culture-bearing stratum some 4 feet below the base of the midden of the village component at the site. Unfortunately, no diagnostic artifacts were found in this stratum and no radiocarbon dates are available for it (Hartle, MS.). The absence of pottery in the lower level suggests that the early component may date from the Foraging Period.

Sites representing the Plains Woodland Period were fairly common in the Middle Missouri subarea. They include both mounds and habitation areas. The only published data on dwellings are from the Scalp Creek and Ellis Creek (39GR1 and 39GR2) sites (Hurt, 1952, pp. 24–25). Associated artifacts consist of stemmed projectile points, chipped stone drills, crude

FIGURE 35 Excavation of
the preceramic component,
Medicine Crow Site.

percussion-flaked axes, and a variety of skin-dressing tools including the characteristic snubnose scraper of the Plains. Pecked and ground celts, bone awls, discoidal shell beads, and several other artifact types are also present. It is interesting to note that a few scapula hoes have been reported from Woodland components in the Middle Missouri (Hurt, op. cit., pp. 18–19). Several kinds of pottery appear to have been made. Exterior surfaces are characteristically cord roughened or plain, but some simple stamped pieces have been reported (Neuman, 1960a). Rims are generally straight and at least some vessels have conoidal bottoms.

The dome-shaped burial mounds are small in comparison to many of those found farther to the east (fig. 36). Although they may range up to 100 feet in diameter, they are rarely over a few feet high. The mounds usually cover a subterranean pit roofed with logs and containing multiple primary and secondary burials and occasional mortuary offerings (figs. 37 and 113).

There are also a number of linear mounds on the high ground outside the Missouri trench in the vicinity of the mouth of the Knife River. Dome-shaped mounds occur near some of the linear structures. The linear mounds are low, usually not more than a foot above the surrounding prairie. Lengths range from 85 feet to almost 600 feet, widths from 30 feet to 40 feet. In two instances they expand into low circular mounds at the south end, raising the possibility that they may have been effigy figures. The cultural association of these features has not been determined. They might be expected to relate to a Woodland occupation. However, Bowers (MS., p. 131) cites traditional evidence that they were built by the Hidatsa.

While the material culture of the Woodland sites is far less elaborate than that of the later villages, the burial mounds do imply a fairly high development of socio-ceremonial organization. The Woodland people were obviously able to coordinate the work of the individuals involved in mound building, and to provide food for the workers while they were diverted from their own subsistence activities.

It is my impression that the Woodland cultures of the Middle Missouri were some-

what better adapted to the Plains environment than those of the Central Plains. The relatively high proportion of refuse bone of bison and the frequent occurrence of bison skulls and other bones at the base of burial mounds, in presumably ritual context, suggest that the Middle Missouri Woodland people had developed the techniques of hunting bison on the uplands far beyond their contemporaries in the Central Plains, who lived chiefly on the deer and smaller game found in the wooded stream valleys.

Radiocarbon dates from Woodland sites in the Middle Missouri range from 430± 150 B.C. to A.D. 750±90 (Missouri Basin Chronology Program, Statements 3 and 4, 1962, Samples M–1080a and I–448).

FIGURE 37 *Multiple Woodland burial.*

FIGURE 36 *Burial mound at the lip of the Missouri River trench.*

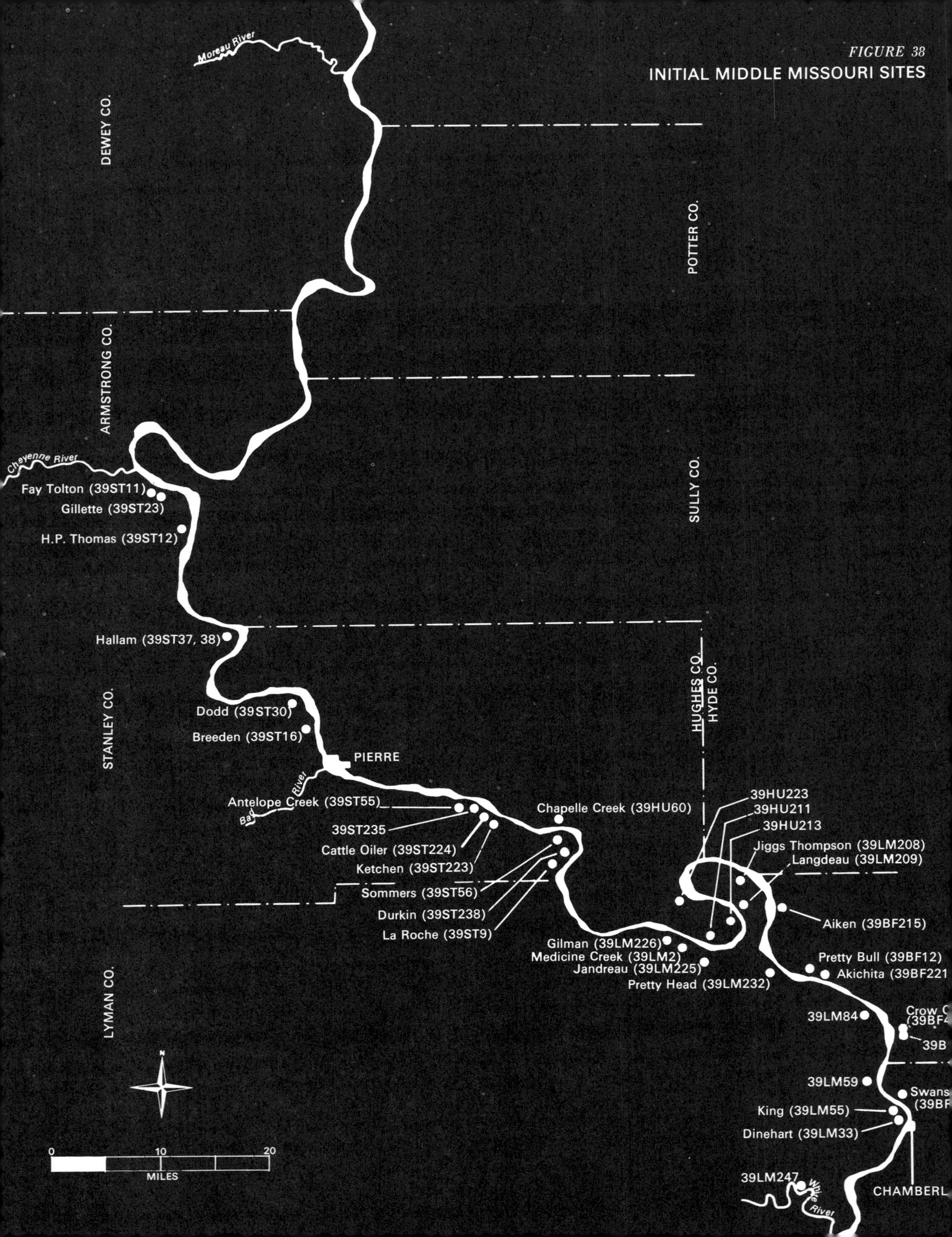

FIGURE 38

INITIAL MIDDLE MISSOURI SITES

DEWEY CO.

POTTER CO.

ARMSTRONG CO.

SULLY CO.

Moreau River

Cheyenne River

Fay Tolton (39ST11)
Gillette (39ST23)
H.P. Thomas (39ST12)

Hallam (39ST37, 38)

HUGHES CO.
HYDE CO.

STANLEY CO.

Dodd (39ST30)
Breeden (39ST16)

PIERRE

Bad River

Antelope Creek (39ST55)
39ST235
Cattle Oiler (39ST224)
Ketchen (39ST223)
Sommers (39ST56)
Durkin (39ST238)
La Roche (39ST9)

Chapelle Creek (39HU60)

39HU223
39HU211
39HU213
Jiggs Thompson (39LM208)
Langdeau (39LM209)

Aiken (39BF215)

Gilman (39LM226)
Medicine Creek (39LM2)
Jandreau (39LM225)
Pretty Head (39LM232)

Pretty Bull (39BF12)
Akichita (39BF221)

LYMAN CO.

39LM84

Crow C
(39BF4

39B

39LM59

Swans
(39BF

King (39LM55)
Dinehart (39LM33)

39LM247

White River

CHAMBERL

N

0   10   20
MILES

EARLY
VILLAGE
CULTURES

The great majority of archeological sites excavated in the Middle Missouri subarea may be identified with the Plains Village Pattern. The Plains villages were geographically intermediate between the transitory camps of the hunting tribes of the Northwestern Plains and the fixed settlements of the Eastern Woodlands peoples. They were also culturally intermediate. Such traits as agriculture, community life in reasonably permanent villages, pottery, and some of the more exotic artifacts were almost certainly derived from the village cultures farther to the east and southeast. The Plains villagers also possessed many of the traits of the migratory western groups, especially a heavy dependence on the hunting of bison and other large game animals, and various implements used in hunting, butchering, and skin dressing.

The Plains Village Pattern was a hybrid which combined diverse traits into a unique configuration in terms of the total assemblage and of the emphasis placed on certain elements. The scapula hoe, for example, occurs in some of the westernmost village complexes of the Eastern Woodlands. It was also used to a limited extent by some of the western Plains tribes. But the large numbers of hoes found in the Plains villages attest to the fact that the trait reached its maximum development in that context.

While similarities link all of the village cultures of the Central Plains and Middle Missouri subareas, distinctive cultural configurations are recognizable within the Plains Village pattern. The most important of these, the Middle Missouri, Central Plains, and Coalescent Traditions, are dealt with in the following pages.

INITIAL AND EXTENDED MIDDLE MISSOURI VARIANTS

The Initial and Extended Middle Missouri Variants were the first village cultures to appear in the Middle Missouri subarea. They were, in effect, the baseline from which later developments proceeded. A substantial number of shared traits indicates that they represent the same cultural configuration, but they are distinguished by differences in geographic distribution, age, and the form of a number of traits. Interactions between the Initial and Extended Middle Missouri groups resulted in changes which are particularly apparent in the late manifestation of the Initial Middle Missouri Variant discussed below as Modified Initial Middle Missouri.

GEOGRAPHIC DISTRIBUTIONS

Sites of the Initial and Extended Middle Missouri Variants show a minimum of overlap. About 25 Initial Middle Missouri village sites are now known, and they are all in the southeastern two-thirds of South Dakota. They lie in a crescent-shaped area which extends westward from the valley of the Big Sioux River near Sioux Falls, across the James River Valley between Mitchell and Twelve Mile Creek, and into the valley of the Missouri River. Initial Middle Missouri sites occur on both sides of the Missouri from Chamberlain to Chapelle Creek, and on up the right bank as far as the Cheyenne River (fig. 38). All the villages within this area appear to be confined to the valleys of the larger streams.

In contrast, the Extended Middle Missouri village sites have a northerly distribution (fig. 39). There are at least 30 of these sites in the Missouri Valley between a point a few miles below the North Dakota-South Dakota line and the mouth of the Knife River, with one northern outlier (Grandmother's Lodge, 32ME59) not far below the mouth of the Little Missouri River. Also, about a dozen Extended Middle Missouri sites are known in the Bad-Cheyenne region, with one southern outlier (Hickey Brothers, 39LM4) well down in the Big Bend. Five sites on the right bank between the mouths of the Grand and the Moreau Rivers are the only Extended Middle Missouri villages in the 90 river miles separating the northern and southern concentrations.

The only area of significant overlap in the distribution of the Initial Middle Missouri and Extended Middle Missouri sites is on the right bank of the Missouri in the Bad-Cheyenne region.

HOUSES

The houses of both variants obviously represent the same architectural tradition (figs. 40 and 41). They were long-rectangular structures in which the length is usually more than 1½ times the width and is sometimes over twice the width. The long axes of the houses are characteristically oriented northeast-southwest, although a few sites have houses oriented from northwest to southeast. House sizes vary considerably. The average seems to have been around 35 by 25 feet, but lengths in excess of 60 feet are known and widths increase more or less proportionately in the larger structures. The size suggests that the larger structures may have had some communal or ceremonial function.

House floors are commonly found to be 3 to 4 feet below present ground surface. The floors are usually the tramped bottom of the pit, although prepared clay floors occur occasionally. Raised benches are sometimes found at one or both ends of the floor, and occasionally around all four sides of a depressed central area. The firepit is a shallow unlined basin in the floor, located near the entrance on the long axis of the house. Cache pits are frequently found in the house floor.

The pit walls were unplastered. The superstructure consisted of a framework of heavy posts. Walls and roof were apparently made of small poles, and I suspect that they were blanketed with earth or sod. The posthole pattern indicates the use of a heavy ridgepole, and parallel stringers on either side of the ridgepole seem to have been used in many of the larger houses. Large numbers of postholes along each of the long walls of the house pit suggest that the side walls were bearing walls which carried most of the roof load.

A few Initial Middle Missouri houses had postholes spaced more or less evenly around all four sides of the floor. It may be that the end walls in this variety of house were also bearing walls. However, this variety of house appears to be an early one, and it may represent a phase in the development of the more common long-rectangular structures before the builders had realized that non-bearing walls do not have to be as solidly constructed as walls which carry a structural load.

The entrance is located at the south end of the house. It consists of a narrow, roofed, and presumably walled antechamber which extends 8 feet or more beyond the end of the house. Earthen steps lead from the entrance into the house pit in Initial Middle Missouri houses and the southern Extended Middle Missouri structures, but this feature

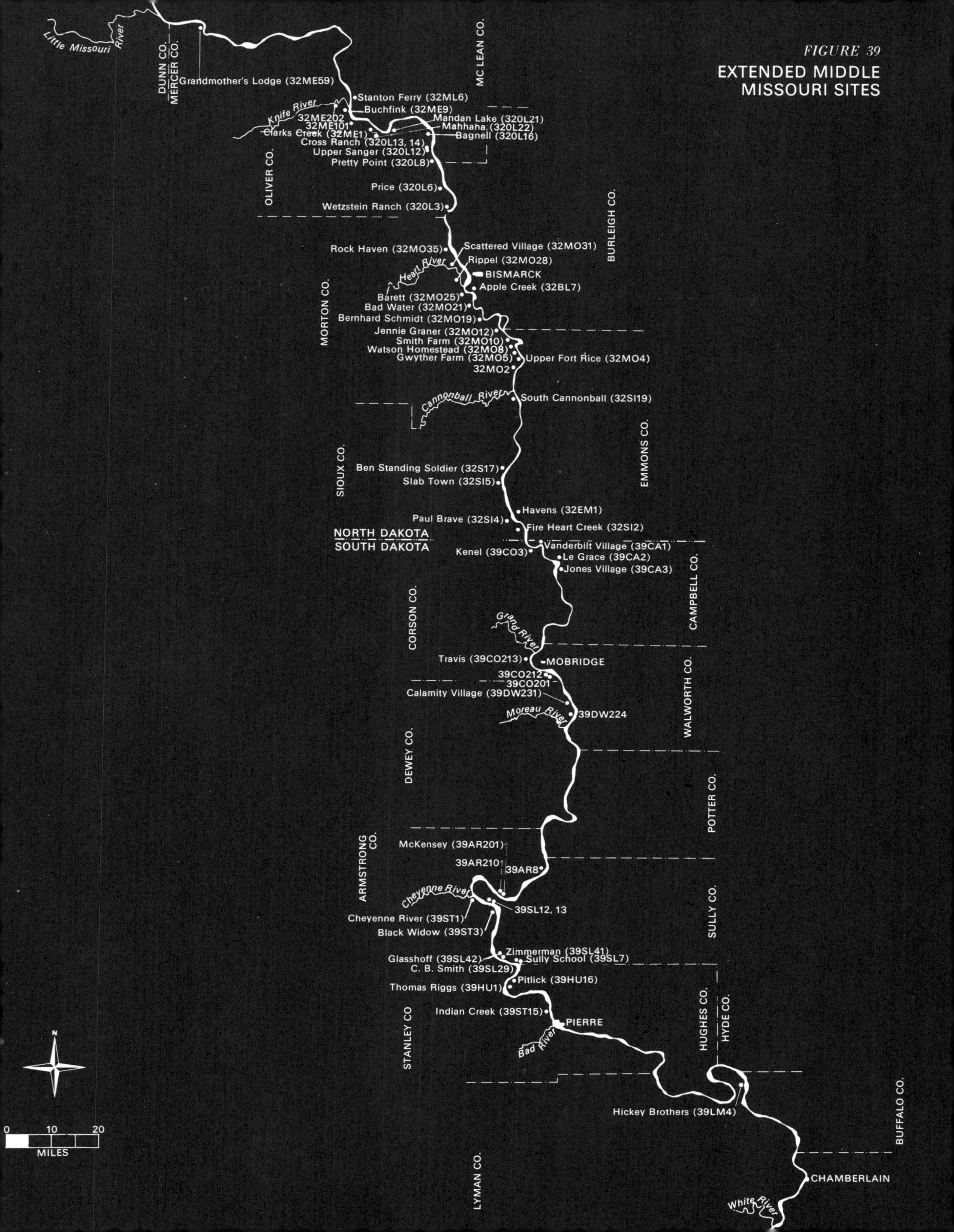

FIGURE 39

EXTENDED MIDDLE
MISSOURI SITES

Little Missouri River

DUNN CO.
MERCER CO.

Grandmother's Lodge (32ME59)

MC LEAN CO.

Stanton Ferry (32ML6)
Buchfink (32ME9)
Knife River
32ME202
32ME101
Clarks Creek (32ME1)
Cross Ranch (32OL13, 14)
Upper Sanger (32OL12)
Pretty Point (32OL8)

Mandan Lake (32OL21)
Mahhaha (32OL22)
Bagnell (32OL16)

OLIVER CO.

Price (32OL6)

Wetzstein Ranch (32OL3)

BURLEIGH CO.

Rock Haven (32MO35)
Heart River
Scattered Village (32MO31)
Rippel (32MO28)
BISMARCK
Apple Creek (32BL7)

MORTON CO.

Barett (32MO25)
Bad Water (32MO21)
Bernhard Schmidt (32MO19)
Jennie Graner (32MO12)
Smith Farm (32MO10)
Watson Homestead (32MO8)
Gwyther Farm (32MO5)
32MO2
Upper Fort Rice (32MO4)

Cannonball River
South Cannonball (32SI19)

EMMONS CO.

SIOUX CO.

Ben Standing Soldier (32S17)
Slab Town (32SI5)

Paul Brave (32SI4)
Havens (32EM1)
Fire Heart Creek (32SI2)

NORTH DAKOTA
SOUTH DAKOTA

Kenel (39CO3)
Vanderbilt Village (39CA1)
Le Grace (39CA2)
Jones Village (39CA3)

CAMPBELL CO.

CORSON CO.

Grand River

Travis (39CO213)
MOBRIDGE
39CO212
39CO201
Calamity Village (39DW231)
Moreau River
39DW224

WALWORTH CO.

DEWEY CO.

POTTER CO.

ARMSTRONG CO.

McKensey (39AR201)
39AR210
39AR8
Cheyenne River
39SL12, 13
Cheyenne River (39ST1)
Black Widow (39ST3)
Glasshoff (39SL42)
C. B. Smith (39SL29)
Zimmerman (39SL41)
Sully School (39SL7)
Pitlick (39HU16)
Thomas Riggs (39HU1)
Indian Creek (39ST15)
PIERRE
Bad River

SULLY CO.

STANLEY CO.

HUGHES CO.
HYDE CO.

Hickey Brothers (39LM4)

BUFFALO CO.

LYMAN CO.

CHAMBERLAIN
White River

N

0   10   20
MILES

FIGURE 40   An excavated
Middle Missouri Tradition
house.

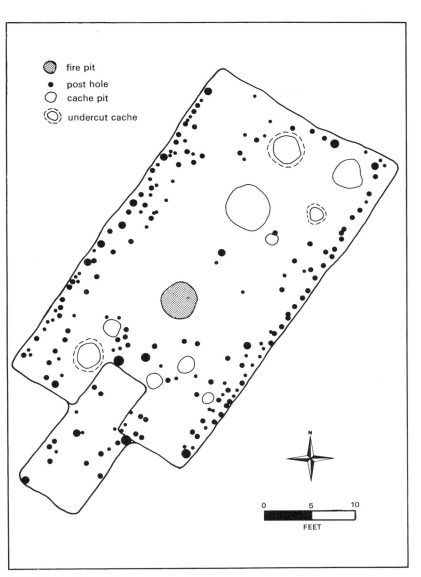

*FIGURE 41 Plan of a
Middle Missouri Tradition
house.*

fire pit
post hole
cache pit
undercut cache

N

0   5   10
FEET

has not been reported for the northern Extended Middle Missouri houses. Where these steps or ramps do occur, they are rectangles of earth left in place when the house pit was dug. They usually measure about 1 foot high by 3 to 4 feet wide, and extend into the pit 5 to 10 feet from the end wall.

CACHE PITS

Cache pits occur in both Initial and Extended Middle Missouri sites. They are found in the house floors and between the houses. Some of the pits are only shallow pockets; others are straight-sided and range from circular to irregular in outline. The most distinctive cache pits are bell-shaped or undercut, with the minimum diameter at or near the mouth and the maximum diameter at the bottom or well down the sides.

MISCELLANEOUS STRUCTURES

Structures, such as drying racks, are indicated by postholes between the houses in both the Initial and Extended Missouri villages. These villages also frequently include shallow irregular pits measuring from 10 to 20 feet across, and usually filled with a heavy concentration of trash. They may have been borrow areas from which earth was removed for various uses.

VILLAGE SIZE AND PLAN

The village size and plan show considerable variation. Initial Middle Missouri and southern Extended Middle Missouri settlements generally consisted of 20 to 30 houses, but many northern Extended Middle Missouri villages contained only a dozen or so.

Most of the houses were arranged side by side in more or less regular rows. Distances between the rows and between the houses vary, apparently as a function of the size of the village and whether or not it was fortified. Houses tend to be closer together in the large fortified communities. Some villages had a central open space or plaza.

FORTIFICATIONS

Fortifications may or may not be present. Initial Middle Missouri villages with fortifications characteristically made use of a combination of the topographic situation and a simple ditch. Sites of this sort were located on points of high ground adjoining the Missouri flood plain between deep tributary channels. The points were protected on three sides by steep natural slopes, and the end away from the river was fortified by a straight ditch dug across the base of the point (fig. 42). Additional protection was often provided by a palisade erected along the inner edge of the ditch.

The northern Extended Middle Missouri villages were not fortified, but most of the southern Extended Middle Missouri villages were protected by ditches and palisades laid out in various ways. A few ran straight across the bases of steep-sided points like those of the Initial Middle Missouri towns. Villages located in the angle between the edge of the Missouri terrace and a deeply incised tributary valley were protected on two sides by steep natural slopes, while the landward sides were defended by an L-shaped ditch, usually backed by a palisade which probably continued all around the village (fig. 42). A fortification ditch of this sort was also present at the Pretty Head Site, which represents the Initial Middle Missouri Variant. Radiocarbon dates from Pretty Head indicate that it was occupied after A.D. 1300, and the fortification plan may well have been copied from the southern Extended Middle Missouri villages. Villages situated at the edge of a straight run of terrace were commonly protected by straight segments of ditch and palisade which formed three sides of a rectangle. Ditches were almost never dug on the side of the village toward the river, presumably because the terrace edge furnished sufficient protection. There may, however, be instances in which a ditch on that side of the village has been eroded away.

The ditches and palisades of many of the southern Extended Middle Missouri sites were studded with rounded bastions. Caldwell has described them as follows:

. . . there are usually strong points in the form of projecting salients or bastions situated at each corner and with others in the intervening sections of wall. Bastions may project outward from the moat line as much as 20 or 30 feet, and in some cases the bastion's surface may be raised by mounded earth or debris presumably to discourage escalade, and to give the defenders the advantage of a plunging fire.

The interval between bastions seems to have been carefully calculated; 50 yards is average, thus providing a reasonable enfilade at all points. . . (Caldwell, 1964, p. 2).

BURIAL CUSTOMS

Burial customs are not known for any of the Middle Missouri variants. Occasional human bones, including calvaria, are found scattered through the village refuse. Rare inhumations found in cache pits or house fill cannot account for all of the deaths that must have occurred during the occupation of the villages. There is a possibility that inhumations were made some distance from the villages, or that platform burial with subsequent scattering of the remains was practiced.

POTTERY

Pottery from all of the sites of the Middle Missouri Tradition has the same basic fabric—a coarse, friable, granular, and rather porous paste, heavily tempered with grit which seems to have been obtained by breaking down chunks of granite from glacial erratics by heating and cooling. The vessels were formed from lumps of clay malleated with paddles. Nearly all the vessels are jars.

Ceramic attributes such as exterior surface finish, rim form, and decoration were much more variable, and they distinguish several pottery traditions within the Middle Missouri Tradition. Cord-roughened bodies, occur in the Initial Middle Missouri sites, as well as in the sites of the Central Plains Tradition. The earliest sites of the Plains Village pattern which contain simple stamped pottery are those of the Extended Middle Missouri Variant. A few cord-roughened sherds have also been found in most of the excavated Extended Middle Missouri villages. Initial Coalescent sites and a group of villages which appear to represent a late manifestation within the Initial Middle Missouri Variant yield both cord-roughened and simple-stamped body sherds. Simple stamping is characteristic of the Terminal Middle Missouri Variant and of sites of the Extended and Post-Contact Coalescent Variants.

The great majority of the vessels from sites of the Middle Missouri Tradition had either flared or S-rims (fig. 43). Flared rims are either straight or curved in cross section, and they project outward above the vessel neck at an angle which is usually between 30° and 60° from the vertical. The flared rims of the Initial Midde Missouri types usually have exterior dimensions from

70

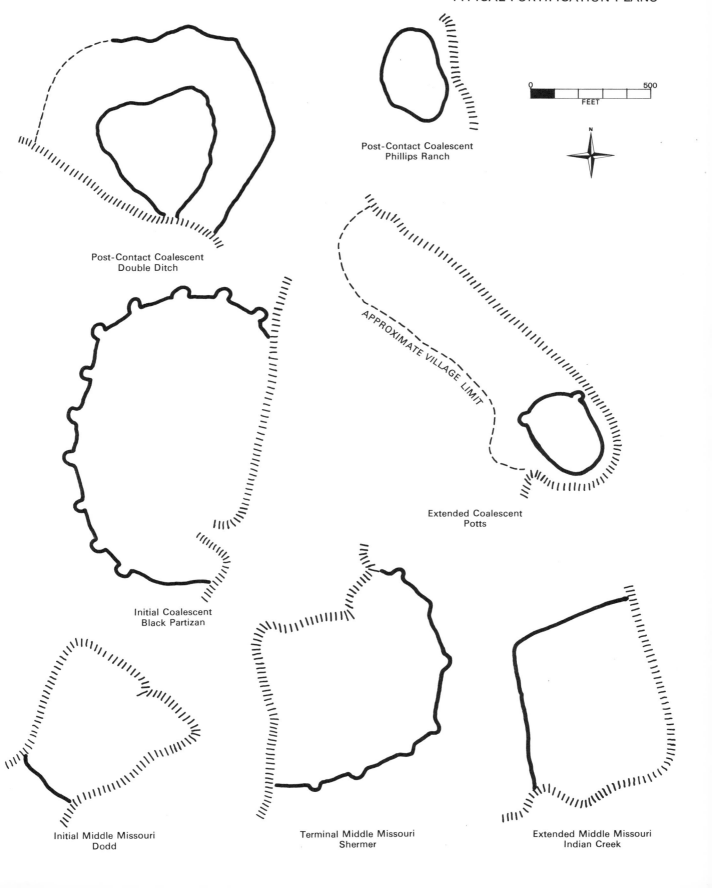

FIGURE 42
TYPICAL FORTIFICATION PLANS

Post-Contact Coalescent
Phillips Ranch

Post-Contact Coalescent
Double Ditch

APPROXIMATE VILLAGE LIMIT

Extended Coalescent
Potts

Initial Coalescent
Black Partizan

Initial Middle Missouri
Dodd

Terminal Middle Missouri
Shermer

Extended Middle Missouri
Indian Creek

0   500
FEET

FIGURE 43

the lip to the juncture of the rim and body which plot out along a bimodal curve. One cluster of measurements lies well above 3.0 cm., while a second cluster lies below that value. The low flared rims occur very rarely in Extended and Terminal Middle Missouri sites. The great majority of the flared rims found in these sites have exterior neck-lip dimensions well in excess of 3.0 cm.

The S-rims from components representing the Middle Missouri Tradition characteristically have inner and outer surfaces which tend to be concentric. The curves of these rims are fairly deep from interior to exterior, and the lower segment of the S usually has a maximum height of less than 2.5 cm. Collared rims are also found in sites of the Middle Missouri Tradition. Their exterior surface tends to be S-shaped, but the form was achieved by thickening the upper segment of the S.

Initial Middle Missouri and early Extended Middle Missouri rims can commonly be distinguished by the form of the lip and the interior surface of the neck. Both S-rims and flared rims from typical Extended Middle Missouri sites have rounded lips, and the interior surface between the rim and the body follows a smooth curve. A majority of the Initial Middle Missouri rims, on the other hand, have flat lips and a sharp angle between the plane of the lip and the inner and outer surfaces of the rim. The transition from the interior of the rim to the inner surface of the vessel body is commonly a sharp angle rather than a smooth curve. It seems likely that these angularities of the Initial Middle Missouri rims resulted from the use of a modeling tool, while the rounded Extended Middle Missouri rims were finger-modeled.

This distinction between Initial and Extended Middle Missouri rims seems to be generally valid for the early Extended Middle Missouri sites. Some angular rims do occur, however, in late Extended Middle Missouri sites and in the Terminal Middle Missouri villages.

Handles are extremely rare on pottery of the Middle Missouri Tradition. When they do occur, they are generally strap or loop handles running from the lip to the shoulder of vessels with flared rims. Triangular to rounded tabs projecting up from the lip in the plane of the flared rims occur with some

10 CM

FIGURE 44

5 CM

frequency, especially on sherds from the Extended and Terminal Middle Missouri sites.

Two decorative treatments were employed. One included incising, punctating, pinching, fingernail indenting, etc. The other involved the use of combinations of single cord impressions or, less frequently, impressions of a rod wrapped with cord or fiber. Both sorts of decoration were applied to the S-rims of all of the variants of the Middle Missouri Tradition. Cord-impressed decoration on flared rims has been found occasionally in Initial Middle Missouri sites, but it is practically nonexistent in sites of the Extended and Terminal Middle Missouri Variants.

STONE, BONE, AND SHELL ARTIFACTS

Artifacts of stone, bone, and shell occur in considerable numbers in the sites representing the Middle Missouri Tradition. Most of them reveal a fairly sophisticated technology. The majority of the artifact types found in these sites also occur in the later villages of the region. This demonstrates a technological continuity throughout the span of the village cultures of the Missouri Valley in the Dakotas, and it also establishes the Middle Missouri Tradition as the complex which provided the technological foundation for the subsequent cultural developments. The following items are the more distinctive artifacts of the Initial and Extended Middle Missouri Variants.

Arrow points (fig. 44) are small, light, generally well-made objects of chipped stone. One basic form has fairly prominent side notches. The outer sections of the notches are characteristically considerably wider than the inner portions. The other basic form is unnotched. Edges of both varieties tend to be convex rather than straight; bases range from concave through straight to convex.

Knives of chipped stone (fig. 45) occur in a variety of forms. The most distinctive ones include long, narrow, well-made pieces which commonly have one convex and one fairly straight edge. These knives were characteristically hafted in slots in the edges of segments of a bison rib or vertebral spine. Leaf-shaped and triangular knives of various sizes occur. The smaller ones were probably hafted. Lanceolate

5 CM

FIGURE 45

pieces, with lengths in excess of 15.0 cm., were usually made from a distinctive bluish or greenish-gray silicified sediment by percussion flaking. One edge is commonly blunted, suggesting that they were used without handles. Other knives were made from thin plates of milky quartz or chalcedony which were broken into rough geometric forms and had one or more pressure-flaked cutting edges. Large side notched and stemmed forms with leaf-shaped or triangular blades also occur in Middle Missouri sites. They were probably knives rather than spear points since one or both edges are commonly blunted.

Drills of chipped stone (fig. 46) are moderately common. A few are pressure-flaked pieces with narrow bits and broad bases. A variant of the broad-based drill has a narrow bit chipped out of a flake, with the unmodified part of the flake serving as a base or handhold. The other basic form has a narrow bit but lacks the expanded base.

Snubnose scrapers (fig. 47) occur in considerable numbers. These artifacts appeared first in the earliest Paleo-Indian complexes, and continued to be used without significant changes in form for well over 10,000 years. They are planoconvex pieces with teardrop or triangular outlines and steep pressure-flaked cutting edges across the broad end. The plane surface is almost invariably a single percussion-flake scar with the bulb of percussion opposite the cutting edge. More than half of the snubnose scrapers found in sites of the Middle Missouri Tradition are fairly small (lengths usually less than 2.5 cm.), with convex surfaces which were carefully shaped by pressure-flaking at right angles to the long axis. Snubnose scrapers with percussion-flaked convex surface occur less frequently and tend to be somewhat larger than the pressure-flaked forms.

Irregular flakes with chipped cutting or scraping edges are common in all village sites of the Middle Missouri subarea.

Stone blanks (fig. 48), percussion-flaked into rough ovals, with lengths which usually fall between 5.0 and 25.0 cm., are found

FIGURE 46

1 CM

FIGURE 47

1 CM

FIGURE 48 Cache of stone blanks.

FIGURE 49

in many sites of the Middle Missouri Tradition. A number of them are often found together in caches. The form and occurrence suggest that they were brought into the villages as raw materials for the manufacture of chipped stone tools. The stone is usually a dark brown cherty chalcedony, known locally as Knife River flint. Most of this material seems to have come from deposits in central North Dakota, and the blanks suggest that it was traded throughout the region by the people of the Middle Missouri Tradition.

Grooved mauls (fig. 49) occur quite commonly in sites of the Middle Missouri Tradition. They were generally waterworn granite cobbles which were modified by pecking a shallow groove for hafting completely or partway around the middle of the stone. The ends, pecked into shape when necessary, usually show signs of battering and spalling. There is a considerable variation in the size and weight of these implements.

5 CM

FIGURE 50

5 CM

Celts (fig. 50), made from diorite or granite, are a common item in the trait inventories of sites of the Middle Missouri Tradition. They are long, approximately cylindrical pieces shaped by pecking, with a wedge-shaped blade at one end and a blunt poll at the other. The greatest width is usually just behind the polished blade, and the size of the body of the celt tends to decrease toward the poll. The poll is often battered in such a way as to suggest that the tool was used as a splitting wedge.

Stone axes are practically nonexistent in Initial and Extended Middle Missouri sites.

5 CM

FIGURE 52

FIGURE 53

|_____|
5 CM

|_____|
5 CM

Arrow shaft smoothers (fig. 51) occur regularly in the Middle Missouri Tradition sites. Made from soft, gritty sandstone, they are relatively narrow with a single longitudinal groove. Lengths tend to exceed 7.5 cm.

Pitted stones (fig. 52), also known as pitted handstones or nut stones, are another artifact type which occurs with fair regularity in Middle Missouri Tradition sites. They are flat, usually about 5.0 cm. thick, and have more or less oval outlines. They rarely show any pronounced wear on the flat faces. Shallow pits, usually 2.5 to 3.0 cm. in diameter, on one or both faces are the distinguishing attribute.

Stone balls (fig. 53), usually made from granite or a hard sandstone, with diameters of about 6.5 cm., are a recurrent trait in Middle Missouri Tradition sites.

Grooved stones (fig. 54), which are more or less cylindrical, about 3.5 cm. in length, with flat or rounded ends and narrow encircling grooves at the center, appear to have been used as weights or sinkers. They occur quite regularly in Extended and Terminal Middle Missouri sites but seem to be rare in the Initial Middle Missouri villages.

Pipes of stone or clay are so rare in sites of the Middle Missouri Tradition and show so much variation in form that they appear to be intrusive from other complexes.

FIGURE 54

FIGURE 51

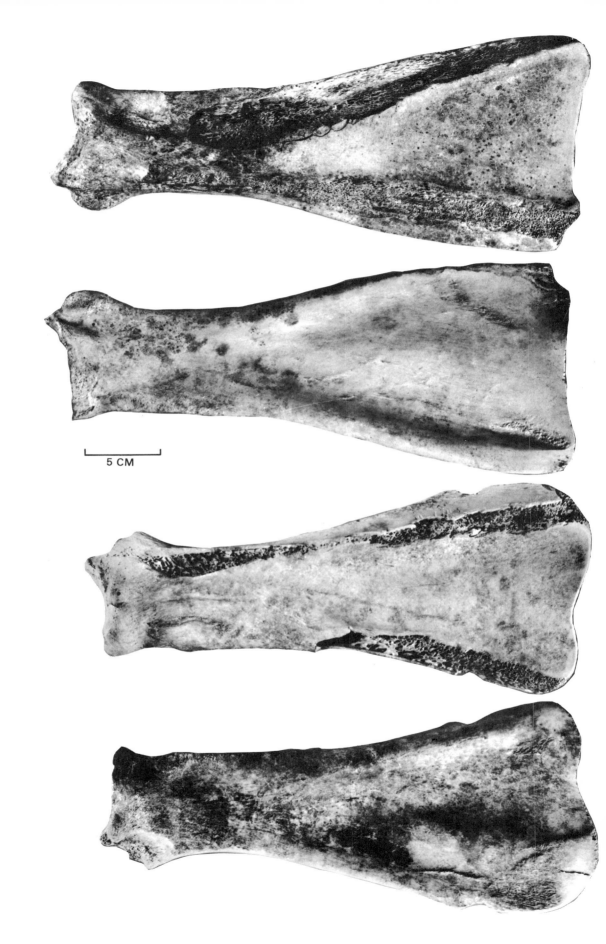

5 CM

FIGURE 55

5 CM

Scapula hoes (fig. 55), made from shoulder blades of bison, or sometimes elk or deer, occur in considerable numbers in Plains village sites. Three styles are common in Middle Missouri Tradition sites. The simplest was made by chopping away the scapular spine and the ridge at the posterior border of the bone, and by removing the scapular cartilage and grinding down the vertebral margin of the bone to a working edge. The second style includes pieces which differ from those in the first group by having a notch in each edge of the blade. These notches presumably served for anchoring a bracing thong which ran diagonally between the bone and a wooden handle set at right angles to it.

The pieces making up the third variety of hoe are quite distinctive. They were made like those in the first two groups, but they have a fairly large hole or socket running longitudinally into the neck of the bone from the glenoid cavity. An intersecting hole was commonly cut through from the medial surface of the neck of the bone. These holes indicate a radically different kind of hafting.

Hoes of the first style occur in sites of all the Middle Missouri variants. Those with notched edges seem to be most common in the northern Extended Middle Missouri and Terminal Middle Missouri sites. The socketed hoes seem to be confined almost exclusively to the southern part of the Middle Missouri subarea.

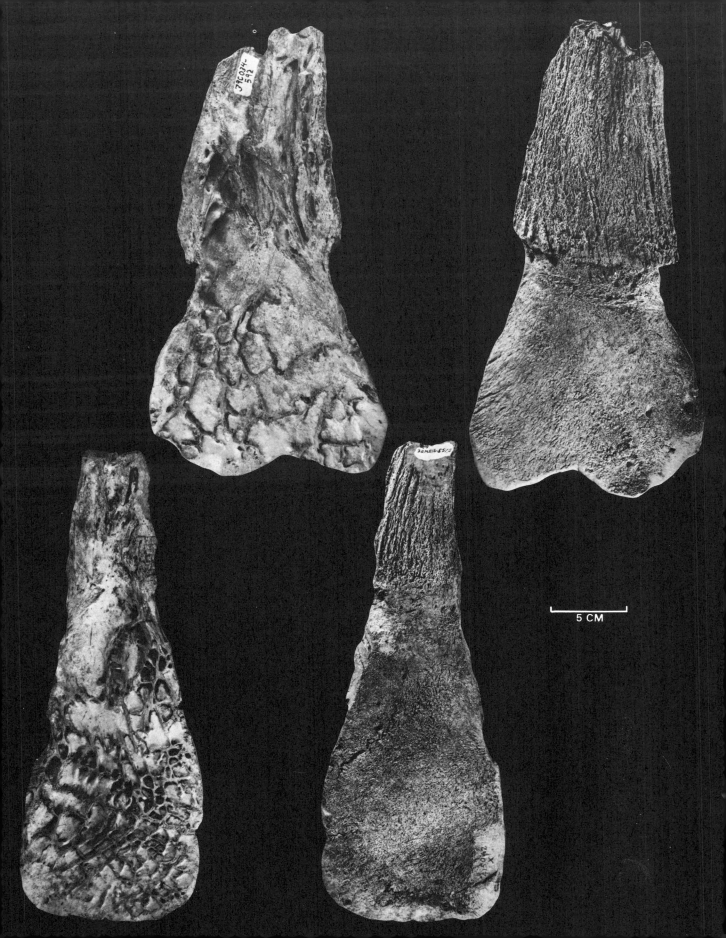

FIGURE 56

Horn scoops (fig. 56), or bison skull hoes, are digging tools made from bison horn cores and the adjacent part of the frontal bone. The horn core appears to have served as a handle. The attached frontal bone was cut into a more or less triangular shape with the apex at the root of the horn. The base of the triangle provided a working edge, which is usually highly polished.

Bone picks (fig. 57) were commonly manufactured from bison radii by cutting away the distal end and part of the shaft. The cut shaft was sharpened to a chisel edge. A longitudinal socket, usually about 2.0 cm. in diameter, was drilled into the proximal end of the bone, presumably for hafting. Some bison ulnae, detached from the radii, show wear at the distal end which may have resulted from using them as picks.

FIGURE 57

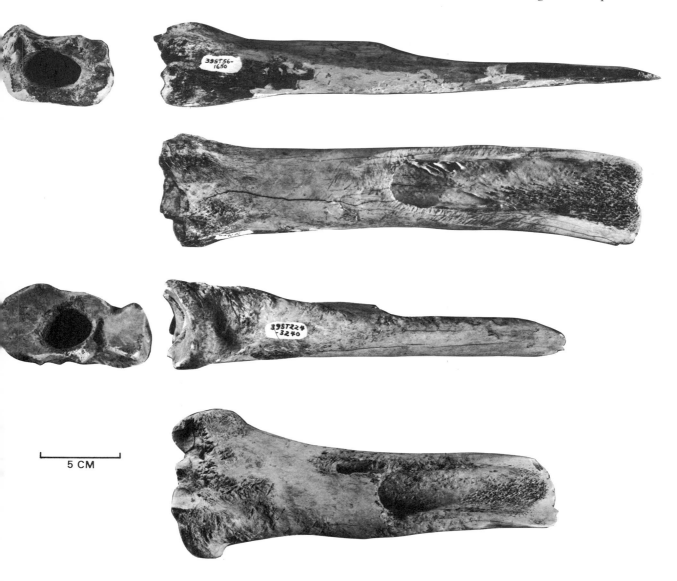

5 CM

Fleshers (fig. 58), made from bison or elk metatarsals, occur in sites of all three variants of the Middle Missouri Tradition. Tools of this type were made by removing the distal end of the bone. In one form, the shaft and the proximal end were split longitudinally and the lower end of the shaft was ground down to a cutting edge. In another form, the head and the upper part of the shaft were unmodified. The lower portion of the shaft was commonly cut on a diagonal to the long axis. In what appears to be an earlier variant, the cut was curved rather than straight, leaving a concave cross section. The cut end was ground down to a chisel edge, which was often notched or serrated. In some cases the tarsals, including the fibular tarsal, were left articulated with the metatarsal. The surrounding hide and tendons were presumably left in place to shrink tightly around the bones and hold them together to provide a handhold.

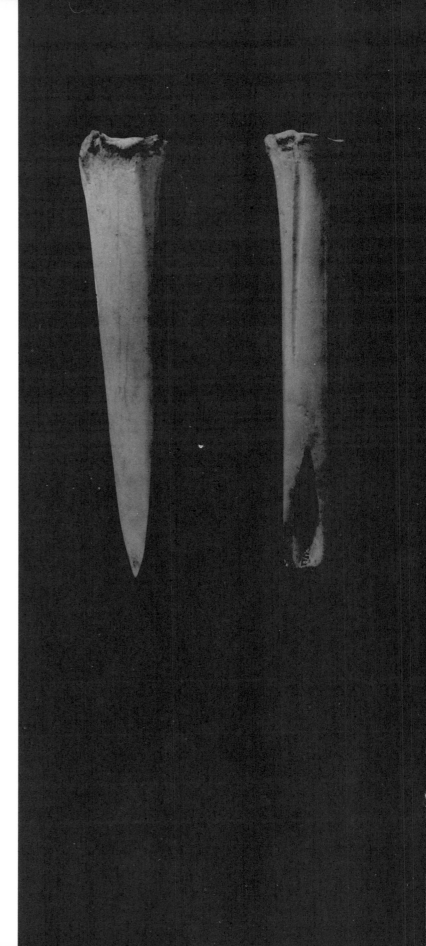

FIGURE 58

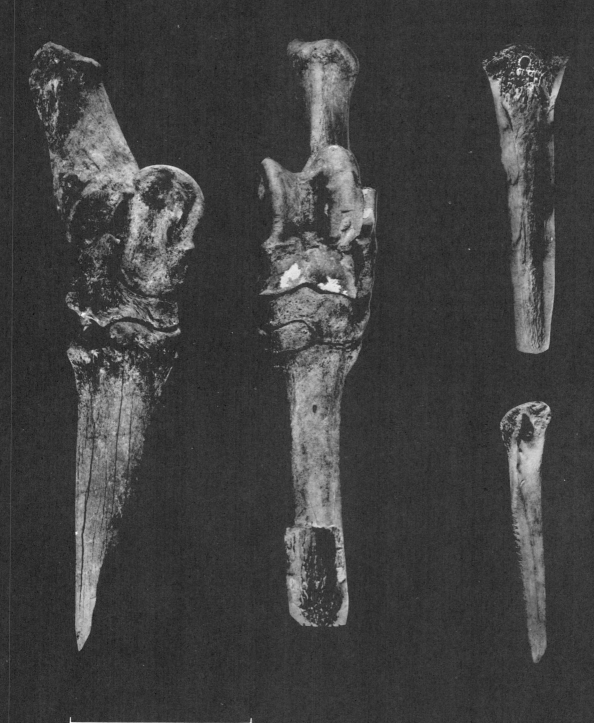

10 CM

Bone spatulas (fig. 59) occur frequently in sites of the Middle Missouri Tradition. They are long flat plates of bone shaped something like the contemporary physician's tongue depressors. Lengths range from less than 8.0 to over 20.0 cm., and widths average about 2.0 cm. Most of the specimens are longitudinally split ribs of large animals, presumably bison. A few appear to have been made by splitting the spinous processes of large vertebrae since they lack the curve of a rib. One of the flat sides is the smooth exterior surface of the bone. The opposite side is cancellous tissue which has been smoothed and partly obliterated on some pieces but has usually been left rough and irregular. Edges of these implements are more or less carefully smoothed. The ends are the most distinctive part of the artifact. Usually rounded, but sometimes tapered to a blunt point, they almost always have a medium to high polish. Microscopic examination commonly shows the occurrence of minute striations apparently developed by use.

The function of these artifacts is not known, but several possibilities have been summarized as follows:

These objects have been called "quill flatteners" in some reports on Plains archeology (Lehmer, 1954b, p. 67). They do show a close resemblance to ethnographic specimens which are identified as having been used in quill working. Wedel (1955, pp. 125–126) has expressed some doubts that this was the only function, and I am inclined to share them. The large number of these objects, in comparison to the other classes of bone artifacts found . . . would certainly seem to indicate some less esoteric use.

Wheeler (1956, pp. 17–20) has suggested that such artifacts may have been used as modeling tools in making pottery. He was unable to find any support for his suggestions in the ethnographic data, but he did demonstrate that tools of this sort could be used to duplicate a variety of elements of form and decoration found in Plains pottery. His argument that the relatively large number of these tools indicates association with a locally important industry also carries conviction.

Ten comparable objects were found by Stirling in the graves which he excavated

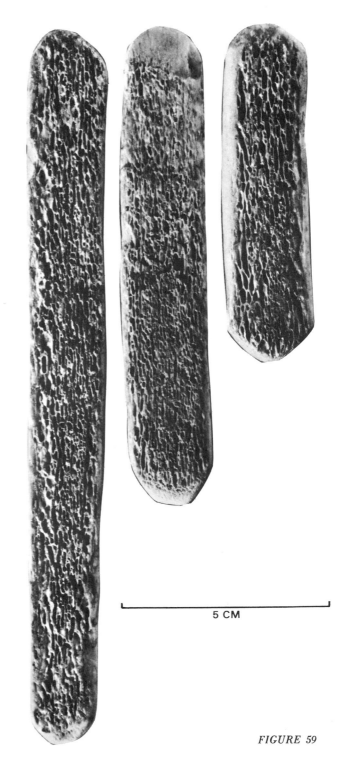

5 CM

FIGURE 59

in the Mobridge area. In no case was more than one found to a grave, and the majority of those found were associated with female skeletons (Wedel, 1955, pp. 125–126). The common association with female skeletons may be an indication that they were model-

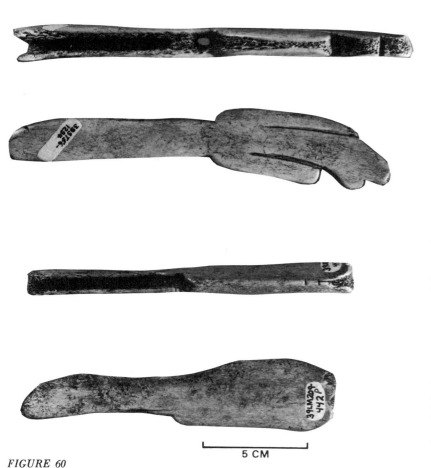

5 CM

FIGURE 60

ing tools which had been buried with the potter who used them.

(Lehmer, 1966, pp. 45–46)

Knife handles (fig. 60), made from segments of large ribs or vertebral spine, are a characteristic trait of the Middle Missouri Tradition. They were made so that stone blades could be set in slots cut into the edge of one end of the bone. Both edges of that slotted end of the bone were frequently cut away to reduce the width. The other end of the handle sometimes carries an elaborately carved decoration.

Bone awls (fig. 61) of various forms occur in Middle Missouri Tradition sites. Awls with broad shafts, rounded butts, and sharply pointed ends were made from the sides of the ventral ends of large ribs. Awls were also commonly made by splitting either the proximal or distal end of deer or antelope metapodials and working the shaft down to a sharp point. A considerable number of bone awls were made from splinters.

Bone and horn punches include blunt-pointed forms similar to the bone awls, and also the tips of antelope horns and the tines of deer antlers.

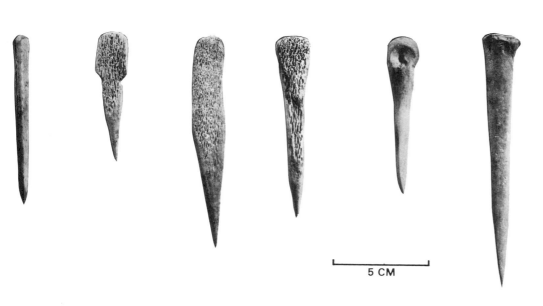

5 CM

FIGURE 61

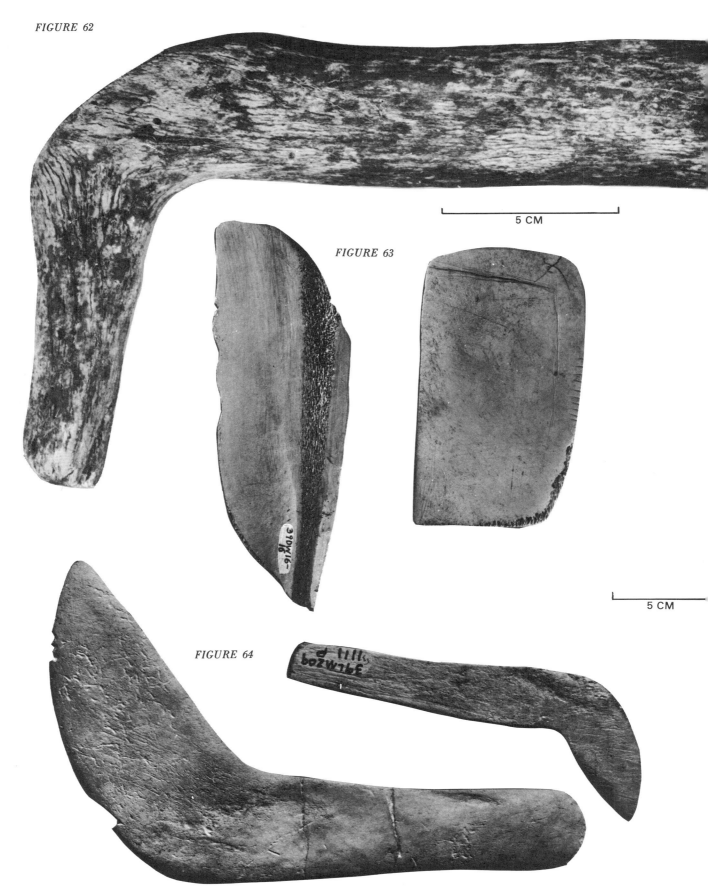

FIGURE 62

FIGURE 63

5 CM

5 CM

FIGURE 64

90

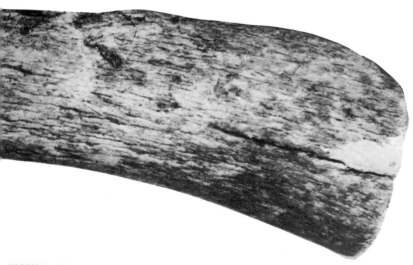

FIGURE 65

Fleshing adzes of elk antler (fig. 62) are another distinctive tool type occurring in all of the variants of the Middle Missouri Tradition. They are L-shaped pieces, with the longer leg consisting of part of the beam of an elk antler and the shorter leg being part of one of the tines. They were almost certainly used for dressing hides like the comparable implements of historic times. The historic pieces had metal blades attached to the short leg of the L. It seems likely that the prehistoric ones were equipped with stone blades, but I know of no instance in which one has been found in place with an antler adz.

Scapula knives (fig. 63) from sites of the Middle Missouri Tradition are roughly rectangular pieces cut from the blades of large scapulae. One edge usually includes either part of the scapular spine or the ridge at the posterior border; the opposite edge was worked down until it was fairly sharp. These pieces are identical with ones in ethnographic collections identified as squash knives (cf. Wilson, 1917, p. 106). The number of tools of this sort which are found suggests, however, that they had more general uses.

Hooked bone knives (fig. 64) were made from the blades of large scapulae. They were cut in a more or less L-shaped form reminiscent of the modern linoleum knife. The end of one leg was rounded and the other was pointed. The edges of the leg with the rounded end were blunt; the inner edge of the leg with the pointed end was fairly sharp. The relative lengths of the two legs vary considerably.

Arrow shaft wrenches (fig. 65) made from the ribs of large animals occur in relatively small numbers in a fair percentage of the sites of the Middle Missouri Tradition. One or more holes are usually drilled from the medial to the lateral surface. The holes have characteristically been worn so they are beveled ovals. The wear surfaces suggest that the arrow shaft was held in the hole at an angle to the long axis of the tool and rubbed or burnished. Comparable pieces made by drilling a single hole through a large deer antler tine are also found. They seem to associate usually with the Initial Middle Missouri Variant.

FIGURE 66

Fishhooks (fig. 66) are a consistent item in the artifact assemblages from the Middle Missouri Tradition sites. They are made of bone, and the hooks are unbarbed. The shanks are generally straight, lack eyes, but often have a few shallow grooves incised near the upper end to prevent slippage of the line. Less frequently, a small knob was carved at the top of the shank.

Miscellaneous bone and antler artifacts (fig. 67) from Middle Missouri Tradition sites include tubes made from bird or small mammal bones. Lengths vary considerably, usually falling between 3.0 and 13.0 cm. Some of the shorter ones were probably beads. Whistles resemble the longer bone tubes, but have a notch cut toward one end of the bone. They are almost always made of bird bone. Antler cylinders about 5.0 cm. long with rounded ends, and L-shaped "sickles" made from scapulae, with a high polish on the upper edge of the foot of the L, are also found. Flat plates of bone shaped like arrowheads occur occasionally. These have previously been considered as ornaments, but references in the ethnographic field notes of the late Gilbert Wilson to the use of horn points suggest that these may have been utilitarian objects.

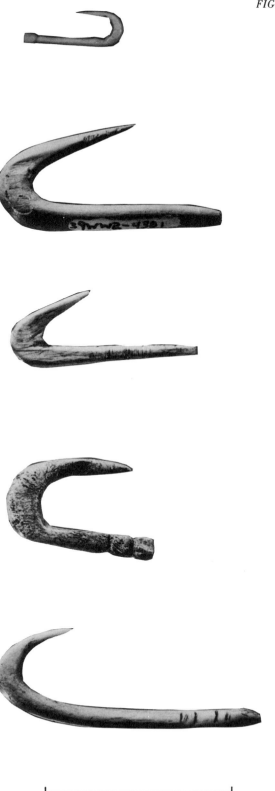

5 CM

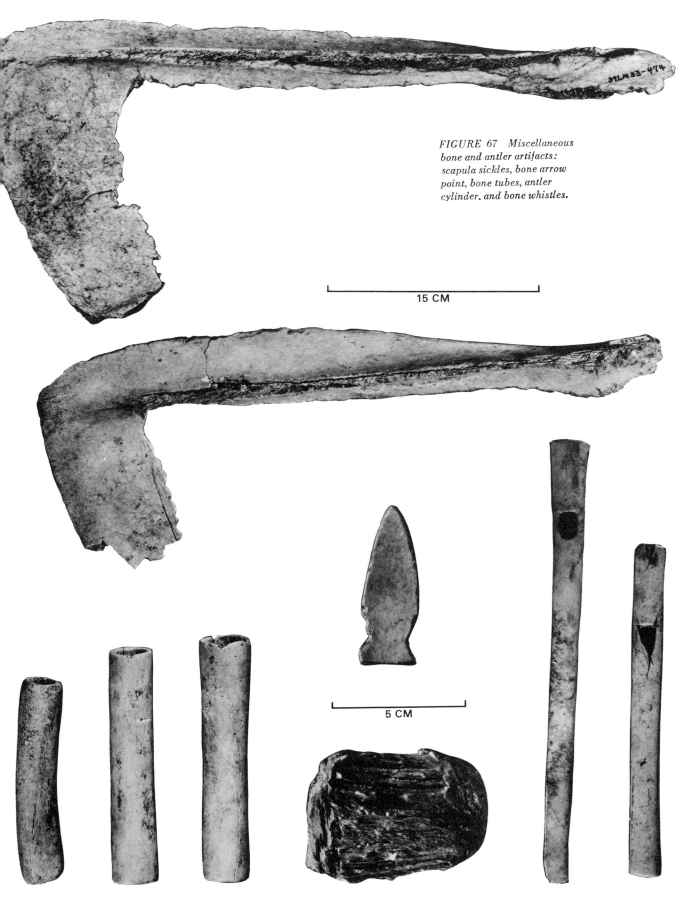

FIGURE 67 Miscellaneous bone and antler artifacts: scapula sickles, bone arrow point, bone tubes, antler cylinder, and bone whistles.

15 CM

5 CM

5 CM

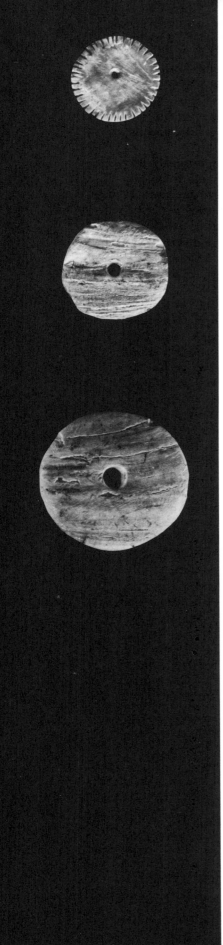

FIGURE 68 *Ornaments:
antler bow guard (?), shell
thunderbird, shell geometrics,
open-center bone rectangle,
and* Busycon columella.

Ornaments (fig. 68) are usually made of bone or shell. They include beads or pendants of *Dentalium*, discoidal beads, and shell or horn disks, from 2.0 to 3.0 cm. in diameter, which may or may not have holes drilled at the center. Horn and antler fragments, apparently parts of bracelets or bow guards, are found. Pendants or gorgets made from *Busycon* columellae occur, mainly in Initial Middle Missouri sites. Small rectangles of bone with open centers are also present.

Small conventionalized bird silhouettes of shell or bone, carved in the traditional thunderbird pattern and decorated with incised lines, are a distinctive item in Middle Missouri Tradition sites.

CHRONOLOGY

Dating of the Initial and Extended Middle Missouri Variants is based almost entirely on carbon-14 determinations. The 19 radiocarbon dates from Initial Middle Missouri components which had been released up to December of 1967 show a considerable time range, but 13 of them (68.4 percent) fall in the period A.D. 950–1300 (fig. 34).

One sample (M–608) from the Breeden Site (39ST16), across the Missouri from Pierre, was dated at A.D. 710±150. It is so much earlier than the others in this group that I am inclined to feel that the true date is considerably later. The next earliest Initial Middle Missouri date was obtained from a sample (M–839) from the Swanson Site (39BR16). It gave a value equivalent to a date of A.D. 850±250. In this case, the standard deviation is so large that there is a good likelihood that the true date falls sometime after the beginning of the 10th century.

The latest published radiocarbon date for an Initial Middle Missouri component, A.D. 1430±80, was obtained from a sample (SI–165) from Pretty Head Site (39LM232). Another Pretty Head sample (SI–166) was dated at A.D. 1300±140. According to Richard E. Jensen, who excavated the site (personal communication, 1968), the sample which yielded the later date came from a lower stratigraphic position than the sample dating A.D. 1300. This certainly casts some doubt on one date or the other. Since the Pretty Head Site does not appear to represent the late manifestation of Initial Middle Missouri culture, I am inclined to accept the earlier date and discount the later one.

Other late radiocarbon dates which appear to relate to Initial Middle Missouri components include two, A.D. 1380 ± 55 and $1390 + 150$ (SI–105 and SI–170), from the La Roche Site (39ST9). The site has also yielded a series of radiocarbon dates which fall in the 16th and 17th centuries. These appear to relate to the Extended Coalescent occupation, which was the main component at the site. A small sample of Initial Middle Missouri pottery also came from the site, suggesting the presence of an early component (Hoffman, 1968). No houses were found which would substantiate this, but the two early La Roche dates can be tentatively assigned to a putative Initial Middle Missouri component there.

An Initial Middle Missouri radiocarbon date of A.D. 1400 ± 100 was determined for a specimen (SI–314) from the Sommers Site (39ST56). Another sample from Sommers (SI–315) was dated at A.D. 975 ± 185. The internal evidence from the site suggests a late occupation and tends to support the later date.

Conversion of the Initial Middle Missouri radiocarbon dates on the basis of Stuiver and Suess' (1966) data tends mainly to raise the earlier dates in the series. A note in their table 1 states that radiocarbon ages for the period A.D. 1000 to 250 B.C. are generally 50 to 100 years older than true ages. This serves as the basis for raising the Breeden and Swanson dates. Other conversions were made graphically. They resulted in appreciable changes for some dates and minimal ones for others. The majority of the converted dates still fall in the period A.D. 950–1300, with a small group clustering around A.D. 1400. Thus there is no appreciable change in the time span indicated for the Initial Middle Missouri Variant.

It should be noted that all but one of the Initial Middle Missouri radiocarbon dates after A.D. 1300 came from sites in a very restricted area across the river from Chapelle Creek. Cultural complexes at most of these sites represent a configuration which may be designated as Modified Initial Middle Missouri. It appears to represent the final stage in the development of the Initial Middle Missouri Variant.

Ward Weakly (MS.) presents a series of tree-ring dates for Initial Middle Missouri from the Sommers (39ST56), H. P. Thomas (39ST12), and Ketchen (39ST223) sites. The Sommers dates range from A.D. $1465 +$ to $1631 +$. Weakly expresses some definite reservations concerning them, and I too feel that all but the very earliest ones in this series are far too late.

The H. P. Thomas Site, on the right bank of the Missouri about 10 miles below the Cheyenne River, was a multicomponent village. While the pottery indicates an Initial Middle Missouri occupation, the one dated specimen was a charred superstructure post from circular House 3 belonging to the Post-Contact component, which could hardly date before A.D. 1700.

Weakly's seven dates from the Ketchen Site form a tight group ranging from A.D. $1433 +$ to $1460 +$. They agree fairly well with the late Initial Middle Missouri radiocarbon dates, allowing for expectable differences inherent in the two techniques. Dendrochronology dates the outside ring of a wood specimen, whereas the radiocarbon method dates the mean of the carbon-14 content of an organic sample. Theoretically, a radiocarbon date for a given specimen would be some years earlier than a tree-ring date for the same specimen.

On the basis of radiocarbon dates, the Initial Middle Missouri Variant proper seems to fall within the period A.D. 900–1300, with the Modified Initial Middle Missouri complex having lasted until shortly after A.D. 1400. This terminal date may be raised to somewhere after the middle of the 15th century if the tree-ring dates from the Ketchen Site are validated by other studies.

Dates for the Extended Middle Missouri Variant are based almost entirely on samples from sites in the Bad-Cheyenne region.

---

*I have used only one date for each of the three specimens from the Cheyenne River Site (39ST1), which was dated more than once. For the specimen which yielded samples I–581, SI–12 and SI–117, I have picked the A.D. 1160 ± 60 date on the basis of the accompanying statement in *Radiocarbon* (vol. 7, p. 247). For the specimen which provided samples SI–17, SI–118, and M–840, I have chosen the date of A.D. 1080 ± 60 from the first two samples in preference to A.D. 1300 ± 200. For the specimen which provided samples I–582 and SI–116, I have selected the latter's date of A.D. 1150 ± 60 as being more in accord with the others in the group than the alternative of A.D. 1600 ± 85.

They include radiocarbon dates from seven specimens and a few tree-ring dates. The one northern radiocarbon date released so far is A.D. 1230±80 on a sample (SI–213) from the Fire Heart Creek Site (32SI2).

Dates for the southern Extended Middle Missouri sites have a definitely bimodal distribution. Six conventional radiocarbon dates range from A.D. 1080±60 to 1220± 200.* One radiocarbon date of A.D. 1520±95 (I–613) and the tree-ring dates indicate occupations between A.D. 1450 and 1550. The only date I am aware of which falls in the period between A.D. 1250 and 1450 is one (SI–119) from the Cheyenne River Site of A.D. 1340±100.

Modification of the conventional radiocarbon dates by the Stuiver and Suess data produces a really striking compression of the apparent time scale. Converted radiocarbon dates in the early group fall in the period A.D. 1195±60 to 1220±200. The two late conventional radiocarbon dates convert from A.D. 1600±85 and 1520±95 to A.D. 1490±85 and 1455±95, respectively. The late converted dates accord very well with the available tree-ring dates.

Statement No. 3 of the Missouri Basin Chronology Program (1962) included tentative tree-ring dates from the McKensey Village (39AR201), Thomas Riggs (39 HU1), and Hickey Brothers (39LM4) sites of A.D. 1471+, 1512, and 1522, respectively. Weakly (MS.) reports a tentative date of A.D. 1501+ for McKensey Village, 13 tentative values ranging from A.D. 1466+ to 1539+ for the Thomas Riggs Site, and one of A.D. 1448+ for the Cheyenne River Site.

All but one of the available Extended Middle Missouri dates from the Bad-Cheyenne region fall into either the early or the late cluster. The almost complete absence of dates for the period A.D. 1250–1450 may well be an accident of sampling, but it does suggest the possibility that the Extended Middle Missouri occupation of the region was a discontinuous one. The earlier stage may be conservatively estimated as lasting from A.D. 1100 to 1250 on the basis of conventional radiocarbon dates, or from A.D. 1190 to 1250 on the basis of the Stuiver and Suess' conversions. The later occupation appears to fall within the span from about A.D. 1450 to 1550.

TAXONOMIC SUBDIVISIONS

Taxonomic subdivisions of the Initial and Extended Middle Missouri Variants have been proposed by a number of workers. For Initial Middle Missouri, these include the Over Focus (Over and Meleen, 1941, p. 41; Hurt, 1951a, pp. 15–16), the Anderson and Monroe Foci (Lehmer, 1954b, pp. 76 and 118–138), and the Grand Detour Phase (Caldwell and Jensen, 1969). Any further attempt to set up phases within the Initial Middle Missouri Variant must wait on the publication of the considerable body of data from unreported Initial Middle Missouri sites. It seems likely, however, that several phases will eventually be recognized within the variant. One may well correspond broadly to the Monroe Focus. Another may include the Grand Detour Phase and the Over and Anderson Foci as subphases. Still another will almost certainly be established to subsume the complex which has been designated here as Modified Initial Middle Missouri.

Proposed subdivisions of the Extended Middle Missouri complex include Will and Hecker's (1944, pp. 53–55) Archaic Mandan, the Thomas Riggs Focus (Hurt, 1953, pp. 47–48 and 51–61; Wood and Woolworth, 1964, pp. 62–63), the Fort Yates Focus (Hurt, 1953, pp. 60–61) and the Fort Yates Phase (Lehmer, 1966, pp. 54–60). Again, any attempt to set up phases would be premature. It seems likely, however, that a unit corresponding to Hurt's Thomas Riggs Focus, which will include the southern Extended Middle Missouri components, will be distinguishable. It may well prove to have early and late subphases. It seems probable that the Fort Yates Phase will continue to be recognizable as a valid cultural entity which includes the northern villages. Again, there is a strong likelihood that it will be possible to distinguish subphases.

CULTURAL INTERACTION, A.D. 900–1400

The Initial Middle Missouri Variant was the first manifestation of the Plains Village pattern to appear in the Middle Missouri subarea. While it is possible that this complex developed *in situ*, it seems more likely that the Initial Middle Missouri peoples migrated into the region from southwestern Minnesota and northwestern Iowa. This is certainly suggested by the distribution of Initial Middle Missouri sites across southeastern South Dakota to the Minnesota border (fig. 69).

The Plains environment has demanded adjustments from every population which has occupied the region (cf. Webb, 1931; Wedel, 1941), and it is probable that a westward movement of the Initial Middle Missouri peoples was preceded by a considerable amount of adaptation to conditions in the Plains. Southern Minnesota and much of Iowa were prairie grassland with wooded stream valleys, and were within the eastern range of the bison. Environmentally, this section was a transition zone between the Eastern Woodlands and the Plains proper. It seems likely that here Eastern farming practices were modified by the addition of new tools such as the bison scapula hoe, and that crop plants were adapted by selection to the climatic conditions of the Northern Plains. I suspect, too, that it was in the prairie margins that the Eastern groups learned to hunt bison herds on foot and acquired new techniques and new tools for hide dressing. The processes of cultural adaptation would have marked the birth of the Middle Missouri Tradition.

Available dates indicate that the Initial Middle Missouri Variant was the only village complex in the Middle Missouri region for perhaps two centuries. But it does not appear to have existed in complete isolation. A number of rather exotic items have been found in Initial Middle Missouri sites

FIGURE 69   Areal distribution of the Initial Middle Missouri Variant.

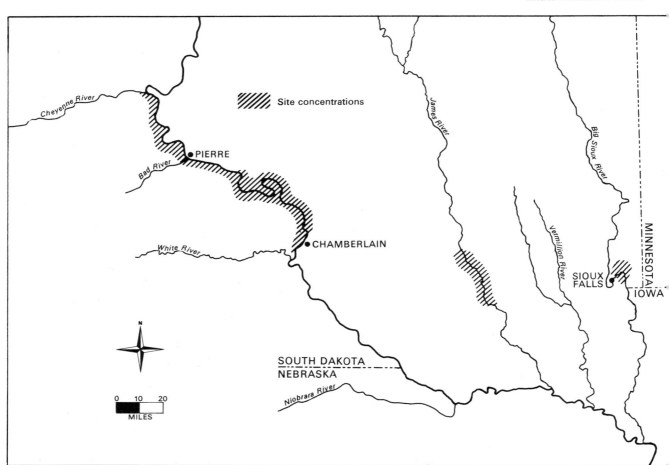

which strongly indicate contacts with the contemporary cultures of the upper and/or central Mississippi Valley. These include pendants made of *Busycon* columellae, pottery decoration incorporating the forked or weeping eye motif (cf. Lehmer, 1954b, pl. 19), and a few artifacts made of native copper (Hill and Neuman, 1966). The shell and bone thunderbirds and the elaborately carved side-blade knife handles have a degree of sophistication which also suggests the contemporary cultures of the Mississippi Valley. A detailed study of all of the collections from Initial Middle Missouri sites will be necessary before this aspect of the contact situation can be dealt with properly.

Wilfred Husted has noted (personal communication, 1967) that collections from Initial Middle Missouri sites include a few arrow points which closely resemble Avonlea points (Kehoe and McCorquodale, 1961; Davis, 1966). Their presence suggests some sort of contact between the Initial Middle Missouri villagers and contemporary migratory hunters of the Northwestern Plains. *Dentalium* beads found in Middle Missouri Tradition villages must have come to the Missouri Valley from the Pacific Coast by way of intermediate groups in the western Plains.

The contact situation between the Initial and Extended Middle Missouri peoples is the best known one for the early period, although it is not yet fully understood. At one time it appeared that the Extended Middle Missouri Variant was a direct outgrowth of the Initial Middle Missouri Variant (Lehmer, 1952a; 1954b, pp. 117–138). This interpretation was based on what was then known of the archeology of the Bad-Cheyenne region and was arrived at without the benefit of radiocarbon dates. It continued to seem reasonable in the light of a wider knowledge of Middle Missouri archeology (e.g. Wood, 1967, pp. 127–131), but today it seems to be an oversimplification of the culture history of the region.

An alternative interpretation was offered in the early 1950's by Wesley Hurt (1953, pp. 60–61, and chart III). Will and Hecker (1944) had previously defined a cultural sequence for the North Dakota villages which ranged from Archaic through Middle Mandan to a Late Heart River complex. Hurt recognized the close similarities between the Thomas Riggs Site in the Bad-Cheyenne region and Will and Hecker's Archaic and Middle Mandan. Hurt organized these complexes in terms of three foci—the Thomas Riggs Focus in the Bad-Cheyenne region; the Fort Yates Focus, equivalent to Will and Hecker's Archaic Mandan; and the Huff Focus, corresponding to Will and Hecker's Middle Mandan. In the terminology used here, the Thomas Riggs and Fort Yates Foci are Extended Middle Missouri, while the Huff Focus is Terminal Middle Missouri. Hurt (1953, chart IV) lumped all three of his foci into an unnamed "northern complex," and he indicated that this complex derived from the Cambrian Aspect of southern Minnesota and the Mill Creek Complex of northwestern Iowa. Hurt's chart also suggested that the Thomas Riggs Focus, the downriver variant of the northern complex, was influenced by the cultures assigned here to the Initial Middle Missouri Variant.

Much of the evidence which has accumulated since 1953 supports Hurt's idea that Extended Middle Missouri Variant was not a direct development out of Initial Middle Missouri. The most telling items include the considerable time overlap between the two variants, the geographic distributions of the sites, and the evidence of interaction between the two complexes.

The overlap in time rules out the possibility of a sequential development from Initial to Extended Middle Missouri. If Extended Middle Missouri did develop out of Initial Middle Missouri, it must have been an offshoot which appeared while the parent complex continued to exist.

The geographic distribution of the majority of the Extended Middle Missouri sites centers in the northern part of the region, while the Initial Middle Missouri sites are located in the south. The heavy concentration of Extended Middle Missouri sites in North Dakota may well indicate that this was the original homeland of the complex in the Missouri Valley, and that the Extended Middle Missouri sites in the Bad-Cheyenne region represent a southern extension of the configuration.

The pattern of interaction between Initial and Extended Middle Missouri groups is also suggestive. Most of that interaction took place in the Bad-Cheyenne region, as summarized below, and there seems to be good evidence that it involved a large-scale conflict between the Initial and Extended Middle Missouri populations.

Similarities between the Initial and Extended Middle Missouri complexes demonstrate that they were closely related. Inadequate evidence, especially the lack of dates from the northern Extended Middle Missouri sites, makes it impossible to form a definite conclusion regarding the nature of these relationships, especially regarding the question of origins. It is possible that the Extended Middle Missouri population was an offshoot which broke away from the parent stock in the Bad-Cheyenne region about A.D. 1100, and pushed upriver to develop in its main center in North Dakota.

It seems somewhat more likely, however, that both Initial and Extended Middle Missouri peoples were rooted in the same, or closely similar, parent stock(s) which centered in southern Minnesota and northern Iowa. Initial Middle Missouri groups would appear to have moved almost due west into the Big Bend and Bad-Cheyenne regions. If the Extended Middle Missouri complex derived from the same area, well to the east of the Missouri Valley, it seems likely that the bearers moved northwest across the eastern part of the Dakotas to the Cannonball and Knife-Heart regions. Such a movement might have followed the chain of glacial lakes which runs along an axis from the Minnesota border just north of Sioux Falls to a point some 40 miles west of Bismarck. If this were the case, the Extended Middle Missouri sites in the Bad-Cheyenne region were probably the result of a downriver movement from the principal Extended Middle Missouri center in North Dakota.

I would, on the basis of presently available evidence, reconstruct the Initial-Extended Middle Missouri contact situation between roughly A.D. 1100 and 1250 along the following lines. The Initial Middle Missouri groups were the original village population in the valley. Their main center of occupation was in the Big Bend region, but they had also pushed upstream on the right bank of the Missouri almost to the mouth of the Cheyenne River. Sometime after A.D. 1100, Extended Middle Missouri groups began to filter downstream from North Dakota, establishing themselves on the left

bank in the upper Bad-Cheyenne region and on the right bank above the mouth of the Cheyenne River. There seem to be good indications that the Extended Middle Missouri groups then pushed southward down the right bank below the Cheyenne and eventually forced the Initial Middle Missouri population out of that locality.

Fortifications at the contemporary Initial and Extended Middle Missouri villages suggest that conflict resulted from the intrusion of Extended Middle Missouri groups into Initial Middle Missouri territory. The construction of fortification ditches and palisades involved both considerable amounts of work and major inroads into the limited supplies of timber available for building purposes. It seems clear that ditches and palisades would only have been provided when the villages required protection against a hostile population. Lacking any good evidence of the presence of a third group in the region during the 12th and 13th centuries, it is reasonable to conclude that the Initial and Extended Middle Missouri populations were fortifying their villages against each other.

Specific evidence of a conflict situation was found at the Fay Tolton Site (39ST11), the northernmost Initial Middle Missouri settlement. The village apparently consisted of more than 30 houses located on a steep-sided point adjoining the Missouri flood plain. It was protected by a ditch dug across the base of the point. The presence of a stockade was not established, but postholes encountered in a trench cross-sectioning the ditch suggest the presence of such a feature. The two houses excavated (Features 2 and 5) were long-rectangular structures, oriented on a northeast-southwest axis, each with an entrance and an entrance ramp at the south end. The houses conform to the basic Initial Middle Missouri type but are unusually small. Feature 2 measured 20.1 by 29.1 feet and Feature 5 measured 24.2 by 32.6 feet. Both houses had been burned.

Three human skeletons were sprawled on the floor in the southeast corner of Feature 2. A considerable amount of debris, including a whole pot and a number of other artifacts, was scattered around the skeletons. William M. Bass, III, who studied the skeletal material, informs me that one of these skeletons was that of a child about 8 years old, and that the other two were females, 12 to 15 and 15 to 17 years old. The skeleton of a male, 29 to 35 years old, had been crammed seat-first into a cache pit in the northeast corner of the house, with the head and shoulders projecting well above the level of the floor. The cache pit also contained a restorable pot, and various artifacts and unworked animal bones were found in and around the mouth of the cache. Most of the bones of each skeleton were in articulation.

The sprawled positions of the remains, the fact that three of them were lying directly on the house floor, and the fact that burned pieces of house superstructure were intermixed with the skeletons combine to rule out the possibility that these were intentional burials. Instead, the four individuals in Feature 2 give mute testimony of some sort of catastrophe.

Remains of a fifth individual were found in Feature 5. They consisted of the post-cranial skeleton of a male, aged 24 to 28 years, which had been dumped into a cache pit in the floor near the west wall of the house. Again, the bones found were in articulation, but the cranium and mandible were not present. The absence of these members suggests the possibility that the head had been carried off as a trophy.

Articulated human skeletons are very rare in Initial Middle Missouri sites. The presence of the unburied skeletons of five individuals in the two burned houses at the Fay Tolton Site strongly suggests a successful enemy raid on the village. While there appears to be no evidence of the identity of the raiders, it is possible that they were a neighboring Extended Middle Missouri population.

The occurrence of Initial and Extended Middle Missouri components in the Bad-Cheyenne region also bears on the relationships between the two complexes. To the best of my knowledge, Initial and Extended Middle Missouri components have never been found in the same site. In contrast, evidence of two superimposed Initial Middle Missouri occupations was found at the Dodd Site (39ST30), along with a Post-Contact Coalescent component (Lehmer, 1954b). The Cattle Oiler Site (39ST224) apparently had two components (David T. Jones, personal communication, 1967). One was Initial Middle Missouri; the other was what is referred to here as Modified Initial Middle Missouri. Initial Middle Missouri components have also been found in sites which had one or more other components representing the Initial, Extended, or Post-Contact Coalescent Variants. Extended Middle Missouri components have been found in sites with Extended and/or Post-Contact Coalescent components. Some factor seems to have operated against the reoccupation of Initial Middle Missouri villages by Extended Middle Missouri populations. This situation is particularly striking in view of the frequent reoccupation of abandoned towns by other village groups of the area.

The distribution of the Initial and Extended Middle Missouri sites in the Bad-Cheyenne region is also significant (figs. 70 and 71). A number of typical Initial Middle Missouri sites occur on the right bank of the Missouri between the mouths of the Bad and the Cheyenne Rivers, and typical Extended Middle Missouri sites are found on both banks of the Missouri down to the mouth of the Bad River. Radiocarbon dates from each group of sites indicate that the Initial Middle Missouri occupation preceded the Extended Middle Missouri occupation. There are no mean radiocarbon dates from the Initial Middle Missouri sites north of the Bad River which are later than A.D. 1150. This suggests that the Initial Middle Missouri groups had been displaced from this section by Extended Middle Missouri peoples by the middle of the 12th century. But in the Big Bend region the Initial Middle Missouri occupation seems to have lasted on through the middle of the 13th century.

There is evidence of some cultural interchange between the two populations, and it probably took place during the period from about A.D. 1150 to 1250. The consistent occurrence of entrance ramps in the southern Extended Middle Missouri structures and the absence of this feature in the north suggests that it was borrowed from the Initial Middle Missouri groups.

Extended Middle Missouri pottery is characterized by simple stamped or plain bodies, while pottery from the early Initial Middle Missouri sites has either cord-roughened or plain bodies. The technique of simple stamping begins to appear, however, in

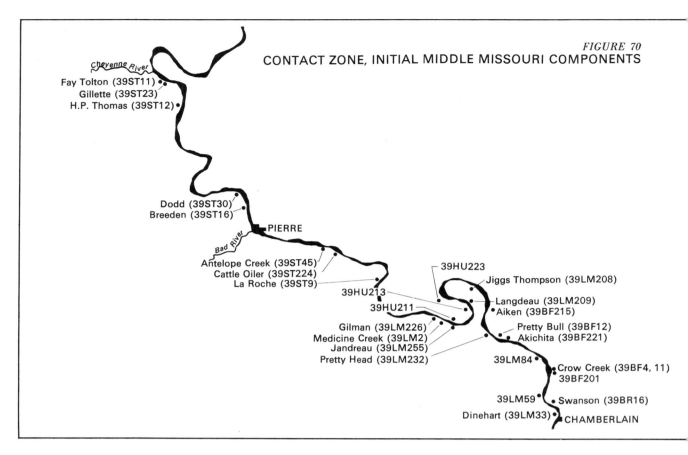

FIGURE 70

CONTACT ZONE, INITIAL MIDDLE MISSOURI COMPONENTS

Cheyenne River

Fay Tolton (39ST11)
Gillette (39ST23)
H.P. Thomas (39ST12)

Dodd (39ST30)
Breeden (39ST16)

PIERRE

Bad River

Antelope Creek (39ST45)
Cattle Oiler (39ST224)
La Roche (39ST9)

39HU223

39HU213

39HU211

Jiggs Thompson (39LM208)

Langdeau (39LM209)
Aiken (39BF215)

Gilman (39LM226)
Medicine Creek (39LM2)
Jandreau (39LM255)
Pretty Head (39LM232)

Pretty Bull (39BF12)
Akichita (39BF221)

39LM84

Crow Creek (39BF4, 11)
39BF201

39LM59

Swanson (39BR16)

Dinehart (39LM33)

CHAMBERLAIN

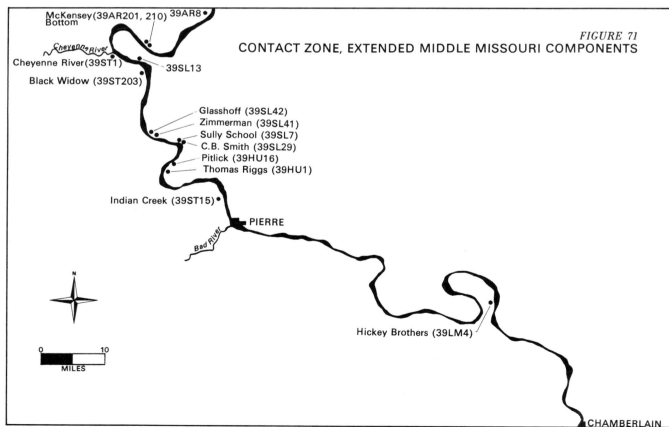

McKensey (39AR201, 210)
Bottom

39AR8

FIGURE 71

CONTACT ZONE, EXTENDED MIDDLE MISSOURI COMPONENTS

Cheyenne River

Cheyenne River (39ST1)

39SL13

Black Widow (39ST203)

Glasshoff (39SL42)
Zimmerman (39SL41)
Sully School (39SL7)
C.B. Smith (39SL29)
Pitlick (39HU16)
Thomas Riggs (39HU1)

Indian Creek (39ST15)

PIERRE

Bad River

N

Hickey Brothers (39LM4)

0   10
MILES

CHAMBERLAIN

102

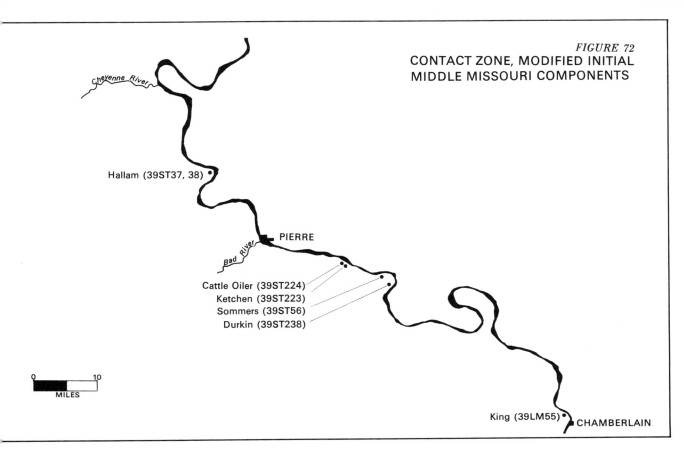

FIGURE 72
CONTACT ZONE, MODIFIED INITIAL
MIDDLE MISSOURI COMPONENTS

Cheyenne River

Hallam (39ST37, 38)

Bad River

PIERRE

Cattle Oiler (39ST224)
Ketchen (39ST223)
Sommers (39ST56)
Durkin (39ST238)

0   10
MILES

King (39LM55)
CHAMBERLAIN

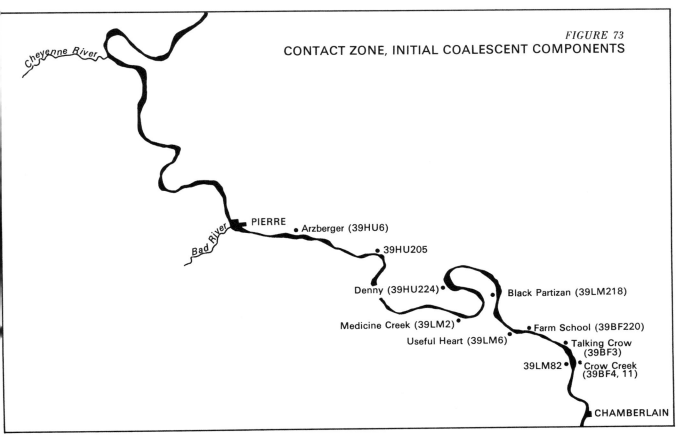

FIGURE 73
CONTACT ZONE, INITIAL COALESCENT COMPONENTS

Cheyenne River

Bad River

PIERRE

Arzberger (39HU6)

39HU205

Denny (39HU224)

Black Partizan (39LM218)

Medicine Creek (39LM2)

Farm School (39BF220)

Useful Heart (39LM6)

Talking Crow
(39BF3)

39LM82

Crow Creek
(39BF4, 11)

CHAMBERLAIN

103

Initial Middle Missouri sites in the border zone between the Bad-Cheyenne and Big Bend regions. Caldwell reports that "recently, simple stamped bodies have been found attached to typical Initial Middle Missouri rims at the Sommers (39ST56) and Cattle Oiler (39ST224) villages in the Big Bend District" (1966a, p. 154). The adoption of simple stamping by all of the late village groups in the Northern Plains suggests that the use of the grooved and ridged paddle had some technological superiority over the cord-wrapped paddle. This seems to have been recognized by the Initial Middle Missouri peoples, and to have resulted in their borrowing simple stamping from their Extended Middle Missouri neighbors.

The nearly complete absence of dates for the period between A.D. 1250 and 1450 from southern Extended Middle Missouri sites suggests the possibility that this group abandoned the Bad-Cheyenne region early in the 13th century. This possibility may be confirmed by the archeological situation in a group of unreported Initial Middle Missouri villages which were probably occupied until a fairly late time. They include the Sommers (39ST56), Ketchen (39ST223), and Durkin (39ST238) sites, and the late component at Cattle Oiler (39ST224). They make up a fairly compact group on the right bank of the Missouri some 20 miles downstream from the mouth of the Bad River (fig. 72). These sites were excavated for the River Basin Surveys by Richard E. Jensen, David T. Jones, and Daniel E. Moerman between 1964 and 1966. My information regarding them comes mainly from conversations with Jensen and Jones. Another site, King (39LM55), located well down toward the southern end of the Big Bend region, seems to represent the same cultural complex. The King Site was excavated by Thomas R. Garth of the River Basin Surveys in 1950 and by C. S. Smith of the University of Kansas in 1953. Two unexcavated sites, 39ST37 and 39ST38, located near each other on the right bank of the Missouri about halfway between the mouths of the Bad and Cheyenne Rivers, appear to belong to this category also.

The archeological complex at each of these sites falls well within the Middle Missouri Tradition. But it is not properly either Initial or Extended Middle Missouri as these terms are generally used. The pottery can best be described as a hybrid. Body sherds include numbers of both cord-roughened and simple-stamped pieces; rims of both the rounded Extended Middle Missouri and the angular Initial Middle Missouri varieties are present. Both rim varieties seem to occur with simple-stamped or cord-roughened bodies.

None of the sites in this group appears to have been fortified, except Sommers (which I would guess was relatively early), where part of the area of occupation was enclosed by a ditch. I would classify these sites as Modified Initial Middle Missouri, regarding them as relatively late manifestations of the Initial Middle Missouri Variant. This is based mainly on the fact that the pottery appears to represent the original Initial Middle Missouri ceramic tradition, modified by borrowing from the Extended Middle Missouri pottery complex. These sites might be regarded as a transitional stage in the development of Extended Middle Missouri out of Initial Middle Missouri, but the available dates indicate that they are much too late to be considered in this connection.

The general lack of fortifications, the virtual absence of dates for the period A.D. 1250–1450, and the location of sites 39ST37 and 39ST38 in what had been Extended Middle Missouri territory suggest the possibility that the Extended Middle Missouri groups temporarily abandoned the Bad-Cheyenne region shortly after A.D. 1250. This would have left the groups carrying the Modified Initial Middle Missouri complex in undisputed possession of the southern districts until an Extended Middle Missouri population returned around the middle of the 15th century.

To recapitulate, cultural interactions affecting the Middle Missouri villages from approximately A.D. 900 to 1400 involved poorly defined contacts with migratory hunting groups of the western Plains and with sedentary peoples of the upper and/or central Mississippi Valley. They also appear to have included a downriver movement of Extended Middle Missouri groups from central North Dakota into the Bad-Cheyenne region. This movement seems to have precipitated open warfare between the Extended Middle Missouri newcomers and the older

Initial Middle Missouri settlers. The Initial Middle Missouri populations seem to have been driven out of the section north of the Bad River. This would have left the Big Bend region in Initial Middle Missouri hands, while the Extended Middle Missouri groups occupied the Bad-Cheyenne region.

There are indications of some diffusion of culture traits between the Initial Middle Missouri groups occupying the Big Bend region and Extended Middle Missouri groups in possession of the Bad-Cheyenne region. The Extended Middle Missouri people appear to have borrowed entrance ramps inside the house pit from their Initial Middle Missouri neighbors, while the Initial Middle Missouri population took over simple stamping and the Extended Middle Missouri version of the basic flared and S-rims of the Middle Missouri Tradition. There are suggestions that the Extended Middle Missouri occupation of the southern districts was interrupted during the period from about A.D. 1250 to 1450.

The close correspondence between the dates for the early periods in the history of the Middle Missouri villages and those proposed for a series of climatic episodes suggests that climatic factors may have exerted a strong influence on culture history in the Northern Plains. Reid A. Bryson has defined a Neo-Atlantic episode which began around A.D. 900 (Baerreis and Bryson, 1965; Bryson and Wendland, 1967). The Neo-Atlantic climate was characterized by influxes of moist tropical air into the Plains. This produced a situation which was very favorable for corn agriculture. The correspondence between the beginning dates for the Neo-Atlantic episode and the Initial Middle Missouri Variant strongly suggests that the first westward movement of the village tribes was encouraged by the Neo-Atlantic climatic conditions.

Less favorable conditions developed at the inception of the Pacific I episode. It was characterized by circulation patterns which brought an increased flow of the westerlies into Northern Plains. Pacific I conditions may well have been responsible for the apparent abandonment of the southern Extended Middle Missouri villages around A.D. 1250, and for the concentration of the remnant population in a handful of Modified Initial Middle Missouri sites.

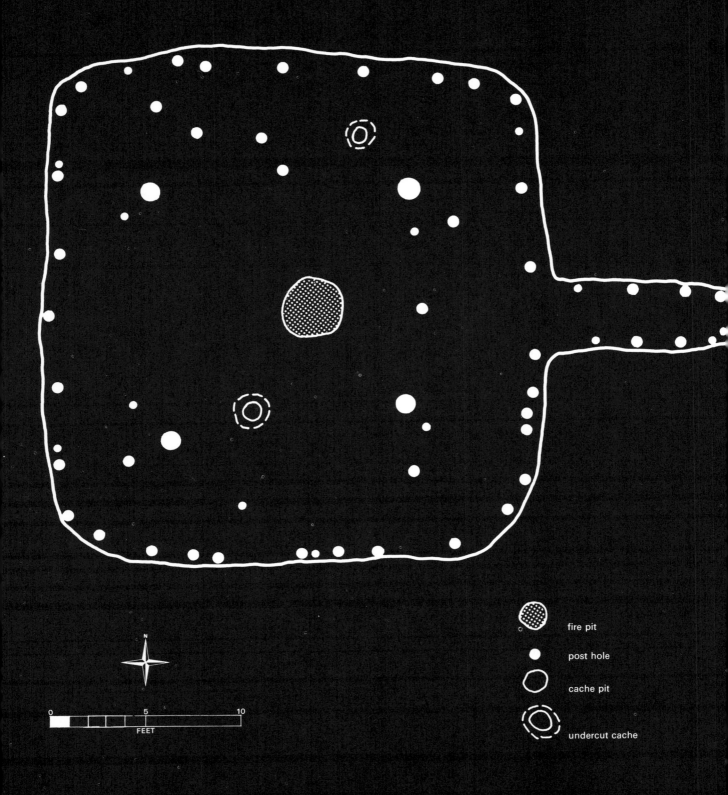

fire pit

post hole

cache pit

undercut cache

N

0   5   10
FEET

THE MIDDLE MISSOURI, A.D. 1400-1675

The culture history of the Middle Missouri became more involved after the beginning of the 15th century. Prior to that time, only the Middle Missouri Tradition was represented in the region. Subsequently, there was a population influx from the Central Plains. This new factor in the cultural equation was responsible for a lengthy process of interaction which eventually culminated in the pattern of the historic village tribes of the Northern Plains.

CENTRAL PLAINS TRADITION

The Central Plains Tradition seems to have been approximately contemporary with the Initial and Extended Middle Missouri Variants, but it differed in a number of ways from the northern configurations. The dissimilarities in geographic distribution and in architecture, village plan, burial customs, and several artifact types are particularly evident.

GEOGRAPHIC EXTENT

The geographic extent of the Central Plains Tradition seems to include the westernmost part of Iowa, eastern and south-central Nebraska, and Kansas north of the Arkansas River drainage. This is in obvious contrast to the concentration of Middle Missouri Tradition in the Missouri Valley in the Dakotas.

HOUSES

The houses of the Central Plains Tradition were more or less square with rounded corners (fig. 74). Vertical wall posts were placed around the perimeter of the floor, usually from 6 inches to 2 feet apart. Four primary roof supports were set at the corners of a square around the unlined firepit in the center of the floor. A long enclosed passageway, leading out from the center of one side, had vertical wall posts like the house proper. A few of the houses found in sites of the Central Plains Tradition are circular rather than squarish (e.g., Champe, 1936, pp. 258–259), foreshadowing the house type of the Coalescent Tradition.

The floors of some Central Plains houses were set in fairly deep pits. Others, especially those of the Upper Republican and Smoky Hill villages, had very shallow pits which

FIGURE 74 Plan of a Central Plains Tradition house.

often involved nothing more than stripping away the original sod. Wedel (1959, pp. 565–566) emphasizes the fact that many Central Plains houses were not semisubterranean pit houses, and points out the importance of this fact in connection with the possible relationships of the Central Plains structures to those of the Spiro area in northeastern Oklahoma.

The Central Plains and Middle Missouri houses patently represent two distinct architectural traditions. There are the obvious differences in basic plan, and others which are somewhat less apparent. The Middle Missouri houses are much more likely to have the floors cluttered with extraneous postholes which are probably remnants of partitions or beds and other furnishings. It is my impression that cache pits occur more frequently in the floors of Middle Missouri houses than in Central Plains structures. There was a considerable range in size in both the Central Plains and Middle Missouri houses. However, the average for the Central Plains houses seems to have been smaller. I would estimate that the Central Plains house floors had a mean area in the neighborhood of 500 square feet, while the Middle Missouri houses had a mean area of about 900 square feet. This difference may well have implications regarding the number of occupants of the two types of houses.

VILLAGES

The villages of the Central Plains Tradition usually consisted of a few houses strung out singly or in small clusters for considerable distances along the edge of the high ground bordering a stream. These villages present a striking contrast to the larger, more compact, and more orderly ones of the Middle Missouri Tradition.

FORTIFICATIONS

Fortifications were not characteristic of the Central Plains Tradition. This negative trait contrasts with the frequent occurrence of ditches and palisades enclosing Middle Missouri Villages.

BURIAL CUSTOMS

The burial customs of the Central Plains Tradition are better known than those of the Middle Missouri Tradition. The most distinctive Upper Republican burials are collections of secondary interments in basin-shaped ossuaries which also include a few articulated skeletons. Mortuary offerings of pottery and other artifacts occur frequently. Individual primary interments also seem to have been made by the Upper Republican people, although there are suggestions that at least some of these individuals were later moved to ossuaries.

The burial practices of what has been called the Nebraska Aspect are poorly known, but there are indications that both secondary and primary burial were practiced. A burial pit excavated near Salina suggests that the Smoky Hill groups followed a pattern of massed primary interments, with most of the bodies buried in a flexed position and lying on the side. Mortuary offerings were fairly common (Wedel, 1959, pp. 517–523).

POTTERY

The pottery from the Central Plains sites shows considerable variation, but there are some common characteristics. Bodies are cord roughened or plain. Flared rims, often resembling the high and low flared rims found in Initial Middle Missouri sites, are common. Rims with thickened collars are also common, contrasting with the S-rims of the Middle Missouri Tradition. Cord-impressed decoration seems to be almost completely absent except in the Sweetwater sites of central Nebraska (Champe, 1936).

STONE, BONE, AND SHELL ARTIFACTS

Stone, bone, and shell artifacts of the Central Plains and Middle Missouri traditions show both similarities and differences. A considerable number of forms, such as the scapula hoe and snubnose scraper, are common to both complexes. These represent what might be considered the basic inventory of the Plains Village Pattern. Central Plains Tradition sites yield a few artifacts which occur rarely, if at all, in the Middle Missouri Tradition sites. These include diamond-shaped knives with alternately beveled edges, chipped celts, projectile points with a base notch or multiple pairs of side notches, stone tobacco pipes, and effigy human heads which were often made of clay and attached to vessels.

Middle Missouri Tradition artifacts which do not seem to be typical of the Central Plains Tradition include metatarsal fleshers, elk antler fleshing adzes, plate chalcedony knives, narrow asymmetrical leaf blades, and grooved mauls which served, among other things, for pounding pemmican and breaking up bones to be boiled to extract the fat content. Other Middle Missouri Tradition traits which are rare in Central Plains sites are pecked and polished celts, stone balls, bison skull hoes, bone spatulas, and hooked scapula knives. A number of these items are found in sites of the Central Plains Tradition in the northeastern corner of Nebraska (cf. Cooper, 1936). They appear rarely, if at all, in sites of the Central Plains Tradition which are more remote from the Middle Missouri heartland.

A substantial number of the Middle Missouri traits which are not typical of the Central Plains Tradition relate directly to the adaptation to the Plains environment, especially to the hunting aspects of the economy. The occurrence of these traits in Middle Missouri Tradition sites demonstrates a technology which was better adapted to life in the Plains than that of the Central Plains Tradition. This suggests that the Middle Missouri groups were either more ingenious in adapting to the Plains environment, had been able to borrow more traits from groups occupying the region when they moved into it, or that the antecedent complex was more oriented towards a hunting economy than the one which gave rise to the Central Plains Tradition.

CHRONOLOGY

The chronology of the Central Plains Tradition is based on a series of 42 carbon-14 dates published in *Radiocarbon* through 1967. Twenty-two of them come from a group of sites in the limited area of Frontier County, Nebr. This series includes one improbably early date of A.D. 465±65 (SI–34). The other 21 mean dates range from A.D. 880±70 (SI–50) to A.D. 1510± 40 (SI–72), and all but two of them (90.5 percent) fall in the period between A.D. 1000 and 1450. The means of other radiocarbon dates from Central Plains Tradition sites in Nebraska, Kansas, and western Iowa are more or less evenly distributed through the period between A.D. 900 and 1500, with two late ones of A.D. 1560±75 (M–1069) and 1560±120 (GaK–298). The Frontier County group strongly suggests an occupation of that particular section of the Central

Plains from about A.D. 1000 to at least 1400. The entire series indicates a maximum time span, in at least parts of the subarea, from A.D. 900 to 1500 or later. Conversions on the basis of the Stuiver and Suess chart compress this range so that the mean dates fall between A.D. 955 and 1470.

It is important to note that there are no major gaps in the distribution of the individual dates (fig. 75). This is contrary to what would be expected if there had been a long-term abandonment of the subarea of the sort suggested in the past (Lehmer, 1954b, pp. 148–149). But the fact remains that many Upper Republican sites are thickly blanketed with sterile windblown silt which suggests dust bowl conditions due to a severe drought (Wedel, 1941; Kivett, 1950). This interpretation is supported by Harry E. Weakly's (1950) pioneer tree-ring studies which indicated drought periods lasting for as much as 26 years. These might well have had such adverse affects on both agriculture and pasturage that they forced the abandonment of parts of the Central Plains, even though this would not necessarily be reflected in the radiocarbon dates for the entire subarea.

TAXONOMIC SUBDIVISIONS

The subdivisions for the materials which I have assigned to the Central Plains Tradition have been suggested by a number of workers. Within the last decade Wedel (1959, pp. 558–567) has proposed a Central Plains Phase which includes three aspects: Upper Republican, Nebraska, and Smoky Hill. Champe (1961) has recognized an Aksarben Aspect with four foci: Upper Republican, Nebraska, Sweetwater, and St. Helena. Brown (1966b), following the Willey and Phillips' terminology, has recognized a Central Plains Tradition with four phases: Upper Republican, Nebraska, St. Helena, and Smoky Hill. Krause (*in* Wood, 1969) has presented an excellent analysis. In view of the considerable amount of unpublished new data on the region, any attempt to go beyond these proposals would be premature.

ORIGINS

The origins of the Central Plains Tradition have been dealt with by several writers. Spaulding has suggested that:

Taking into consideration the fundamental

relationship of Upper Republican and the Nebraska Aspect, a possible interpretation is that in post-Hopewell times an ancestral culture arose in the Central Plains characterized by the nonceramic features common to the Upper Republican and Nebraska Aspects and having as a sort of highest common ceramic factor a grit-tempered, cord-wrapped paddle-stamped jar with simple rim and little, if any, decoration. . . . The subsequent bifurcation of the ancestral tradition involved the addition of Middle Mississippi influences to the more easterly sites, resulting in the Nebraska Aspect, and the addition of the collared rim with associated decorative techniques to the more westerly sites to form the Upper Republican Aspect. The source of the collared rim tradition presumably lies to the north and east, where the Late Woodland cultures from Minnesota to the Atlantic coast show basically similar vessels. In the Great Lakes area these collars were most frequently cord impressed rather than incised, as at Aztalan, Wisconsin (Barrett, 1933, pp. 303–313), although the Mill Creek culture of northwestern Iowa and adjacent regions exhibits collared and noncollared rims with incised designs.

(Spaulding, 1956, p. 79)

Wedel has pointed out the importance of the Smoky Hill Aspect to the problem of the origin of the Central Plains Tradition:

The exact relationships of the Smoky Hill materials to those of the Upper Republican and Nebraska Aspects remain, of course, to be demonstrated when larger bodies of controlled data are in hand. That strong relationships exist is clear; and I would expect that the Smoky Hill sites nearest the Upper Republican and Nebraska Aspect localities will exhibit stronger similarities than those more remotely situated. That the Smoky Hill sites can be satisfactorily assigned to either of these aspects I nevertheless doubt. To me, the ceramic remains of the Smoky Hill complex sites, and the meager but provocative hints we have of them yet farther south, suggest a more generalized tradition than either Upper Republican or Nebraska Aspect wares. It is tempting to see in this the "sort of highest common ceramic factor" out of which developed the "classic" Upper Republican pottery to the west and northwest and the Nebraska Aspect pottery to the east—the former perhaps by stimulus from

Late Woodland cultures in the upper Mississippi-Great Lakes area, the latter through contacts with Middle Mississippi influences coming up the Missouri. From here, it is only a short, if at the moment hazardous, step to propose that the Smoky Hill cultural complex generally is not far from the sort of generalized "ancestral culture" which Spaulding (1956, p. 79) aptly suggests may have arisen in the Central Plains in post-Hopewellian times and fathered, so to speak, the Upper Republican and Nebraska Aspects as we now know them. . . .

The suggested southward distribution [of the Smoky Hill Aspect], *as down the Neosho drainage into Oklahoma, should certainly be worked out. As has been noted elsewhere in this paper, locally exotic pottery commonly associated with the Spiro Focus was found in direct association with Smoky Hill burials at the Whiteford Site. This, aside from its obvious connotations of chronological equivalence, suggests the possibility of more fundamental relationships that should not be entirely overlooked because of the wide and obvious differences otherwise between the two manifestations.*

FIGURE 75 Radiocarbon dates for the Central Plains Tradition.

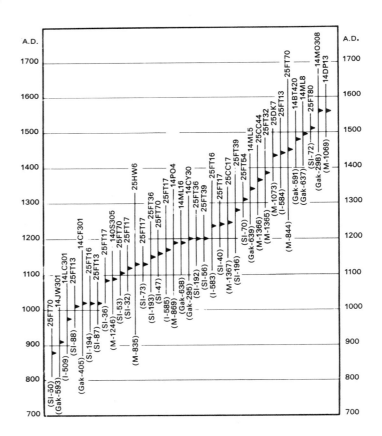

The house types attributed by Orr to the Early and Middle Spiro components, for example, are not far, in respect to floor plan, from the typical Central Plains earthlodge, which appears first in the general time period and cultural stage with which we are here concerned; and the Spiro houses are said (Orr, 1946, p. 230) to have been "a few inches to a foot under the surface." As I have pointed out above, many of the Central Plains earthlodges were not pit houses but were surface or near-surface structures, apparently like those of the lower Arkansas-Red River area. In the Central Plains, moreover, the square or rectangular earthlodge is associated with hoe tillage, direct evidence of fishing, a basically eastern pottery complex, and a way of life generally much more eastern than western in flavor. (Wedel, 1959, pp. 564–566)

INITIAL COALESCENT VARIANT

None of the village sites excavated to date in the Middle Missouri Valley is truly representative of the Central Plains Tradition. However, the sites which are assigned to the Initial Coalescent Variant might well be considered as belonging to a modified Central Plains Tradition. Their basic trait complexes correspond closely to those of the Central Plains sites; the few significant differences between Initial Coalescent and Central Plains are almost certainly the result of borrowing from the contemporary Middle Missouri villagers.

The Initial Coalescent sites represent the first stage in the blending of the older Central Plains and Middle Missouri traditions, a blending which culminated in the village complexes which existed in the Northern Plains during the 18th and early 19th centuries.

GEOGRAPHIC DISTRIBUTION

The distribution of the Initial Coalescent villages is definitely restricted (figs. 73 and 76). The variant is represented by less than a dozen sites in the Big Bend region. Most of them are on the left bank of the Missouri. Only two of the ones which have been excavated, Arzberger (39HU6) and Black Partizan (39LM218), have been reported to

date (Spaulding, 1956; Caldwell, 1966b).

HOUSES

The houses of the Initial Coalescent sites are similar to those of the Central Plains Tradition, while they contrast sharply with the long-rectangular structure of the Middle Missouri Tradition sites. Some details of the Initial Coalescent houses are closely consistent, while others vary considerably. An unlined basin-shaped firepit was typically located at the center of the house floor. The primary element of the superstructure consisted of four heavy posts, or sometimes paired lighter posts, set at the corners of a square which had the firepit located approximately at its center. These posts presumably supported four stringers which carried most of the load of a dome-shaped superstructure. Initial Coalescent houses had an entrance passage from 4 to 5 feet wide which extended out some distance from the house wall. Its walls included a series of small vertical posts set 1 foot or so apart. The centerline of the entrance passage almost always ran at right angles to a line connecting two of the primary support posts of the house. An extension of the centerline passed about midway between those two posts and intersected the central firepit. These features also are characteristic of the houses of the Central Plains Tradition.

Initial Coalescent houses were less consistent in the matters of shape and superstructure. House III at Arzberger had a ground plan which might be described either as a square with deeply rounded corners or a circle with four flattened sides. This plan is nearly identical with that found in the typical houses of the Central Plains Tradition. The rest of the reported Initial Coalescent houses whose shapes are clearly defined are more nearly circular. The shapes of a few Arzberger and Black Partizan houses were not clearly discernible.

Most of the Initial Coalescent houses had numerous postholes spaced more or less regularly around the perimeter of the floor. These presumably held the wall posts of a superstructure like that of the historic earthlodge of the region. The house at Black Partizan designated as Excavation Unit 8 lacked the regularly spaced wall posts. Its ground plan is quite similar to those of the houses excavated at the Extended Coalescent

FIGURE 76
INITIAL COALESCENT SITES

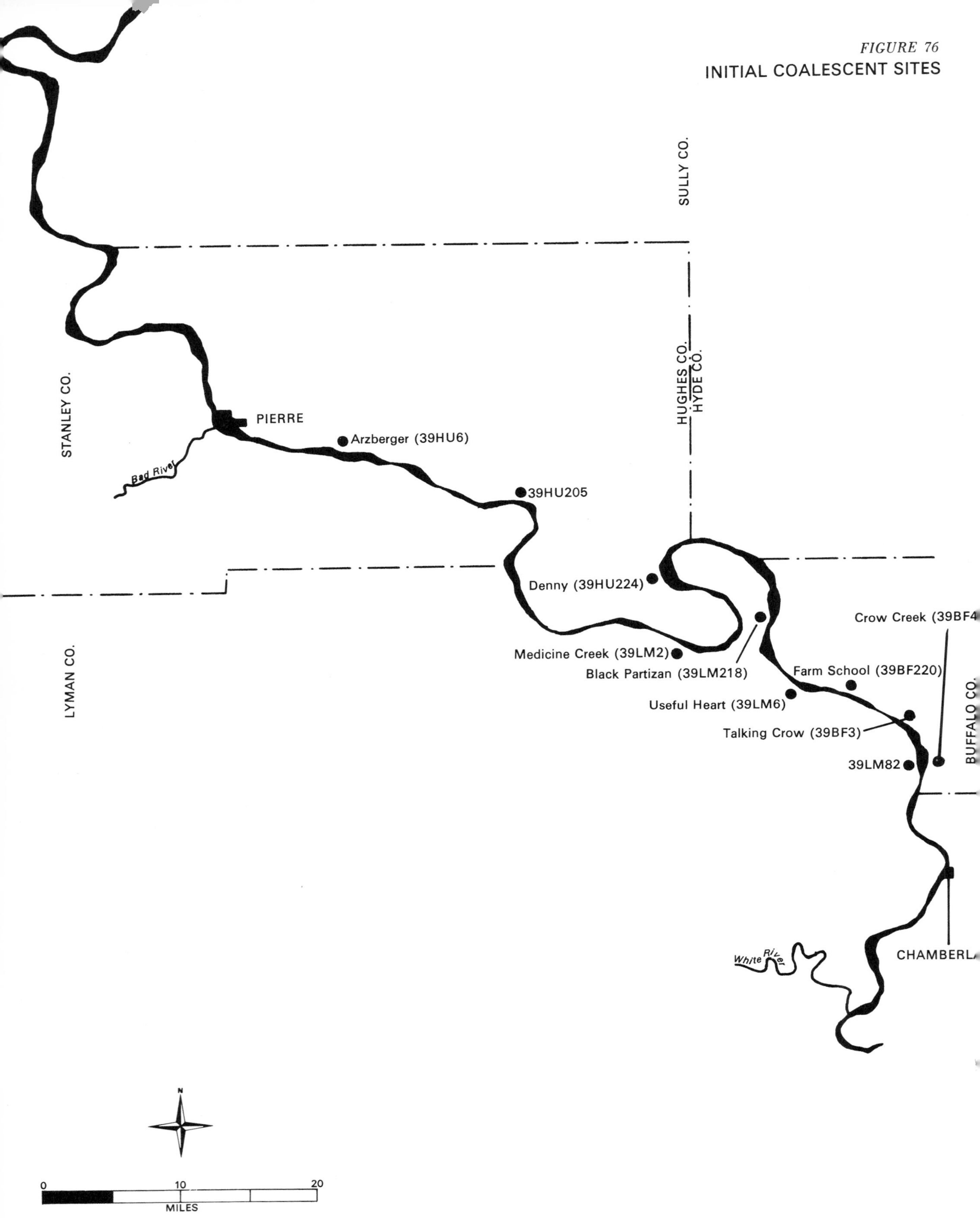

SULLY CO.

STANLEY CO.

HUGHES CO.
HYDE CO.

PIERRE

Bad River

● Arzberger (39HU6)

●39HU205

Denny (39HU224)●

LYMAN CO.

Medicine Creek (39LM2)●

Black Partizan (39LM218)●

Useful Heart (39LM6)●

Talking Crow (39BF3)●

Crow Creek (39BF4

Farm School (39BF220)●

BUFFALO CO.

39LM82●

White River

CHAMBERL

N

0 ——— 10 ——— 20
MILES

Demery Site (Woolworth and Wood, 1964). Similar structures from Post-Contact Coalescent villages include those excavated at the Spotted Bear Site (39HU26) (Hurt, 1954), Feature 27 at the Phillips Ranch Site (39ST14) (Lehmer, 1954b), and the houses of the late component at the Fire Heart Creek Site (32SI2) (Lehmer, 1966). There is good evidence that these houses had conical superstructures resembling those of the historic Mandan and Hidatsa eagle trapping lodges (cf. Wilson, 1934; Bowers, 1950). Their occurrence in Initial, Extended, and Post-Contact Coalescent sites indicates that they were a minority house type which coexisted with the more common earthlodge throughout the life of the Coalescent Tradition.

CACHE PITS

The cache pits of all the Coalescent variants include irregular, straight-sided, and bell-shaped or undercut forms like those of the Middle Missouri Tradition.

VILLAGE SIZE AND PLAN

The size and plan of the Initial Coalescent sites both compare and contrast with the villages of the Central Plains Tradition. As in the Central Plains sites, the houses of the Initial Coalescent villages are widely spaced and scattered in a random fashion through the village area. The Initial Coalescent villages probably contained more houses than those of the Central Plains Tradition, but there was a much lower density per acre than in sites of the Middle Missouri Tradition and those of the late Post-Contact Coalescent villages.

FORTIFICATIONS

The fortifications at the Arzberger and Black Partizan sites consisted of long curving ditches, backed by palisades on the inside of the ditch (fig. 42). Bastions were present in both the ditches and palisades. At Arzberger, the ditch-palisade system appears to have completely enclosed the village. At Black Partizan it did not extend along the steep terrace edge at the east side of the site, although a segment of ditch there may have been destroyed by erosion.

The layouts of both the Arzberger and Black Partizan villages suggest that they may have originally been unfortified (Spaulding, 1956, map 1; Caldwell, 1966b, fig. 2). The enclosed area at Arzberger was a fairly regular ellipse with axes of about 1,300 and 2,000 feet. The roughly oval area enclosed by the ditch at Black Partizan was somewhat smaller, with axes of approximately 750 and 1,250 feet. By way of comparison, the fortifications at the Terminal Middle Missouri Huff Site (32MO11) enclosed a rectangular area measuring 700 by 800 feet (Wood, 1967, p. 23) and the major axes of the elliptical area inside the ditch at the Post-Contact Coalescent Phillips Ranch Site (39ST14) measured only about 230 and 300 feet (Lehmer, 1954b, p. 85). The striking difference between these sites and Arzberger and Black Partizan is not primarily the size of the sites, but rather the number of houses within the fortified area. Wood reports over 100 houses at the Huff Site, making the average density in excess of 11 houses for each acre enclosed by the fortification system. At Phillips Ranch the density is well in excess of 14 houses per acre. In both cases, the builders seem to have intentionally kept the village as compact as possible, with a corresponding reduction in the extent of the fortifications.

In contrast, Spaulding (1956, pp. 5–6) points out that there are surface indications of only 44 houses at the Arzberger Site, which works out to the extremely low density of only one house per acre of fortified enclosure. The presence of two components at Black Partizan makes it impossible to estimate accurately how many houses relate to the Initial Coalescent occupation, but there seems to be every indication that the number of houses per acre was on the order of that at Arzberger.

The situation at Arzberger and the one which presumably obtained at Black Partizan might be explained in several ways. The most likely would seem to be that the villages were originally scattered and unfortified communities like the ones typical of the Central Plains Tradition, and that enemy pressure later necessitated fortifying sprawling villages which had not been developed with that eventuality in mind.

The presence of fortifications as a characteristic trait of the Initial Coalescent villages is a feature which contrasts sharply with the lack of fortifications at villages of the Central Plains Tradition.

BURIAL CUSTOMS

The burial customs of the Initial Coalescent

people are unknown so far as I am aware.

POTTERY

The pottery from the Initial Coalescent sites shows a blending of Central Plains and Middle Missouri attributes. Vessel form and decoration are strongly reminiscent of the varieties found in the Upper Republican sites. Cord-impressed decoration is practically nonexistent. Rims include flared, collared, and vertical forms. Vertical rims range from straight to curved in cross section; the important characteristic is the orientation.

Surface finish of the Initial Coalescent vessels shows a considerable range of variation. There is almost always a high percentage of plain body sherds. Other body sherds are cord roughened, simple stamped, or occasionally check stamped. Cord-roughened sherds made up approximately 12 percent of the sample from the Arzberger Site (Spaulding, 1956, p. 122). They comprised 20 percent of the total body sherds from the two-component Black Partizan Site (Caldwell, 1966b, p. 31), 18 percent of the bodies from the two-component Farm School Site (Neuman, 1961c, p. 193), and 23 percent of all the body sherds found during the first season's work at the Talking Crow Site, which includes an Initial Coalescent component (C. S. Smith, 1951, p. 32).

Cord-roughened bodies of Initial Coalescent pottery almost certainly hark back to the cord roughening of the Central Plains Tradition. The presence of this surface finish should be considered as a diagnostic of the Initial Coalescent Variant. The simple-stamped finish on Initial Coalescent pottery presumably represents borrowing from the Middle Missouri Tradition. It is one of the hallmarks of the coalescence of the Central Plains and Middle Missouri Traditions.

STONE, BONE, AND SHELL ARTIFACTS

The stone, bone, and shell artifacts from Initial Coalescent sites also point to a blending of cultural traditions. While some items, such as scapula hoes and snubnose scrapers, were common to both the Central Plains and Middle Missouri Traditions, a few Initial Coalescent traits, including diamond-shaped knives with beveled edges and tobacco pipes, almost certainly derived from the Central Plains Tradition. Other artifacts found in Initial Coalescent sites occur rarely or not at all in Central Plains contexts. They include grooved mauls, knives made of plate chalcedony, and horn scoops or bison skull hoes. These were presumably borrowed from Middle Missouri groups.

CHRONOLOGY

The chronology of the Initial Coalescent Variant is based on three radiocarbon determinations and a number of tree-ring dates. The Initial Coalescent component at the Crow Creek Site (39BF11) has yielded a single radiocarbon date of A.D. 1390 ± 150 (M–1079a), and dates of A.D. 1450 ± 150 (M–1126) and 1520 ± 200 (M–1126a) have been reported from Arzberger (fig. 34). These convert to 1395 ± 150, 1410 ± 150, and 1455 ± 200, respectively, on the basis of the Stuiver and Suess curve. Tree-ring dates of A.D. 1441 for a sample from the Crow Creek Site and 1468+ for a sample from Black Partizan have been reported (MBP Chronology Program, Statement No. 3). Weakly (MS.) lists a series of 11 tree-ring dates from the Crow Creek Site. An indeterminate number of outside rings was missing from 10 of the specimens, and only one of them was definitely associated with the Initial Coalescent component at the site. Weakly's dates, ranging from A.D. 1385+ to 1508+, accord very well with the others available for the variant.

On the basis of presently available evidence, I would estimate a beginning date of roughly A.D. 1400 for the Initial Coalescent Variant. The terminal date would be marked by the transition from Initial to Extended Coalescent. Dates from sites representing each variant indicate that it could not have taken place later than A.D. 1550.

TAXONOMIC SUBDIVISIONS

The subdivisions of the Initial Coalescent Variant are not now readily apparent. In his recent analysis, Caldwell (1966b, p. 85) recognizes an Arzberger Phase which includes the Arzberger Site and the early component at Black Partizan, and he suggests that other Initial Coalescent components in the Big Bend region should probably be included as well. He goes on to suggest that the Lynch Village (25BD1) and several other sites in northeastern Nebraska are closely related to the Arzberger Phase, although they are set apart from it by lack of fortifications and certain positive traits. It may be that the Lynch complex, which Witty (1962) grouped with Arzberger in an Anoka Focus, should be included in a separate Initial Coalescent phase or subphase.

ORIGINS

The origins of the Initial Coalescent Variant are traceable, in part, to the Central Plains Tradition. It is possible that Initial Coalescent resulted from a diffusion of Central Plains traits to some group in the Missouri Valley, with a consequent displacement of their pre-existing culture. It seems much more likely, however, that the Initial Coalescent Variant represents an actual population influx from the Central Plains subarea. It has been suggested that a movement of this sort might have been in response to drought conditions in the Central Plains (Lehmer, 1954b, pp. 148–150; Wedel, 1961, pp. 182–184). Any consideration of Initial Coalescent origins must also take account of the fact that the complex includes a number of traits which are rare or nonexistent in sites of the Central Plains Tradition. These elements are part of the Middle Missouri Tradition. Their occurrence in Initial Coalescent sites appears to represent the first stage of an amalgamation of Central Plains and Middle Missouri into the Coalescent Tradition.

EXTENDED COALESCENT VARIANT

The Extended Coalescent Variant appears to have been a direct outgrowth of Initial Coalescent. Differences between Initial and Extended Coalescent seem to be primarily the result of modifying and expanding the Initial Coalescent culture by a series of changes which originated within the configuration itself.

GEOGRAPHIC DISTRIBUTION

The distribution of Extended Coalescent sites contrasts markedly with that of the Initial Coalescent sites. There is evidence of an explosive increase in the number of villages and in the extent of the area occupied (fig. 77). Well over 100 sites represented in the River Basin Surveys' collections from the Middle Missouri subarea show evidence of an Extended Coalescent occupation, either as a single component or as one of several components. Extended Coalescent sites have a nearly continuous distribution throughout the 475 river miles between the North Dakota-South Dakota border and the White River. Similar sites also occur as far downstream as the Nebraska line. It should be emphasized that many of these sites are small and show evidence of a relatively short occupation. It seems likely that there was some growth in population after Initial Coalescent times, but it was probably not nearly so great as the number of Extended Coalescent sites would suggest.

HOUSES

The houses of the Extended Coalescent sites seem to perpetuate the basic Initial Coalescent architectural tradition, but with considerable individual variation. The ideal house was a circular structure having a central firepit, four primary superstructure support posts set in a square around the firepit, and an enclosed entrance passage. Available ground plans indicate that this ideal was realized in only a relatively small proportion of the houses built. Indications of an entrance passage are often sketchy; the firepit (or firepits) is commonly not in the center of the floor; and postholes indicating four primary superstructure supports are often impossible to recognize.

House shapes also show considerable variability. An active imagination may discern rectanguloid forms with rounded corners and entrance passages in the posthole arrangements of the three structures uncovered at the Molstad Site (Hoffman, 1967, figs. 5, 6, and 7). This raises the possibility that the old Initial Coalescent house form lasted on as a minority style in the Extended Coalescent architectural complex. Outlines indicated by the wall posts of other Extended Coalescent houses include a few approximate circles, ovals, and lopsided curvilinear forms. It seems probable that there was a corresponding range of variation in the details of the superstructure construction. Some Extended Coalescent houses may have had tepee-like pole superstructures.

Extended Coalescent houses give the impression of having been hurriedly built and intended for only short occupation. They also suggest that the builders were struggling with the problem of relating the square of the primary superstructure supports to the circle of the outer wall of the house.

CACHE PITS

Cache pits in the Extended Coalescent villages include undercut and straight-sided forms and pocket caches. For the most part, they tend to be small and few in number.

VILLAGE SIZE
AND PLAN

Village size and plan vary appreciably within the Extended Coalescent Variant. The most common type of village seems to have been a small, irregular cluster of houses. Some settlements consisted of houses strung out singly and in small groups for considerable distances along the terrace edge at the margin of the Missouri floodplain, or on high ridges at the edge of the valley. This arrangement is essentially the same as that of a great many of the villages of the Central Plains Tradition. At least some Extended Coalescent Villages, such as the Spain Site (39LM301), were located on the floodplain proper, suggesting that they may have been winter villages (Smith and Grange, 1958).

Most of the excavated Extended Coalescent villages had very thin refuse deposits and yielded smaller numbers of artifacts than the majority of sites of the Middle Missouri Tradition. This implies that they were occupied for only short periods of time and that the Extended Coalescent population was generally a rather mobile one.

A few Extended Coalescent sites, mostly in the Grand-Moreau region, depart radically from the other villages representing this complex. Sites of this sort are typified by the Davis Site (39CO14). The houses are closely packed inside an extensive fortification system and heavy deposits of refuse point to a long occupation. Internal evidence indicates that these sites were late within the total span of the Extended Coalescent Variant.

FORTIFICATIONS

Fortifications seem to be restricted to the northern and the southernmost parts of the Extended Coalescent range. The Extended Coalescent component at the Scalp Creek Site (39GR1), located near the South Dakota-Nebraska line, was protected by a ditch across the base of the point on which the village was situated, and the cluster of some 15 houses appeared to have been surrounded by a palisade (Hurt, 1952, pp. 3–5). Fortified Extended Coalescent sites are not known to occur in the Big Bend region nor in the Bad-Cheyenne region below the mouth of the Cheyenne River.

Johnston and Hoffman (1966) have assigned five fortified Extended Coalescent sites on the right bank of the Missouri, from just north of the Cheyenne River to a point a few miles above the Moreau, to the Le Compte Focus. Each of these villages consists of a number of houses scattered for some distance along the terrace edge. A few houses, usually near the center of the village were surrounded by a curved fortification ditch and seem to have served as a defensive strongpoint within the community (fig. 42). A palisade with one or two bastions was found inside the ditch at the excavated sites.

The Hosterman Site (39PO7) should also be included with those listed by Johnston and Hoffman. Located on the left bank of the Missouri about halfway between the Cheyenne and the Moreau Rivers, it had about 15 houses enclosed by a semicircular fortification ditch and palisade that terminated at the terrace edge. This was evidently the fortified nucleus, for as Miller (1964, p. 225) noted, "While the main portion of the [Hosterman] settlement was surrounded by a palisade and ditch . . . other houses together with their trash areas occurred to the east and north of the palisaded area unsurrounded by any protective devices." Aerial photographs in the Department of Agriculture's 1938 series show a number of other settlements of this type on both the right and left banks of the Missouri. Sites 39CO205 and 39WW204 and one component at Site 39WW8 are the most clearly defined.

The Payne Site (39WW302) is another small Extended Coalescent site on the left bank of the Missouri. Wilmeth (1958) found that this village was completely surrounded by an oval palisade but lacked a fortification ditch. This suggests the possibility that some unexcavated Extended Coalescent sites which appear to be unfortified may have been provided with a fortification system.

The Davis Site exhibits still another com-

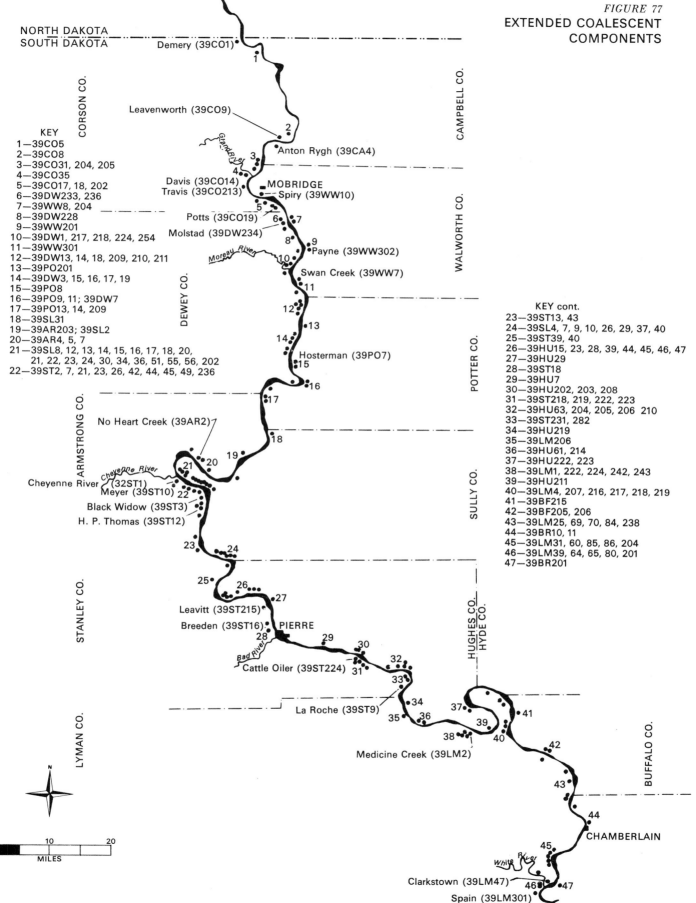

FIGURE 77
EXTENDED COALESCENT
COMPONENTS

bination of village plan and fortification system. The occupation area adjoins a steep bank, and the village is enclosed on the other three sides by a well-defined ditch. The ditch, in contrast to those at most other fortified Extended Coalescent sites, was laid out in irregular lines which form a rough rectangle. Aerial photographs indicate that Site 39WW8, a few miles below Davis on the opposite side of the Missouri, had a similar fortification ditch, in addition to a smaller one like the Le Compte sites.

BURIAL CUSTOMS

The burial customs of the Extended Coalescent Variant are poorly known. At the two-component Swan Creek Site (39WW7), Hurt found both individual primary inhumations in graves, often covered with wooden slabs or poles, and multiple burials which frequently contained partial and disarticulated skeletons. There were indications that at least some of the group burials were later than some of the primary inhumations (Hurt, 1957, pp. 14–22). Because of this, the primary individual burials were equated with the Akaska Focus (Extended Coalescent) and the group burials with the Le Beau Focus (Post-Contact Coalescent). Hurt points out, however, that this conclusion is weakened by the apparent association of a tubular copper bead with one of the primary inhumations and a glass bead with another one (Hurt, op. cit., pp. 17 and 22–23).

Perhaps both types of burial at Swan Creek were associated with the Post-Contact Coalescent occupation. It is possible that the primary inhumations in the covered graves represent the standard burial pattern, and that the mass burials were made in the wake of one of the smallpox epidemics that ravaged the village populations of the Middle Missouri during the 18th century.

POTTERY

The pottery from Extended Coalescent villages is easily distinguished from that of other complexes in the Middle Missouri subarea. It is grit tempered, like the other native wares, but the temper is comparatively sparse and has a somewhat smaller average grain size. The compact paste seems to be harder than the other Middle Missouri varieties, and I suspect that it may have been fired at a higher temperature. Vessel walls are typically thin; in some cases, they are extremely thin for the size of the vessel. Colors range from buff through light orange to dark gray, but there is a tendency for brownish and reddish shades to predominate. Vessel exteriors are characteristically simple stamped or plain. Cord roughening is so rare that it cannot be considered an integral part of the ceramic tradition.

Rim forms are varied. Rims with straight or curved cross sections and a nearly vertical orientation predominate. A few flared rims and deeply curved S-rims, like those of the earlier complexes, occur. Another variety of S-rim also makes its appearance during Extended Coalescent times. Both the upper and lower segments of the S are relatively high. The lower segment almost always has a shallow curve, and this is also commonly true of the upper segment. This high shallow S-rim was an important addition to the Coalescent pottery tradition, and it spread from Extended Coalescent complexes to other variants in the region.

Some Extended Coalescent vessel lips were no thicker than the vessel walls, some were slightly thickened when decorative elements were impressed into the lip. It was also a common practice to thicken vessel lips in various ways. Some of the thickened rims have the T-shaped or inverted L-shaped cross section of Smith's Iona series (Smith and Grange, 1958). Other thickened Extended Coalescent lips foreshadow the braced rim which is an important attribute of Post-Contact Coalescent pottery.

Most Extended Coalescent vessels had incised decoration on the rims, lips, and shoulders, and much of the decoration was very skillfully executed. Cord-impressed rim decoration does occur, but it is generally a minority element and seems to be almost entirely confined to the sites in the northern part of the Extended Coalescent range. Vertical striations or brushing on the vessel necks also occurs on some of the northern Extended Coalescent pottery. This trait is another one which becomes much more common in the pottery of the succeeding Post-Contact Coalescent Variant.

STONE, BONE, AND SHELL ARTIFACTS

Artifacts of stone, bone, and shell from Extended Coalescent sites tend to duplicate those of the Initial Coalescent Variant.

1 CM

FIGURE 78

Unnotched arrow points are more common than notched forms. Pecked and polished grooved axes occur rarely. Catlinite is present more often than in sites of the earlier complexes, and pipes seem to be somewhat more common.

Two distinctive artifacts of the Middle Missouri Tradition also appear in late Extended Coalescent sites. These are the metatarsal flesher and the L-shaped antler fleshing adz. Bone sliders (fig. 78), which are common in Post-Contact sites, also occur occasionally in Extended Coalescent contexts (cf. Wilmeth, 1958, p. 9, and fig. 21). In its classic form, the bone slider is a segment from a large rib, usually about 13 cm. long. One end is cut square, with the cancellous tissue hollowed out to leave a fairly deep socket. The other end has a triangular shape, which was produced by making a transverse cut on the concave side of the bone and a pair of intersecting diagonal cuts on the opposite surface. These objects are nearly identical to gaming pieces which Culin (1907, pp. 399–419) reports from ethnographic collections.

Materials used for chipped stone artifacts from both the Extended and Initial Coalescent sites contrast strikingly with those used by the people of the Middle Missouri Tradition. A very high proportion of the chipped pieces from the Middle Missouri Tradition sites (often up to about 75 percent) were made of Knife River flint. This material is decidedly rare in Initial and Extended Coalescent assemblages, where light colored varieties of chalcedony, jasper, chert, quartzite, and quartz predominate.

CHRONOLOGY

The chronology of the Extended Coalescent Variant is based on radiocarbon dates from three sites and tree-ring dates from three other villages. The six dated sites have a geographic range from the upper Big Bend region through the Bad-Cheyenne to the lower Grand-Moreau region.

Four radiocarbon dates have been reported from the Molstad Village (39DW 234). They are 1475±100 (SI–25), 1565 ±95 (I–720), 1590±50 (SI–59), and 1675 ±85 (I–721). Internal evidence from the site indicated a relative short occupation. The excavator discounted the 1675±85 date because of inferred contamination and concluded that the occupation took place be-

tween 1540 and 1575 (Hoffman, 1967, p. 45). However, I believe that a slightly later time of occupation can be estimated on the basis of the standard deviations of the radiocarbon dates. Increasing the earliest mean date by one sigma raises it to A.D. 1575, and reducing the latest mean date by one sigma lowers it to A.D. 1590. Leaving the other two mean dates unchanged, we have dates for Molstad Village of 1565, 1575, and 1590 (twice), a range of 25 years.

Five radiocarbon dates have been reported which appear to associate with the Extended Coalescent component at the La Roche Site (39ST9) in the upper Big Bend region. They are 1500±120 (SI–169), 1520±60 (SI–104), 1640±55 (SI–106), 1660±60 (SI–97), and 1680±50 (SI–95). The mean dates fall into two groups, one at the beginning of the 16th century and the other well into the 17th century. The distribution of dates appears to confirm the excavator's suggestion that there were two Extended Coalescent components at the site. It should be noted, however, that the specimens that yielded the 1500 and 1680 dates appear to have been part of the superstructure of the same house (Hoffman, 1968, p. 64).

Hoffman (idem.) also reports two dates from the nearby Bowers' La Roche Site (39ST232) of 1240±90 (SI–215) and 1400±210 (SI–214). The former is so early that it is discounted as an anomaly. The latter has such a large standard deviation that the date could fall anywhere between A.D. 1190 and 1610, making it almost valueless for comparative purposes.

The last Extended Coalescent radiocarbon date available is one from limited excavations at Site 39SL24 across the Missouri from the mouth of the Cheyenne River. This date of 1710±80 (I–614) seems somewhat too late for the complex represented there, since it would place the site well within the early years of the contact period. It, too, should probably be reduced within the range of its standard deviation.

Conversion of the mean radiocarbon dates for the Extended Coalescent Variant by the Stuiver and Suess curve throws four of them back into the 15th century, gives five others values between 1510 and 1575, and reduces the latest one to 1645±80. Such a modification makes the group far

FIGURE 79

too early to accord with available dates for the other cultural complexes in the region.

The tree-ring dates for the Extended Coalescent Variant show a much closer grouping than the radiocarbon determinations. Statement No. 3 of the Missouri Basin Chronology Program included a bark date of 1566 for the No Heart Creek Site (39AR2) and a date of 1650+ for the Medicine Creek Site (39LM222). Weakly (MS.) lists three additional dates from the Medicine Creek Site which range from 1574+ to 1593+. Weakly also reports a series of seven dates from the Sully Site (39SL4) which range from 1663+ to 1694+. These dates suggest that an Extended Coalescent component existed at Sully, but this cannot be established until all the information from the site has been analyzed.

The three early radiocarbon dates from Molstad and the La Roche sites raise the possibility that the transition from Initial to Extended Coalescent began sometime before the middle of the 16th century. The transition probably lasted over a number of years, but every indication points to its having been completed by the mid-1500's. The end of the Extended Coalescent Variant is marked by the interchange of traits with the Terminal Middle Missouri Variant, which is discussed below. This probably took place in the latter half of the 17th century.

The duration of the Extended Coalescent Variant may be estimated to have covered the period from A.D. 1550 to 1675.

TAXONOMIC SUBDIVISIONS

The subdivisions of the Extended Coalescent complex, like those of the other precontact complexes of the region, cannot be defined with any precision at this time. The basic Extended Coalescent culture corresponds generally with that of the Chouteau Aspect proposed earlier (Stephenson, 1954; Hoffman, 1967). Five foci centering in the Middle Missouri subarea have been included in the Chouteau Aspect at various times: La Roche (Hurt, 1952), Bennett (Stephenson, 1954), Akaska (Hurt, 1957), Shannon (Smith and Grange, 1958), and Le Compte (Johnston and Hoffman, 1966). The Redbird Focus of northeastern Nebraska has also been included in the Chouteau Aspect

(Wood, 1965).

While the phases which are coming to be recognized in the Middle Missouri subarea are not strictly equivalent to the foci which have been defined in the past, the two kinds of taxonomic units will inevitably show some correspondence since both phases and foci recognize essentially the same order of cultural complexes. Smith and Johnson (1968, p. 49) have proposed a Shannon Phase which would include most of the Extended Coalescent manifestations from the Big Bend southward. The most obvious distinguishing characteristic is the pottery, which tends to be somewhat coarser and heavier than that found farther upstream. It also seems likely that phases will be established which correspond generally to the Le Compte and La Roche Foci. The Le Compte configuration has a distinctive settlement pattern characterized by small fortified centers in fairly large and scattered house clusters. The La Roche sites include the majority of the ones assigned to the Extended Coalescent Variant—fairly small unfortified villages with widely separated houses. It appears that at least two subphases, previously assigned to the Bennett Focus, will be recognized. A fourth phase will almost certainly be needed for the late Extended Coalescent developments in the Grand-Moreau region which embrace elements borrowed from the Terminal Middle Missouri peoples. This configuration will presumably include the materials assigned to the Akaska Focus, toegther with others such as those from the Davis Site. Again there is a possibility of divisions at the subphase level.

ORIGINS

The origins of the Extended Coalescent Variant appear to involve a direct development out of the older Initial Coalescent Variant.

TERMINAL MIDDLE MISSOURI VARIANT

The culture of the Terminal Middle Missouri Variant, the final manifestation of the Middle Missouri Tradition, seems to have coexisted with the Extended Coalescent

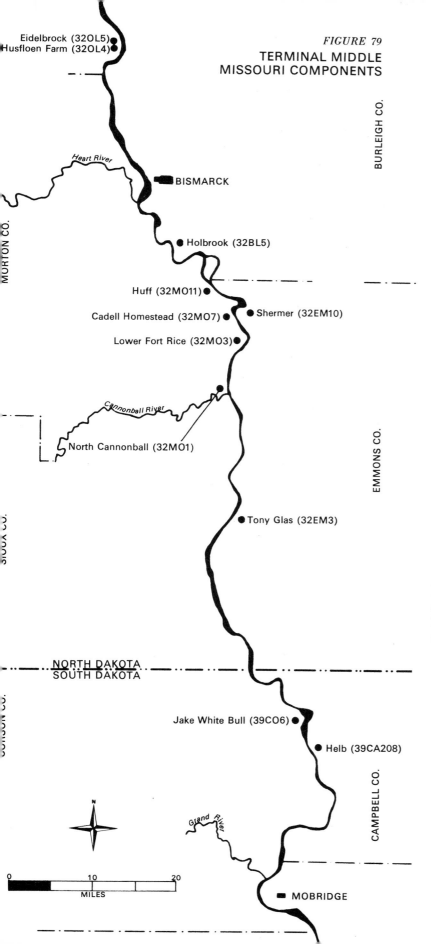

FIGURE 79

TERMINAL MIDDLE
MISSOURI COMPONENTS

Eidelbrock (32OL5)
Husfloen Farm (32OL4)

Heart River

BURLEIGH CO.

MORTON CO.

BISMARCK

Holbrook (32BL5)

Huff (32MO11)

Cadell Homestead (32MO7) Shermer (32EM10)

Lower Fort Rice (32MO3)

Cannonball River

North Cannonball (32MO1)

EMMONS CO.

SIOUX CO.

Tony Glas (32EM3)

NORTH DAKOTA
SOUTH DAKOTA

CORSON CO.

Jake White Bull (39CO6)

Helb (39CA208)

CAMPBELL CO.

N

Grand River

0   10   20
MILES

MOBRIDGE

Variant during the time from roughly A.D. 1550 to 1675. The Coalescent groups occupied the southern part of the Middle Missouri subarea, whereas the Terminal Middle Missouri peoples were restricted to the northern section.

GEOGRAPHIC
DISTRIBUTION

The distribution of the Terminal Middle Missouri villages is definitely more restricted than that of the Extended Middle Missouri settlements (fig. 79). Will and Hecker (1944) classify over 40 sites as "Middle Mandan." This category is approximately equivalent to Terminal Middle Missouri. Determining how many of these sites can be counted as Terminal Middle Missouri has required the establishment of criteria which are diagnostic for that variant. Will and Hecker's site categorization was based almost entirely on pottery. This trait still provides the primary criterion for distinguishing Terminal from Extended Middle Missouri, but house type, village size, the presence of fortifications, and geographic area are also of considerable importance in this connection.

A number of the sites which Will and Hecker include in their inventory are listed as "probable sites." Sherd collections from them are not available, nor from other relatively insignificant localities. Also, refinements in the pottery typology for the region indicate that other sites which they classify as Middle Mandan should be considered as Extended rather than Terminal Middle Missouri, or as having both Extended Middle Missouri and Post-Contact Coalescent components.

Sites counted here as Terminal Middle Missouri have pottery assemblages of the sort described below. All of them appear to have long-rectangular houses as the dominant architectural form. All of them are located well to the north of the Grand River, in the Cannonball and Knife-Heart regions. They were characteristically large, and their size contrasts sharply with that of the northern Extended Middle Missouri villages. The Cannonball and Knife-Heart regions contain more than twice as many Extended as Terminal Middle Missouri sites. The increase in size and the reduction in the number of sites combine to suggest that the populations of the small Extended Mid-

121

dle Missouri villages were later concentrated in the larger Terminal Middle Missouri towns. The Terminal Middle Missouri sites also differ from the northern Extended Middle Missouri villages in having strong fortification systems.

The pottery, village size, fortifications, and location in the northern part of the Middle Missouri subarea provide the basis for recognizing 11 Terminal Middle Missouri sites in the Cannonball and southern Knife-Heart regions. Three of them—Tony Glas (32EM3), Jake White Bull (39CO6), and Helb (39CA208)—are scattered along the Missouri below the Cannonball River. While they are large fortified villages, the pottery found in them lacks a number of characteristics of the other Terminal Middle Missouri assemblages. This suggests that these three sites date from the earliest years of the Terminal Middle Missouri span and may be transitional between the Extended and Terminal Middle Missouri complexes. The classic Terminal Middle Missouri sites lie between the Cannonball River and Square Buttes.

It is not possible, at this time, to recognize with any certainty Terminal Middle Missouri sites in the Knife-Heart region upstream from Square Buttes. A high incidence of check-stamped body sherds in the early villages there demonstrates that the ceramic tradition differed somewhat from that of contemporary sites downstream. None of the Middle Missouri Tradition sites north of Square Buttes were fortified, and none of the sites which appear to have only long-rectangular houses are particularly large. It is possible that this section of the valley was abandoned during Terminal Middle Missouri times. However, it seems more likely that the population remained there and concentrated in large villages only on the eve of the emergence of the Post-Contact Coalescent complex.

HOUSES,
CACHE PITS, AND
MISCELLANEOUS
STRUCTURES

The houses, cache pits, and miscellaneous structures of the Terminal Middle Missouri villages generally show a close similarity to those of the other variants of the Middle Missouri Tradition, but the long-rectangular houses characteristically did not have the interior earthen entrance ramp of the southern Middle Missouri structures.

Another kind of house appears as a minority type in at least one of the Terminal Middle Missouri sites. Wood (1967, pp. 51, 52) reports finding one structure at the Huff Site (32MO11) which had the central firepit, four primary support posts, and entrance passage of the Coalescent architectural tradition.

VILLAGE SIZE
AND PLAN

Village size and plan are diagnostic features of the Terminal Middle Missouri villages. The villages are consistently large; several of them include over 100 houses. Houses were arranged in rows, and the village layout often exhibits a remarkable regularity. A central open area or plaza seems to be a common characteristic of these communities.

FORTIFICATIONS

Fortifications are definitely present at the Terminal Middle Missouri sites south of Square Buttes, and they were the strongest and most elaborate ones provided by any of the village groups in the region. Both ditches and palisades inside the ditch were used. In most cases, the segments of the fortification followed reasonably straight lines rather than pronounced curves. Villages located in the angle between the Missouri terrace edge and a deeply incised tributary were protected by L-shaped ditches and palisades on the landward sides; those on the Missouri terrace edge were protected by U-shaped ditches and palisades on the other three sides. Most of the Terminal Middle Missouri fortification systems were studded with bastions spaced more or less evenly along the entire line of the works (fig. 42).

BURIAL CUSTOMS

The burial customs of the Terminal Middle Missouri people are unknown.

POTTERY

The pottery from the Terminal Middle Missouri sites is a direct carryover from the Extended Middle Missouri ceramic complex. Paste, temper, and form are like those of the earlier wares of the Middle Missouri Tradition. Most of the rims are either the flared forms of the Riggs series or the S-shaped forms of the Fort Yates series, which were first described on the basis of collections from Extended Middle Missouri sites (Hurt, 1953; Wood and Woolworth, 1964; Lehmer, 1966). Fillets were often added to the exterior of the flared rims, either just below the lip or near the middle of the rim. This trait is extremely rare in the northern Extended Middle Missouri sites. S-rims usually make up from 30 to over 70 percent of the samples from Terminal Middle Missouri sites. A minority of the flared and S-rims have lips and interior neck-body junctures which exhibit the angularity characteristic of the Initial Middle Missouri wares. This trait seems to have reappeared in the late northern Extended Middle Missouri sites, and to have been continued on the pottery of some of the Terminal Middle Missouri villages such as the Shermer Site (32EM10) (Sperry, 1968).

Two new rim forms occur in what are presumably the later Terminal Middle Missouri sites. One is a high, shallow S-rim similar to that already described for Extended Coalescent pottery but executed in the coarser paste of the Middle Missouri Tradition. The other is a braced form on a rim with a straight or curved cross section and nearly vertical orientation. The exterior of the rim just below the lip was thickened, often by the addition of a fillet of clay bonded to the surface. The forms of these pieces show a close resemblance to many of the Extended Coalescent rims except for the coarser paste of Middle Missouri Tradition pottery. The rim forms fall well within the range of the Stanley Braced Rim Ware (Lehmer, 1954b, pp. 42–46), but they surmounted higher, narrower

FIGURE 80   Full-grooved stone ax.

5 CM

bodies which lacked the well-defined Stanley shoulder.

STONE, BONE, AND SHELL ARTIFACTS

Stone, bone, and shell artifacts from the Terminal Middle Missouri sites are direct carryovers from the earlier variants of the tradition. The Terminal Middle Missouri sites seem, on the whole, to be richer in specimens than the earlier Extended Middle Missouri villages. There is also a noticeable elaboration of certain forms, especially those made of bone. This may reflect a greater degree of craft specialization within the larger communities of the Terminal Middle Missouri Variant.

A distinctive trait of the Terminal Middle Missouri sites, which may have appeared first in the late northern Extended Middle Missouri villages, is a long, wide, and relatively thin full-grooved ax with a definite ridge on each side of the groove (fig. 80). These axes are uniformly very well made. They do not occur in large numbers, and I suspect that they may have been traded into the region.

CHRONOLOGY

The chronology of the Terminal Middle Missouri Variant is based primarily on a series of radiocarbon dates from the Huff Site (fig. 34). Wood (1967, p. 115) lists five of them. He finds two of these unacceptable, SI–183, with a mean value after A.D. 1810, and SI–182, dated at A.D. 1180 ±140. In the latter case, even the mean date plus one standard deviation is entirely too early. The other three determinations, and three more released since the Huff report appeared (Wood, personal communication, 1968), give dates ranging from A.D. 1350±300 (SI–448) to 1770±120 (SI–180). The mean dates themselves cover a period of 420 years, which is impossibly long for the occupation of a single site. Adjusting the Huff dates (except SI–182 and SI–183) to plus or minus one standard deviation gives a greatly reduced span of A.D. 1570 to 1650. These dates make sense on the basis of other evidence.

George Will dated 11 wood specimens from Huff as part of his pioneer studies of dendrochronology in the Dakotas. His dates range from A.D. 1485 to 1543 (Will, 1946, pp. 15–16). While the indicated 58-year time span is reasonable, the dates

themselves seem to be too early to fit the overall Middle Missouri chronology.

The radiocarbon dates from Huff suggest that the Terminal Middle Missouri Variant may be tentatively assigned to the period between A.D. 1550 and 1675.

TAXONOMIC SUBDIVISIONS

The taxonomic subdivisions proposed to date are limited to a single Huff Focus. Reports by Wood (1967, pp. 131–139) and Sperry (1968, pp. 79–84) provide excellent summaries. It is possible that all of the Terminal Middle Missouri manifestations will prove to be assignable to a single phase. However, the pottery and other specimens from the Shermer Site suggest that differences between Shermer and Huff exist at the subphase level.

ORIGINS

The origins of the Terminal Middle Missouri Variant are firmly rooted in the earlier developments of the Middle Missouri Tradition.

CULTURAL INTERACTION, A.D. 1400–1675

Cultural interaction in the Dakotas became increasingly complex after the beginning of the 15th century. Prior to A.D. 1400 the contact situations involving the village cultures of the Middle Missouri subarea were primarily within the Middle Missouri Tradition. Subsequently, such *intra*-tradition contacts were far less important than contacts between the Middle Missouri and the Coalescent traditions. These *inter*-tradition contacts resulted in much more conspicuous changes in the native culture patterns.

The available evidence indicates that there were two concentrations of villages in the Middle Missouri at the beginning of the 15th century. One included the considerable number of Extended Middle Missouri villages in the Cannonball and Knife-Heart regions in central North Dakota. The second group was made up of the Modified Initial Middle Missouri communities in the Big Bend and lower Bad-Cheyenne regions.

A new factor was added to the cultural equation shortly after A.D. 1400, when the population which was responsible for the remains assigned to the Initial Coalescent Variant arrived in the southern part of the Middle Missouri subarea. These people established a few villages in the Big Bend region, but they apparently did not move into the area of the Modified Initial Middle Missouri villages on the right bank below the mouth of the Bad River. The close similarities in houses, pottery, and other artifacts between the Initial Coalescent Variant and the Central Plains Tradition leave little doubt that the Initial Coalescent groups were immigrants from the Central Plains.

It seems likely that the Modified Initial Middle Missouri villages continued to be occupied for at least a time after the Initial Coalescent Variant was established in the Big Bend region. If this was the case, the Modified Initial Middle Missouri and Initial Coalescent populations must have had some contacts after the beginning of the 15th century. The late dates from some of the Extended Middle Missouri sites in the Bad-Cheyenne region suggest that they too were occupied during the late 15th and early 16th centuries. Thus three different populations—Initial Coalescent, Modified Initial Middle Missouri, and Extended Middle Missouri—must have been in fairly close contact in the Big Bend and Bad-Cheyenne regions during the late 15th and early 16th centuries (figs. 69–73).

Some diffusion of Middle Missouri traits to the Initial Coalescent groups is apparent. The simple stamped pottery made by the Initial Coalescent people almost certainly represents copying of a Middle Missouri Tradition trait. Artifacts such as grooved mauls, plate chalcedony knives, and bison skull hoes or horn scoops were presumably borrowed from the same source, although their occurrence in the St. Helena sites of northeastern Nebraska (Cooper, 1936) may indicate that they had passed to peripheral Central Plains groups at a somewhat earlier time.

The elaborate bastioned fortifications at Initial Coalescent sites such as Arzberger and Black Partizan represent a striking addition to the trait list of the old Central Plains Tradition. The Middle Missouri Tradition is the obvious source of the idea of bastioned fortifications. The presence of fortifications at a village seems to be an excellent indication that the population lived under the threat of enemy attack. The most likely enemies in pre-horse times would have been other village populations. It also seems likely that any population which exerted sufficient pressure on another population to cause it to fortify its villages would be susceptible to reprisals and would have to fortify villages in turn. The one likely exception would be a case in which some of the group's villages lay well away from the scene of hostilities. Then, one would expect to find that only the border towns were fortified. The presence of fortifications at the southern Extended Middle Missouri sites and their absence from the northern Extended Middle Missouri towns would appear to be a case in point.

The lack of fortifications at the Modified Initial Middle Missouri sites suggests that the first Initial Coalescent settlers in the Big Bend region were fairly well received by the resident villagers.

The small numbers of houses and the great extent of the fortified areas at Arzberger and Black Partizan suggest that these villages were originally scattered and unfortified communities, like those of the Central Plains Tradition, and that enemy pressure later necessitated fortifying them. The need for fortifying the Initial Coalescent villages may well have resulted from a southward movement of Extended Middle Missouri groups during the latter part of the 15th century.

A second Extended Middle Missouri intrusion into the Bad-Cheyenne region is indicated by findings at the Thomas Riggs Site (39HU1). In his 1947 excavations here, Meleen (1949b) discovered evidence of the superposition of one long-rectangular house on another, suggesting that the site had been abandoned and later reoccupied. The tree-ring dates which Meleen reported from George Will support the inference of two occupations, while the artifact content indicates that they were both manifestations of the Extended Middle Missouri Variant.

The situation at the Hickey Brothers Site (39LM4) may have a bearing on cultural interaction around A.D. 1500 (Caldwell et al, 1964). The site lay well down

125

in the neck of the Big Bend of the Missouri. The three sides of the village away from the terrace edge were enclosed by a clearly marked, roughly rectangular ditch with seven evenly spaced bastions, and a palisade followed the inner line of the ditch at least part way around the habitation area. The houses have been described as "diffuse." Actually, there was nothing which could be identified as a permanent structure, but there were suggestions of temporary shelters. In the concluding section of their site report the authors state: "It is worth noting that the situation at the Hickey Brothers site suggests that the village defenses were completed prior to the large-scale building of houses" (Caldwell et al, 1964, p. 288).

A similar situation seems to have obtained at the Pitlick Site (39HU16), on the left bank of the Missouri some 15 miles upstream from Pierre. It was situated on a steep-sided point in the terrace edge, with a distinct ditch across the base of the point. Aerial photographs indicate two bastions near the center of the ditch, one pointed away from the village and the other toward it. Depressions which appear to indicate the presence of long-rectangular house pits are reported as being observable on the ground (Hurt, 1953, p. 61) and can also be seen on aerial photographs. A trench was cut across the ditch in 1958 by Charles H. McNutt for the River Basin Surveys. Here, as at Hickey Brothers, the fortification system seems to have been completed. House pits also appear to have been dug at Pitlick, but there is no evidence that superstructures were put up. The negligible specimen return and the general absence of charcoal and animal bone reported by Hurt and recorded in McNutt's field notes indicate an extremely brief occupation.

The artifact yield from Hickey Brothers was also extremely low, supporting the idea of a transient occupation. While the artifacts found leave no doubt that the Hickey Brothers Site represents the Middle Missouri Tradition, it is difficult to assign it to a particular variant. The bulk of the rim sherds are Extended Middle Missouri varieties. Seven rims (six from the same vessel) were classified as the Initial Middle Missouri type Anderson Low Rim, and 36 body

sherds are cord roughened (Caldwell et al, 1964, pp. 284–285). If these earlier sherds belong to the main occupation of the site, Hickey Brothers is Modified Initial Middle Missouri. On the other hand, if this pottery represents a fleeting occupation which preceded the attempt to establish the village, as the authors of the site report suggest, the main occupation is a manifestation of the Extended Middle Missouri Variant. In either case, Hickey Brothers seems to represent an unsuccessful attempt to establish a Middle Missouri settlement less than a mile upstream from the Black Partizan Site. A provisional tree-ring date from Hickey Brothers of A.D. 1522 falls well within the time span of the Initial Coalescent Variant.

It seems likely that the occupation of the southern regions by people of the Middle Missouri Tradition was terminated not later than A.D. 1550 because of Initial Coalescent pressure. This would have cleared the way for the northward expansion of the Coalescent peoples, which is one aspect of the transition from the Initial to the Extended Coalescent Variant.

The Extended Coalescent villages in the Big Bend and lower Bad-Cheyenne regions are scattered groups of houses with no signs of fortifications. They represent a return, after the fortified Initial Coalescent sites, to the older village plan of the Central Plains Tradition. Their characteristics and their numbers argue for a lack of enemies and an opportunity for unopposed expansion of the variant in the southern sections of the valley.

The fortifications of the Le Compte Focus sites (Johnston and Hoffman, 1966) suggest that there was opposition to the Extended Coalescent expansion upstream from the Cheyenne River. This suggestion is reinforced by the five Extended Middle Missouri sites which cluster on the right bank of the Missouri between the Grand and the Moreau Rivers. The only one excavated, Calamity Village (39DW231), produced pottery and other artifacts which definitely link it to the Middle Missouri Tradition. The village had a massive fortification system with a double ditch line. The houses were long-rectangular structures, but the floors seem to have been nearly at ground surface instead of in deep pits. The shallow pits and a simple posthole pattern suggests that this village, like Hickey Brothers, was occupied only long enough for the fortification system to be completed and never achieved the status of a permanent settlement. It seems likely that the Calamity Village population was driven out by the northward-moving Extended Coalescent groups, and that the Extended Middle Missouri villages in the lower Grand-Moreau region represent a sort of way station on the northward withdrawal of the Middle Missouri peoples.

The Demery Site (39CO1), just below the North Dakota-South Dakota line, is the northernmost known Extended Coalescent village, and the Helb Site (39CA208), a few miles downstream from Demery, is the southernmost Terminal Middle Missouri village. These sites indicate that a slight overlap existed in the maximum Extended Coalescent and Terminal Middle Missouri ranges, with the former groups dominating the southern Middle Missouri regions and the latter peoples holding the northern regions. The fact that there are only three Terminal Middle Missouri sites known south of the Cannonball River indicates that this section was lightly held. There are suggestions, moreover, these sites were abandoned during the first half of the 17th century, to leave the southern Cannonball region as an unoccupied buffer zone between the Terminal Middle Missouri and Extended Coalescent groups.

The settlement patterns of the two groups are markedly different. The numerous Extended Coalescent villages were scattered house clusters, usually unfortified or with minimal fortification systems and seemingly occupied for relatively short periods of time. The Terminal Middle Missouri population was concentrated in a few large, compact, and heavily fortified centers which appear to have been lived in for long periods.

The population of the Terminal Middle Missouri centers was presumably drawn mainly from the earlier northern Extended Middle Missouri sites. It probably included a substantial number of refugees from the Extended Middle Missouri towns in the Bad-Cheyenne region and also from the Modified Initial Middle Missouri communities. The occupants of the Extended Coalescent towns were presumably descend-

ants of the Initial Coalescent groups.

The differences in community pattern between Extended Coalescent and Terminal Middle Missouri seem to have implications regarding social organization and social control. The diffuse and transient Extended Coalescent towns could have gotten along with a minimum of formal sociopolitical organization. The large, compact, and fairly permanent Terminal Middle Missouri communities would almost certainly have required much stronger social controls. These would have been necessary both for day-to-day living and to organize the work parties which built the elaborate fortification systems. The unusual elaboration of many of the artifacts from Terminal Middle Missouri sites suggests a fair amount of individual craft specialization which does not seem to be in evidence for the Extended Coalescent communities.

The fortifications at the Terminal Middle Missouri sites and at some of the northern Extended Coalescent sites suggest that there was a fair amount of raiding back and forth between the two groups. There is also evidence of a significant amount of cultural interchange. This process led to the final crystalization of the Coalescent Tradition and to the disappearance of the Middle Missouri Tradition as a recognizable cultural entity. Evidence of these trait interchanges is most apparent in the Terminal Middle Missouri and the northern Extended Coalescent sites.

The late northern Extended Coalescent villages include the sites which Hurt (1957) assigned to his Akaska Focus, together with others such as the Davis Site (39CO14) and probably the early village at the multicomponent Anton Rygh Site (39CA4). All of them seem to have been more compact and to have been occupied for a greater length of time than the majority of the Extended Coalescent villages. Davis was definitely fortified, and the fortification system at Anton Rygh is probably related, at least in part, to its Extended Coalescent component. The compact settlement pattern, the long occupation, and the fortification at the northern Extended Coalescent sites closely parallel traits of the Terminal Middle Missouri communities and probably represent ideas borrowed from the north.

Pottery with cord-impressed decoration

is extremely rare in the majority of Extended Coalescent sites, but it becomes progressively more common upstream from the Cheyenne River, and seems to occur most frequently in the Akaska Focus sites and at the Davis Site. This trait was almost certainly borrowed from the Middle Missouri Tradition, along with the distinctive L-shaped antler fleshing adz, the metatarsal flesher, and the bone slider.

The Coalescent house, with its central firepit, four primary superstructure supports, side entrance passage, and roughly circular form, passed north to the Terminal Middle Missouri groups some time before the end of the 17th century. An example of this basic type was found at Huff (Wood, 1967), and it became the typical dwelling in the northern Post-Contact Coalescent villages. Shallow S-rims and braced rims are found in Terminal Middle Missouri sites. They are counterparts of those of the Extended Coalescent Variant, but are executed in the coarse Middle Missouri Tradition paste. The paste differences seem to rule out any possibility that these were intrusive Extended Coalescent pieces. Rather, the Terminal Middle Missouri potters seem to have borrowed the rim forms from their southern neighbors.

It seems likely that the idea of the rectilinear fortification ditches and the use of bastions were derived from the southern Extended Middle Missouri groups. Their presence at Terminal Middle Missouri sites presumably represents borrowing within the Middle Missouri Tradition.

To recapitulate, the main themes of Middle Missouri culture history between A.D. 1400 and 1675 were the influx of the Initial Coalescent population from the Central Plains, the period of cultural exchange between this population and the peoples of the Middle Missouri Tradition, the withdrawal of the Middle Missouri groups from the southern regions, and a Coalescent movement upstream almost to the North Dakota line in the wake of their retreat. The geographic distributions of the two populations became stabilized, with Coalescent groups occupying most of the Missouri Valley in South Dakota and Terminal Middle Missouri people restricting themselves to the upper Cannonball and Knife-Heart regions. Further trait exchanges between the two groups went far toward erasing differences in their cultural traditions.

Climatic factors appear to have been operative during this period too. The unfavorable conditions of the Pacific I episode began to moderate after the beginning of the 15th century. By 1450 climatic conditions had reverted in part to those of Neo-Atlantic times, ushering in the Pacific II episode (Baerreis and Bryson, 1965; Bryson and Wendland, 1967). This is the time when the Extended Middle Missouri populations seem to have reoccupied the Bad-Cheyenne region, and it seems reasonable to assume that their movement was linked with the improved climate. The Pacific II episode lasted for only about 100 years. By 1550 changed circulation patterns had produced the cool summers which characterized Bryson's Neo-Boreal episode. This was also the time when the southern villages of the Middle Missouri Tradition were finally abandoned and Extended Coalescent groups began to spread upstream to the North Dakota border.

The Extended Coalescent settlement pattern of small villages occupied for only a short time may represent a response to marginal economic conditions, which in turn were the product of a less favorable climate. If this were the case, the sections of the valley between the Cannonball and Knife Rivers must have been less affected since the Terminal Middle Missouri settlements there were large communities occupied for considerable periods of time. Bryson has suggested (Baerreis and Bryson, 1965) that the Neo-Boreal conditions were modified somewhat during the first half of the 18th century. The larger and more permanent Post-Contact Coalescent settlements in South Dakota may represent a response to this improvement in the climate.

39SL4
F421 B40
BASS 7 2 62

LATE VILLAGE CULTURES

The archeological materials in the Middle Missouri Valley which date after approximately A.D. 1675 reflect events which took place far beyond the borders of the Plains. The European settlement of North America had a profound effect on the Indian populations and their cultures. Many times those effects ran far ahead of the penetration of the continent by the Europeans themselves, and this was particularly true in the Great Plains.

Beginning as early as A.D. 1541, European explorers made their way into the Great Plains. But there was no significant European settlement in the Northern Plains until well into the 19th century. While settlers themselves were absent, their presence in other parts of the continent had a tremendous impact on the Plains tribes. The horse, taken over from the Spaniards in New Mexico and Texas, revolutionized the patterns of resource exploitation in the Northwestern Plains and provided the basis for the development of the culture of the mounted bison hunters of the Equestrian Period. The fur trade in Canada and eastern United States was responsible for the addition of a host of new traits—especially metal, glass, and manufactured items—to the material culture of the Plains tribes. It was also responsible for major changes in the native economic patterns. Finally, white-introduced epidemic diseases such as smallpox were responsible for profound demographic changes in the area.

The pattern of European-Indian contacts in the Plains was a unique one. In most other parts of the Americas, European settlement followed close on the heels of European influences. In the Northern Plains, settlement lagged behind influences by nearly a century and a half. As a result, the native population had a long time in which to accommodate its way of life to European innovations, without having to cope with major intrusions of settlers into the area. The result was a hybrid culture which is clearly evidenced by the archeological remains of the Post-Contact Coalescent sites.

FIGURE 81 A typical Post-Contact Coalescent burial.

FIGURE 82

POST-CONTACT COALESCENT
COMPONENTS OF THE 18TH CENTURY

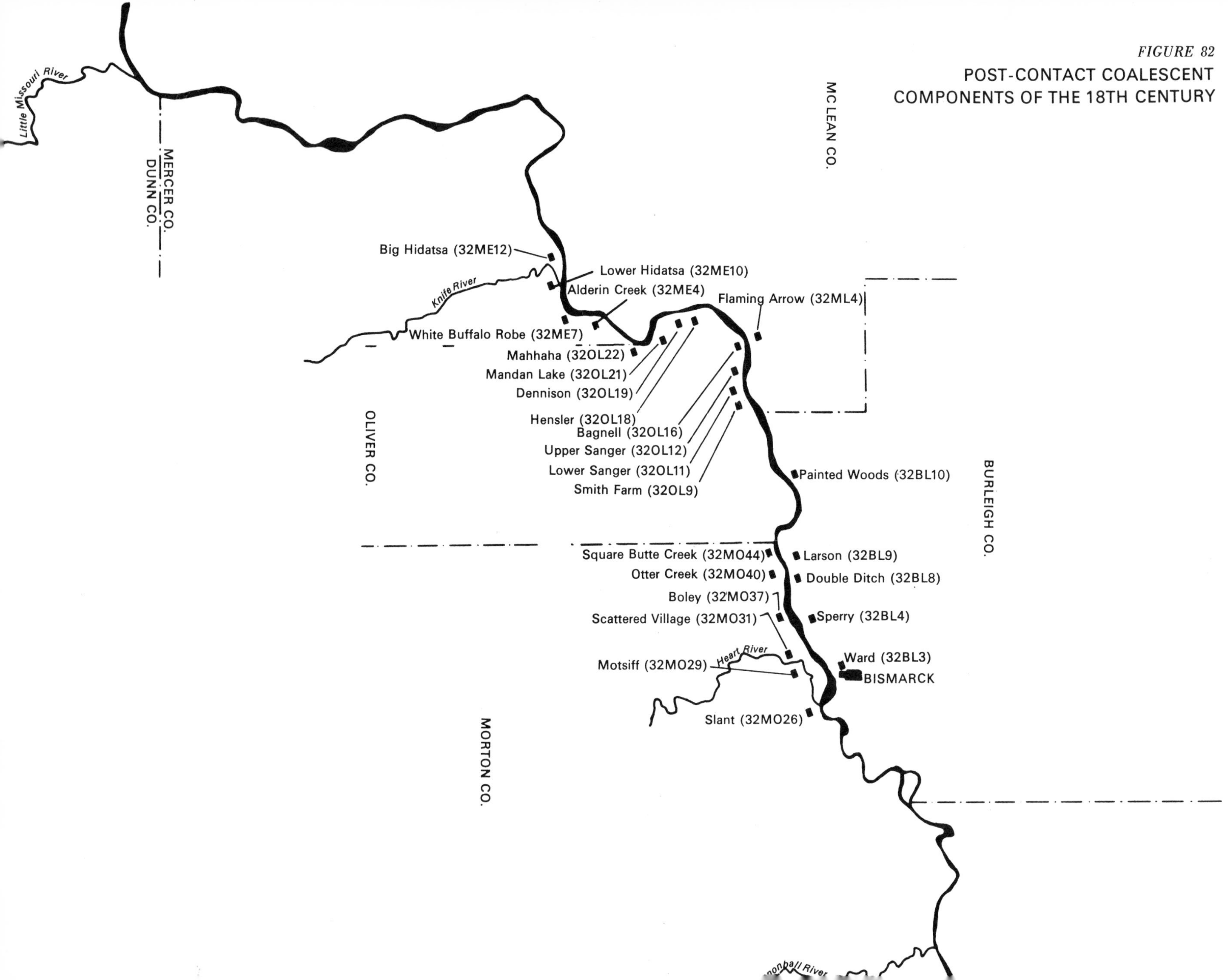

BURLEIGH CO.

MC LEAN CO.

MORTON CO.

OLIVER CO.

MERCER CO.
DUNN CO.

Little Missouri River

Knife River

Heart River

Apple River

BISMARCK

Flaming Arrow (32ML4)
Painted Woods (32BL10)
Larson (32BL9)
Double Ditch (32BL8)
Sperry (32BL4)
Ward (32BL3)

Big Hidatsa (32ME12)
Lower Hidatsa (32ME10)
Alderin Creek (32ME4)
White Buffalo Robe (32ME7)
Mahhaha (32OL22)
Mandan Lake (32OL21)
Dennison (32OL19)
Hensler (32OL18)
Bagnell (32OL16)
Upper Sanger (32OL12)
Lower Sanger (32OL11)
Smith Farm (32OL9)

Square Butte Creek (32MO44)
Otter Creek (32MO40)
Boley (32MO37)
Scattered Village (32MO31)
Motsiff (32MO29)
Slant (32MO26)

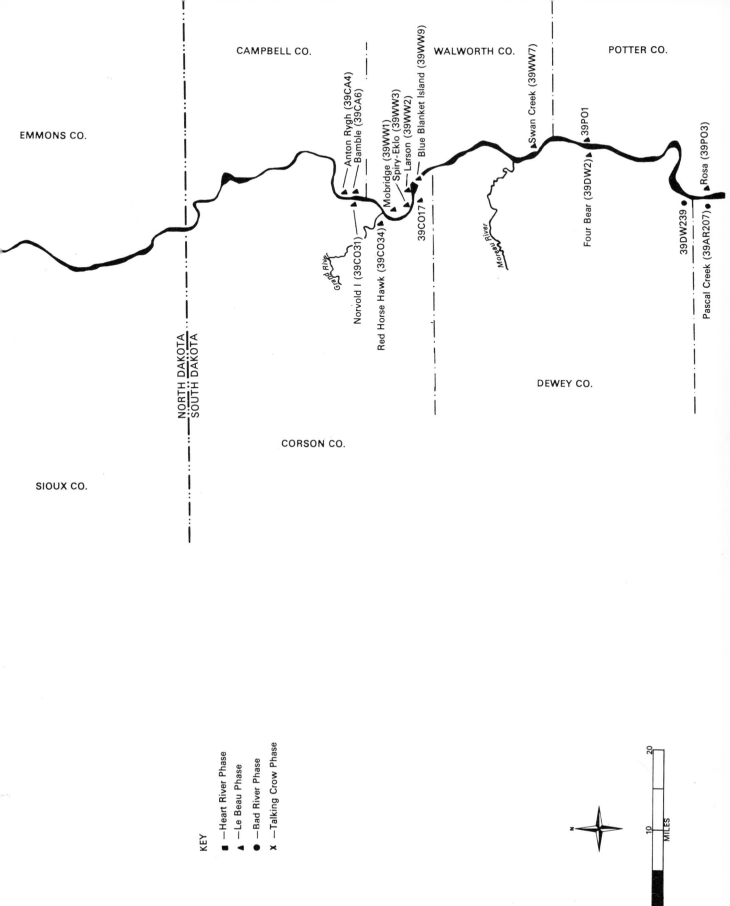

FIGURE 82

POST-CONTACT COALESCENT
COMPONENTS OF THE 18TH CENTURY

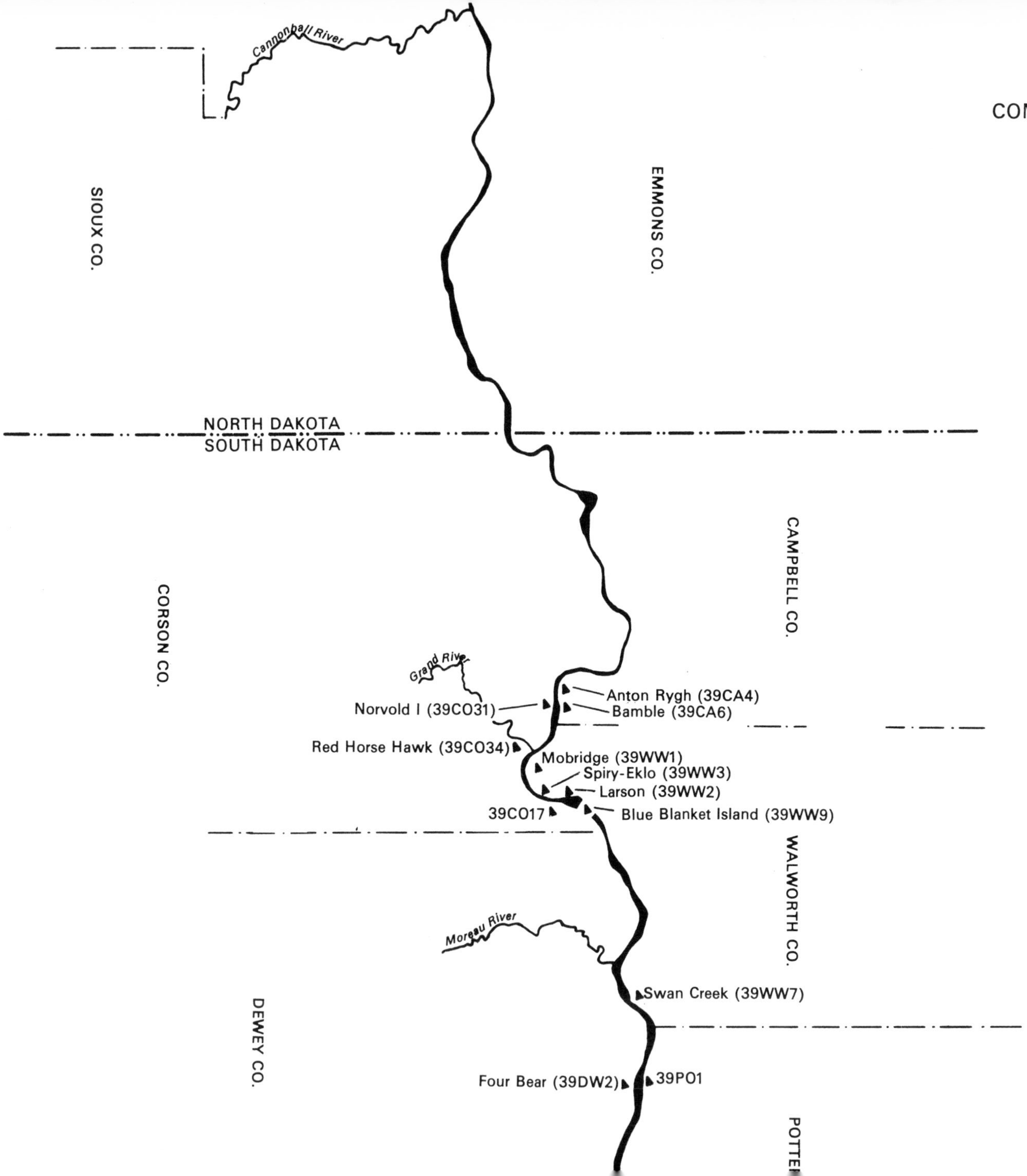

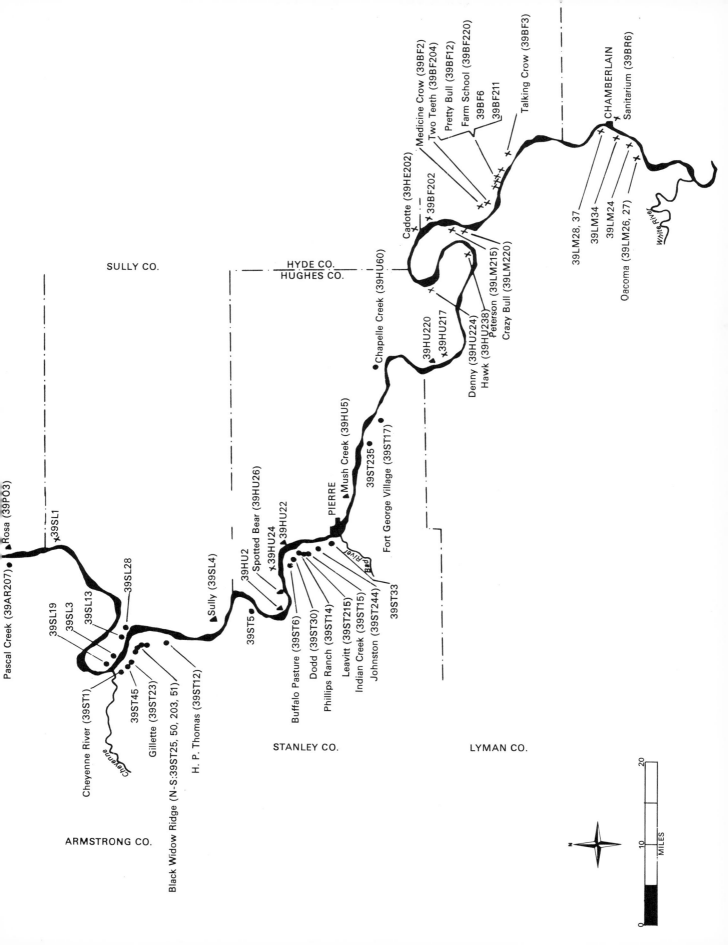

POST-CONTACT COALESCENT VARIANT

The 18th century was the heyday of the Middle Missouri villagers. Historical sources document the presence of three major tribal groups in the area: the Arikara, who occupied most of the valley in South Dakota, and the Mandan and Hidatsa, who had their settlements farther upstream in North Dakota. Nearly all of the work done in Post-Contact sites under the salvage program has been in areas which relate to the Arikara, since the great majority of the historic Mandan and Hidatsa villages were located between the head of Oahe Reservoir and Garrison Dam. There are enough data available, however, to give a fair picture of Mandan and Hidatsa archeology during this period.

Ethnology and ethnohistory document some significant distinctions between the three tribal groups in the late 18th and early 19th centuries. The Arikara spoke a Caddoan dialect. The Mandan and Hidatsa languages were both Siouan, but they differed from each other to the point of mutual unintelligibility. David Thompson, describing the situation in 1797–98, wrote:

Fall Indians [Hidatsa] who also have Villages, are strictly confederate with the Mandanes, they speak a distinct language . . . very few of the Mandanes learn it; the former learned the language of the latter. (Glover, 1962, p. 177)

There were other differences in the nonmaterial culture of the 19th-century villagers. These, unfortunately, tend to be only dimly reflected in the materials with which the archeologist has to work. On the basis of the archeological record alone, the uniformities of Post-Contact Coalescent culture are much more apparent than the tribal differences.

The similarities which characterize the cultures of the late village tribes were undoubtedly the product of a convergence of the Middle Missouri Tradition and the earlier manifestations of the Coalescent Tradition. The culture of the historic Mandan and Hidatsa was directly rooted in the Middle Missouri Tradition, but the northern village tribes had lost enough old traits

and had added a sufficient number of new ones to place them well within the Coalescent range. Post-Contact Arikara culture was an outgrowth of the Extended Coalescent complex. But there were changes there too, especially in pottery and village plan. Those changes all worked to increase the similarity between 18th-century Arikara and Mandan-Hidatsa cultures.

GEOGRAPHIC DISTRIBUTION

The distribution of the Post-Contact Coalescent sites varied considerably through time, with a marked reduction in both the total extent and in the number of villages during the later years of the variant. Throughout most of the 18th century, there were two main centers (fig. 82). A southern group of villages had a nearly continuous distribution along both sides of the Missouri from the White River to a point a few miles above the mouth of the Grand. The stretch of over 100 river miles from above the Grand almost to the mouth of the Heart River seems to have lacked any important permanent villages during Post-Contact times. The second major concentration of Post-Contact Coalescent villages extended along the Missouri through the Knife-Heart region. These were the Mandan and Hidatsa towns. There were a few permanent villages in the Garrison region, but most of them seem to date after 1780.

HOUSES

The houses of the 18th-century villages are known mainly from excavations in sites in South Dakota which presumably relate to the Arikara. The great majority of them conform to a single basic pattern which ultimately traces back to the houses of the Central Plains Tradition (figs. 83–85). Post-Contact Coalescent structures were almost always circular. They were characterized by a firepit at the center of the floor; four postholes, which held the primary superstructure supports, set at the corners of a rectangle enclosing the firepit; and an entrance passage. Many entrances were bounded by rows of vertical posts set fairly close together, with heavier posts at the inner and outer ends of the rows. Others seem to have had a four-post-and-stringer framework, with small poles leaning against the stringers. There was a considerable variation in the length of the passage

FIGURE 83 A Post-Contact Coalescent house.

FIGURE 85 Plan of a Post-Contact Coalescent house.

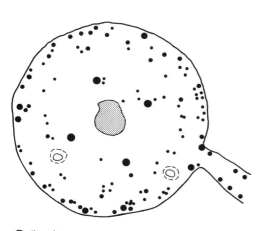

fire pit

post hole

cache pit

undercut cache

0   5   10

FEET

FIGURE 84 *An excavated
Post-Contact Coalescent
house.*

Two plans were used in building the lower walls of the superstructure. A great many of the houses had heavy posts (most often from 9 to 12) set at fairly regular intervals around the edge of the floor. Stringers were presumably placed on top of these posts to support the outer ends of the poles used in the upper part of the superstructure. The spaces between the heavy posts were filled with lighter posts set vertically. When a house was constructed in a pit, these posts were set just inside the pit wall.

The other variety of superstructure also had heavy posts set at intervals around the edges of the floor, but the lighter posts were lacking. The tops of the heavy posts were again presumably connected by stringers. Both archeological evidence and 19th-century descriptions indicate that the walls of these houses were formed by light poles whose butts were set outside the circle of heavier posts and whose tops were inclined against the stringers.

Bowers (1965, pp. 480–481) has suggested that the slanted lower walls and the presence of a floor (*atutish*) area between the wall support posts and the base of the wall proper was a northern trait which dif-

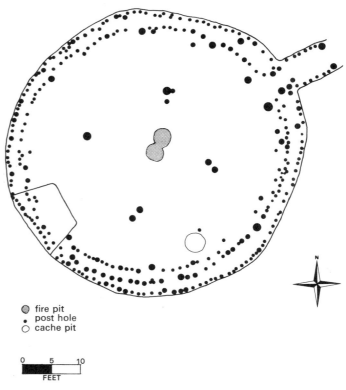

⊙ fire pit
• post hole
○ cache pit

0   5   10
FEET

FIGURE 87 Plan of a Post-Contact Coalescent ceremonial lodge.

FIGURE 86 *An excavated Post-Contact Coalescent ceremonial lodge.*

fused downstream from the Mandan-Hidatsa area in North Dakota. It should be noted, however, that many of the Extended Coalescent houses lack any evidence of vertical wall members, and that they may well have had the slanted lower walls.

Other superstructure details seem to have paralleled those of the well-documented earthlodges of the 19th century. Sgt. Patrick Gass of the Lewis and Clark party had been an apprentice carpenter before joining the army. He was a meticulous observer of the buildings he saw, and his description of an Arikara earthlodge, one of the earliest to be published, follows.

In a circle of a size suited to the dimensions of the intended lodge, they set up 16 forked posts five or six feet high, and lay poles from one fork to another. Against these poles they lean other poles, slanting from the ground, and extending about four inches above the cross poles; these are to receive the ends of the upper poles, that support the roof. They next set up four large forks, fifteen feet high, and about ten feet apart, in the middle of the area; and poles or beams between these. The roof poles are then laid on extending from the lower poles across the beams which rest on the middle forks, of such a length as to leave a hole at the top for a chimney. The whole is then covered with willow branches, except the chimney and a hole below they pass through. On the willow branches they lay grass and lastly clay. At the hole below they build a pen about four feet wide and projecting ten feet from the hut; and hang a buffaloe skin at the entrance of the hut for a door. This labour like every other kind is chiefly performed by the squaws.

(Gass, 1958, p. 61)

Tabeau's description, based on the same village seen at the same time as Gass' visit, differs in some respects. After remarking that earthlodges should be inhabited only by Arikaras, dogs, and bears, he says:

Four posts, thirteen feet above the ground, are fixed in a square, twelve feet apart, and hold up in their notches four joists. Eight other poles, five feet long above the ground, are then fixed in an octagon twelve feet from the first and hold up also eight joists. These latter sustain the frame of little stakes and, being themselves inside and outside propped upon the forks, which prevents

them from falling, they serve as a support for the rafters. The rafters touch each other by being joined at the top and they also rest upon the four joists which form the inner square. Only one opening is left. This, being in the middle, forms a point which, consequently, allows only one fire in the center of the lodge. Upon this frame are spread mats of willow or of osier, covered first with a layer of straw and then with earth five to six inches deep. Thus, at a distance, all these cabins, built without order, appear to be small natural elevations. Notwithstanding this triple covering, which would be sufficient were it not for the poor workmanship of the builders, the rain comes in a great deal in all the lodges and each one is obliged to make a camp above his bed. There is but one door and the opening at the top is in place of window and chimney. (Abel, 1939, pp. 146–147)

The most common structure was the domestic earthlodge. The average diameter was about 30 feet, but diameters varied a good deal and seemingly increased somewhat through time. I believe that when the ground plans of all excavated houses are available for study several subtypes will be recognized within this general category.

Specialized houselike structures also occur in the Post-Contact Coalescent villages. What appear to have been communal or ceremonial lodges are found in many of the South Dakota sites (figs. 86 and 87). Like the houses, they had four primary posts, central firepit, and walled entrance passages. Diameters were generally in the 50- to 60-foot range. The outlines were often octagonal rather than circular, and in some cases a low earth platform or altar was set against the wall opposite the entrance.

The earliest references I have found to structures of this sort date from 1811. Brackenridge mentions an Arikara "magic, or medicine lodge, in which they have a great collection of magic, or sacred things" (Thwaites, 1966, vol. 6, p. 126), and Bradbury (Thwaites, 1966, vol. 5, pp. 175–176) also speaks of a ceremonial structure in an Arikara village.

Bowers (1950, fig. 14) illustrates a type of Mandan ceremonial lodge, dating from the contact period, which is horseshoe-shaped with the entrance in the flat side. It has a central fireplace and eight primary superstructure supports set in two rows, one on either side of the long axis. This sort of structure seems to perpetuate some of the characteristics of the older long-rectangular houses of the Middle Missouri Tradition in a ceremonial setting, a situation comparable to the relationships of the Anasazi pithouse and kiva in the Southwest.

Another variety of Post-Contact Coalescent house was the so-called eagle trapping lodge. It seems to have been made in several forms. One involved the use of the central firepit and four primary superstructure supports, but the superstructure itself was made by leaning poles tepee-fashion against the central square of stringers. These structures commonly had a walled entrance passage. Other lodges in this category seem to have had the conical shape but lacked the four primary superstructure posts near the center of the floor (cf. Wilson, 1934, pp. 411–415; Bowers, 1950, pp. 207–208 and 232–235; Metcalf, 1963a, pp. 22–25; Lehmer, 1966, pp. 16–24). Houses of this general type occur most commonly in settlements which appear to have been seasonal hunting camps used year after year.

Some sites show evidence of considerable rebuilding of the earthlodges. In some cases, new structures may have been erected on the sites of older ones which had burned; in others, the rebuilding seems to have been necessitated by rotting of the superstructure timbers. Wilson (1934, p. 358) states that the usual life span of an earthlodge was 10 to 12 years, and he gives a number of details of the rebuilding process.

The circular Post-Contact Coalescent structures represent a continuation and formalization of the architectural tradition of the Initial Coalescent and Extended Coalescent Variants. There are suggestions, however, that the long-rectangular house of the Middle Missouri Tradition may have persisted in some villages into early Post-Contact times.

Sherd collections from both the Ward (32BL3) and Sperry (32BL4) sites consist almost entirely of types which are characteristic of the Post-Contact Coalescent Heart River Phase. Surface indications and aerial photographs indicate the presence of circular houses. However, the aerial photographs appear to show at least one row of long-rectangular structures along the east edge of each site. Furthermore, Will and Hecker (1944, p. 81) report that early excavations exposed "sub-rectangular" house floors at Ward. While there may be both Terminal Middle Missouri and Heart River components at these sites, this is not indicated by the sherd collections. Instead, present evidence suggests that the earlier house form lasted on there into Post-Contact times.

CACHE PITS

Cache pits (fig. 88), especially the undercut variety, occur in considerable numbers in the Post-Contact Coalescent villages. It is my impression that the villages occupied during the 18th century had a greater total storage capacity than those of any other period. If this is actually the case, it would presumably be a reflection of increased agricultural production to provide crops for the villagers' intertribal trading operations.

MISCELLANEOUS STRUCTURES

Miscellaneous structures in the Post-Contact Coalescent villages are indicated by irregular pits, which were probably borrow pits for dirt used in house building, and by large numbers of postholes in the areas between the houses. The postholes themselves are not particularly informative, but some of the early 19th-century accounts describe features which most likely also were present in the 18th-century villages. One category includes the drying racks which are such a prominent feature in Bodmer's paintings of the Mandan village at Fort Clark (Thwaites, 1966, vol. 25, pls. 48, 49, and 60). In describing the village, Maximilian wrote:

. . . *among the huts are many stages of several stories, supported by poles, on which they dry the maize.*

(Thwaites, 166, vol. 23, p. 269)

Another feature of the 19th-century villages may also have been present earlier. Catlin's drawings of the Arikara, Mandan, and Hidatsa villages (1965, vol. I, pls. 47, 48, 58, 59, 67, 69, 70, and 80) and Bodmer's paintings of the Mandan village (Thwaites, 1966, vol. 25, pls. 48 and 60) show numerous tall poles projecting well above the top of the houses. Catlin (1965, vol. I, p. 88), with his usual talent for the sensational, speaks of these poles as displaying enemy scalps. Maximilian writes:

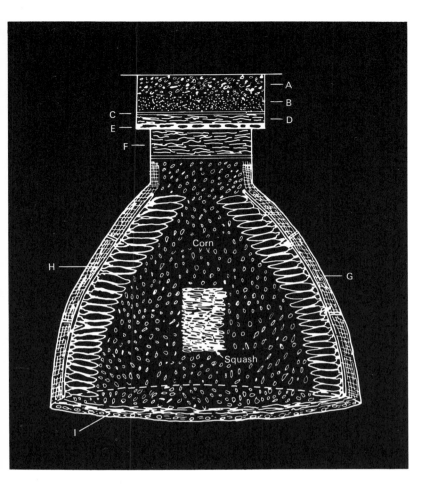

A
B
C
D
E
F
H
Corn
Squash
G
I

At the top of a high pole, a figure is here placed, made of skins, with a wooden head, the face painted black, and wearing a fur cap and feathers, which is intended to represent the evil spirit, Ochkih-Hadda (corresponding with the devil), or a wicked man, as they affirm, who once appeared among them, had neither wife nor child, and vanished, and whom they now stand greatly in dread of. Other grotesque figures, made of skins and bundles of twigs, we saw hanging on high poles, most of them being offerings to the deity.

(Thwaites, 1966, vol. 23, p. 269)

The 19th-century Mandan villages had one feature which apparently did not occur in Arikara or Hidatsa towns. This was the so-called sacred cedar and its surrounding cylindrical wall of cottonwood logs or planks bound with a water willow (cf. Maximilian in Thwaites, 1966, vol. 23, p. 269; Bowers, 1950, pp. 111 and 113). So far as I know, there is no direct archeological evidence for such a feature in the earlier villages, but it may go back at least as far

as the 18th-century communities.

Trash or refuse mounds between the houses are distinctive features of some of the villages occupied during the 18th and early 19th centuries. They only seem to occur in villages in the Knife-Heart and Grand Moreau regions, and they are not present in all of them. When they do occur, they tend to fill most of the village area between the house depressions. These refuse mounds suggest that the northern communities were occupied for longer periods than the villages downstream, which have only sheet refuse between the houses.

VILLAGE SIZE AND PLAN

Village size and plan show considerable variation. Some of the South Dakota sites, apparently dating from the first half of the 18th century, contain only a dozen or so houses, but the Sully Site (39SL4), occupied into Post-Contact Coalescent times, is the largest village in the Middle Missouri Valley, and the Double Ditch Site (32BL8), north of Bismarck, is shown on early maps at the State Historical Society of North Dakota as having over 150 houses. The majority of the Arikara sites occupied during the 18th century seem to have averaged about 35 houses. The Mandan and Hidatsa towns of the same period were larger, apparently averaging over 90 houses.

None of the Post-Contact Coalescent villages had houses arranged in rows like the settlements representing the Middle Missouri Tradition. Instead, the individual structures were scattered more or less at random throughout the occupation area. Many of the Mandan towns had a central open space or plaza, a feature carried over from the Terminal Middle Missouri village plan. Arikara villages do not seem, as a rule, to have had a central plaza, but many of them show surface indications of a large ceremonial lodge commonly located near the center of the house cluster. Hidatsa towns do not seem to have had plazas or ceremonial lodges (cf. Libby, 1908; Bowers, 1950, pp. 111, 113).

FORTIFICATIONS

Fortifications occur at many 18th-century villages in the Missouri Valley. But a number of the Post-Contact Coalescent sites show no evidence of having been fortified. There are indications that the majority of the unfortified sites date from early Post-Contact Coalescent times. The later sites in the southern regions seem to have been fortified with roughly oval ditches and palisades inside the ditch line. The curvilinear ditches of the Post-Contact Coalescent sites contrast with the straight-line segments of the earlier Middle Missouri Tradition ditches, and the contrast is heightened by the almost complete lack of bastions in the Post-Contact Coalescent fortifications.

Most of the Post-Contact Coalescent villages in the Grand-Moreau region show traces of more or less oval fortification ditches without bastions. Excavation there has shown that palisades were usually put up inside the ditch line. Some of the 18th-century villages in the Knife-Heart region, especially the northern ones, show little if anything in the way of encircling ditches. Others were clearly enclosed by ditches and presumably palisades.

BURIAL CUSTOMS

Burial customs are well documented for the Post-Contact Coalescent village tribes. The Arikara characteristically practiced primary inhumation in individual graves (fig. 81), although a few multiple interments are found. Bodies were usually at least partly flexed and laid either on the back or side. It seems to have been a common practice to place poles or split logs over the interments, with the ends higher at the head than at the feet. Tools and ornaments were sometimes buried with the dead. Most of the Arikara burials seem to have been grouped in a cemetery near the village. Rare burials are found also in the villages themselves.

The Mandan and Hidatsa usually practiced scaffold burial rather than inhumation during the 19th century (fig. 89). I suspect that this custom existed well back in prehistoric times, and that it accounts for the lack of skeletal remains in sites of the Middle Missouri Tradition.

Some inhumation was also practiced by the Mandan and Hidatsa. There are surface indications of burial areas near the historic Hidatsa villages on the Knife River. In 1938 Strong excavated at the old Mandan town now called Slant Village (32MO26), which he referred to as the Old Fort Abraham Lincoln Site. In summarizing his work there, Strong writes:

. . . we found 11 burials; all were flexed, several in pits covered with slabs of wood, and several in the deepest and oldest cache pits. One of the latter contained a large, mature man who had met a violent death through a blow on the skull. He had his medicine bag alongside his head as well as his arrow-making tools on the other side. This was apparently a prehistoric burial but several of the other graves had limited white contact materials. There were no evidences of an intrusive culture, for example Arikara, and large numbers of similar burials around and beneath house floors were encountered here in a previous W.P.A. project. We were inclined to attribute these burials to emergency conditions created by the smallpox epidemic which caused the abandonment of the village about 1764, but the apparent care manifested as well as the antiquity of certain burials makes this assumption dubious.

(Strong, 1940, pp. 362–363)

POTTERY

Pottery from the Post-Contact Coalescent sites (fig. 90) has some characteristics which occur only in certain cultural contexts and others which are more or less uniform throughout the entire region. The majority of the common characteristics show a resemblance to the pottery of the Middle Missouri Tradition and contrast sharply with the ware found in the Extended Coalescent villages.

FIGURE 89 A Mandan village, with skin-wrapped bodies on scaffolds in the middle distance and a circle of skulls in the foreground. Oil painting by George Catlin.

142

The fabric of all late ceramics is generally uniform. Paste tends to be granular and somewhat porous, liberally tempered with rather coarse grit (usually decomposed granite), buff to dark gray in color. Vessels were almost invariably jars, with walls ranging from fairly thin to thick. Decorative techniques include cord impressing, incising, punctating, fingernail indenting, and pinching at the lip.

Body exteriors are either simple stamped or plain, with the former predominating. Maximilian described 19th-century Mandan pottery making in these words:

The work-woman forms the hollow inside of the vessel by means of a round stone which she holds in her hand, while she works and smoothes the outside with a piece of poplar bark.

(Thwaites, 1966, vol. 23, p. 279)

The late Gilbert Wilson's unpublished field notes in the collections of the Minnesota Historical Society include drawings of cottonwood bark paddles used in Hidatsa pottery making. One of these implements, with a series of parallel grooves cut diagonally across the smooth concave inner surface of the bark, would have produced the characteristic simple-stamped finish.

Another surface treatment occurs on the necks of much of the Post-Contact Coalescent pottery. It consists of a series of deep, closely spaced, vertical striations which look as if they had been made by brushing the plastic clay with something comparable to the modern whiskbroom. This neck treatment seems to have made its first appearance in the Middle Missouri at some of the Extended Coalescent sites in the Grand-Moreau region. By Post-Contact Coalescent times it had come into use throughout the whole region, but was most common in South Dakota. It is an excellent variant marker.

These attributes, with the exception of vertical neck brushing, show a close resemblance to the pottery from sites of the Middle Missouri Tradition. Post-Contact pottery differs from that of the earlier Coalescent Variants in the extensive use of cord impressed decoration and in the lack of the distinctive paste and thin walls of the Extended Coalescent vessels. Thus the basic fabric of Post-Contact Coalescent pottery appears to have been derived primarily from the Middle Missouri Tradition.

Rims show a closer resemblance to the Extended Coalescent than to the Middle Missouri Tradition forms. Three important rim forms, one minor one, and a group of intermediate rim forms occur in the 18th-century sites in the Middle Missouri Valley. One of the major categories consists of what Hurt (1957, pp. 40–43) originally called Le Beau S-shaped Rim. What is today generally designated as Le Beau S-rim has a high, shallow S-shaped rim profile. It is similar to the one which appeared in sites of the Extended Coalescent Variant and is also found as a minority element in the Terminal Middle Missouri sites. The Le Beau S-rim sherds from the Post-Contact Coalescent sites typically have a darker and somewhat coarser paste than the Extended Coalescent variety, and cord impressing is the dominant decorative technique. Much of this pottery is extremely well made, with thin walls, meticulous decoration, and considerable elaboration of the lip area. I would rate it as the best Post-Contact Coalescent pottery.

A small proportion of the Post-Contact Coalescent rims are collared, falling within the type which has been called Colombe Collared Rim (Lehmer, 1954b, p. 102). The collar proper is usually from 2.5 to 5.5 cm. high. The exterior surface of the collar slopes sharply outward below the lip, and is straight or concave in contrast to the convex exteriors of the S-rims. There is a fairly abrupt angle at the base of the collar, with the exterior surface curving in sharply to a concave neck area. Interior surfaces are concentric to the exterior surfaces. Decoration is usually cord impressed, although some incising does occur. Colombe Collared Rim seems to be largely confined to sites of the Bad River Phase (Lehmer and Jones, 1968), where it appears as a minority element in the total assemblage.

Another major rim form encompasses what C. S. Smith (1951) has called Talking Crow Ware. Cross sections of the rim-neck area range from straight to curved, and the rims are approximately the same thickness from top to bottom. The distinguishing feature is the vertical or near-vertical orientation of the rim. This contrasts with the flared rims of the Middle Missouri

5 CM

FIGURE 90

Tradition vessels. Both form and orientation are similar to many of the Extended Coalescent rims.

Another important rim form characterizes Stanley Ware (Lehmer, 1951; 1954b, pp. 42–46). The form and orientation of the rim-neck area is nearly identical with the Talking Crow rims. The distinguishing feature is a thickening or brace on the rim exterior just below the lip. This was usually made by bonding a fillet of clay to the surface of the rim. A similar treatment was applied to about a third of the 18th-century rims from the Knife-Heart region. The Stanley and Knife-Heart rims represent the same technological tradition, but differences in the bracing and the overall vessel forms are great enough to justify assigning them to different wares.

In his report on the Swan Creek Site, Wesley Hurt set up a series of types under the name Le Beau. These included both the Le Beau S-rims, already described, and a series of rims which fall between Stanley and Talking Crow in the matter of bracing. Hurt stated, in his discussion of the undecorated sherds in the series:

The types classified as Talking Crow Brushed and Stanley Plain appear to form two ends of a series with Le Beau Plain as the intermediate type.

He also said:

The major difference between Le Beau Ware and Stanley Braced Rim Ware is the lack of the braced rim in the former. This difference is not clear cut, however, for some of the thickened and rolled rims of the Le Beau Ware are transitional to braced rims.

(Hurt, 1957, pp. 40, 37)

Baerreis and Dallman faced the same problem of classification in reporting their work at late sites in the Mobridge area. They rejected Hurt's concept of recognizable Le Beau types on both typological and interpretative grounds, and classified their rim sherds under three categories—Talking Crow, Stanley, and "Intermediate." They characterized the latter category as:

a group of sherds that seem to represent a mid-point or transitional form between Talking Crow and Stanley wares. The difficulty of placing these intermediate forms in either of the two categories led to the establishment of a provisional Intermediate category which we visualized might sub-sequently be included with either of the two wares should it seem justified.

(Baerreis and Dallman, 1961, pp. 439–440)

NON-POTTERY ARTIFACTS

The non-pottery artifacts of the Post-Contact Coalescent Variant provide a far more obvious index to the impact of White culture on the 18th-century Middle Missouri villages than do other aspects of the material culture. The introduction of metal, glass, and manufactured goods by the fur trade not only greatly enlarged the assemblage but produced changes in the native artifacts themselves. The latter effect was particularly evident with regard to items made of bone and antler, which could be worked much more readily into a variety of forms with metal than with stone tools.

Arrow points (fig. 91) from the 18th-century Post-Contact Coalescent sites include substantial numbers of chipped-stone pieces. Like the points from the earlier variants, they are small, fine, and usually well made. Bases may be convex, straight, or concave. Both side-notched and unnotched forms occur; the notches are usually deep and narrow with parallel sides in contrast to the tapered notches of the Middle Missouri Tradition. Points from the late South Dakota sites characteristically have straight edges which give them a triangular form. Those from the villages in North Dakota more commonly have convex edges like the points of the Middle Missouri Tradition, but they usually have the narrow side notches.

A few long tenoned, split base, or socketed bone points are also found in the 18th-century village sites.

Points of iron, and less commonly of brass and copper, occur in considerable numbers in the Post-Contact Coalescent villages. Many of the metal points were made by the Indians themselves, but some may have been products of white manufacture. Most of these points have triangular blades. Some have straight bases, others have stems which are straight-sided or flare out slightly at the proximal end. The metal points are consistently heavier than their stone counterparts, and many of them tend to be appreciably longer. Mean lengths for the stone points are approximately 2.5 cm. A collection of some 200 metal points from the Deapolis Site (32ME5), which was occupied by the Mandan during the 19th century, had lengths ranging from 2.2 to 7.4 cm., with a mean length of about 4.2 cm.

Knives (fig. 92) occur in a variety of forms. The commonest in Post-Contact Coalescent sites are those made of plates of milky quartz or chalcedony, and triangular or leaf-shaped forms. Large side-notched stone knives, usually with triangular blades, also occur. They are particularly common in the North Dakota sites. Stone knives seem to have been replaced by metal ones as rapidly as the group's resources permitted.

Metal knives fall into two general categories. The first includes the ones made by the Indians themselves. Many of these were ovoid or rectangular pieces of iron or brass which were hafted in the edges of segments of large ribs, counterparts of the side-blade stone knives. Less commonly, large metal scraps were used as blades and fitted with bone or wooden handles at one end, in imitation of the trade knives. A few rectangular pieces of sheet metal seem to be counterparts of the aboriginal scapula knives. The second category includes the manufactured items traded into the area. Many were heavy butcher knives. Sometimes the original wooden handle was re-placed by a native-made bone handle. Some clasp knives with fairly large blades occur. *Drills* chipped from stone are relatively rare in the Post-Contact Coalescent sites. When they do occur, they are usually the expanded base variety. It seems likely that the stone drill was quickly replaced by metal counterparts.

Snubnose scrapers continued to be a common item in the Post-Contact Coalescent artifact inventory. Forms are identical with those found in the pre-contact villages in the region. The larger pieces with percussion-flaked convex surfaces are the most common form in the South Dakota villages. Both the percussion-flaked variety and the more carefully made scrapers with pressure flaking on the convex surfaces, like those from the Middle Missouri Tradition sites, are found in the Post-Contact villages in North Dakota.

Irregular flakes with chipped cutting or scraping edges occur in Post-Contact Coalescent sites, as in earlier contexts. They seem to be proportionately somewhat less common in the later sites than in the pre-contact villages.

Stone blanks, presumably raw materials for making chipped stone artifacts, occur in some of the 18th-century Post-Contact

FIGURE 91 Most of the specimens in the following figures were made available by Mr. Ralph Thompson and Mr. Roger Holkesvik who recovered them while conducting their own salvage program at the Deapolis Site (32ME5), a historic Mandan Village which was destroyed by gravel pit operations and power-plant construction.

5 CM

FIGURE 92

10 CM

5 CM

FIGURE 93

FIGURE 95

5 CM

5 CM

FIGURE 94

5 CM

5 CM

FIGURE 96

Coalescent sites. They seem to be much less common than in the earlier sites in the region.

Gunflints (fig. 93) of both white and native manufacture are found in some quantities. The ones of European origin are usually distinguishable both by the types of stone used and by subtle characteristics of the chipping process. Native-made pieces are obvious copies of the European forms.

Grooved mauls like those found in earlier sites are common in the Post-Contact Coalescent villages. The form of this artifact type seems to have undergone no change during the contact period, and the considerable numbers found indicate that there was little or no attempt to substitute an iron equivalent for the stone maul.

Saws (fig. 94) may have been traded into the region, but I am not aware of any instance of a manufactured tool of this sort being found in one of the 18th-century villages. A native-made equivalent is present in roughly rectangular scraps of iron or brass with shallow slits or notches along one edge forming a series of teeth.

Pitted stones, like those found in the earliest sites in the area, occur in the 18th-century villages.

Arrow shaft smoothers (fig. 95) made from soft sandstone occur with some frequency. They are characteristically bun-shaped, with a single longitudinal groove in one fairly flat surface. Lengths generally are less than 7.5 cm.

Axes (fig. 96) from Post-Contact Coalescent sites are almost always iron trade pieces. Some of the trade axes were factory-produced items, others seem to have been hammered out by blacksmiths. The Lewis and Clark journals for the winter of 1804–5 include numerous references to the party's blacksmith making and repairing axes for the Mandan and Hidatsa, and Lewis indicates that many of them were made to the Indians' specifications (Thwaites, 1959, vol. 1, pp. 254–255).

FIGURE 97

5 CM

Pipes (fig. 97) occur in fair numbers in the Post-Contact Coalescent sites. Most of them were made from catlinite, but other stones were used, especially by the Mandan and Hidatsa. The commonest form was a prowed or calumet pipe with a projection of the stem extending in front of the bowl. Bowls were either barrel-shaped or truncated cones. Elbow pipes occur with some frequency, and tubular forms are present but rare. A late elaboration of the catlinite pipe was made by carving grooves in the soft stone, usually in the stem, and inlaying them with a lead or white metal.

Stone disks and rectangles (fig. 98) are found, mainly in the northern Post-Contact Coalescent sites. These pieces are usually made from fairly soft sedimentary rock, often a tabular sandstone. Disks average 5.0 to 6.0 cm. in diameter and 1.0 to 1.5 cm. in thickness. The rectangular pieces are of about the same size. Edges are sometimes ground smooth, but usually they are roughly chipped. Some rectangular pieces are made of catlinite or other red stone, show very

FIGURE 98

5 CM

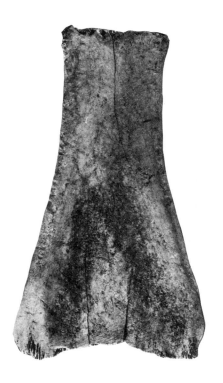

FIGURE 99

⊢———————⊣
5 CM

good workmanship, and bear incised geometric designs on one or both faces. Many disks are unperforated, but some have holes about 1.0 cm. in diameter drilled in the center. The drilled disks resemble spindle whorls, but the large numbers of undrilled pieces and the general lack of spinning in Plains culture seem to rule out this function. It is possible that many of these stones were game pieces.

Scapula hoes (fig. 99) are among the commonest artifacts in Post-Contact Coalescent sites. The styles with the glenoid cavity intact and with notched or unnotched edges continued to be made. The early variety with a socket running from the glenoid cavity into the neck seems to have disappeared completely from the Missouri Valley north of the White River by Post-Contact times.

New forms of bone hoes appear in the late sites. In one of these the whole inferior end of the bone, including the glenoid cavity, was removed by chopping through the neck of the scapula. In another form the area of the glenoid cavity was reduced by chopping away large sections of the inferior end of the bone. This variety is common in late sites throughout the whole Middle Missouri subarea. Still another new form usually has the inferior end of the bone left intact, but the anterior edge and a considerable part of the supraspinous fossa were chopped away to materially reduce the width of the blade.

Creating these new styles of hoes involved cutting away considerably more of the bone than in the older hoe forms. The appearance of the new varieties almost certainly reflects the greater efficiency of metal knives and axes in working green bone.

Metal trade hoes (fig. 100) were also brought into the area and incorporated in Post-Contact Coalescent assemblage. These hoes do not seem to have become common, however, until after the route up the Mis-

5 CM

FIGURE 100

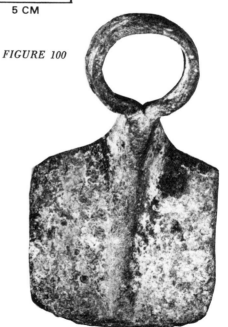

souri from St. Louis began to be extensively used during the 19th century.

Horn scoops, or bison-skull hoes, occur in considerable numbers in the Post-Contact Coalescent villages. They have the same form as those found in sites of the Middle Missouri Tradition. A clue to one use of these scoops is contained in Wilson's description of the setting of the four primary support posts in a Hidatsa earthlodge:

The postholes were carefully dug with digging-sticks which were similar to but longer than those used in agriculture. The loose earth was cleared from the holes with the hands. When the holes became too deep and the bottom could not be reached easily the earth was removed with large buffalo horn or Rocky Mountain sheep horn scoops.
(Wilson, 1934, p. 357)

Bone awls generally resemble those found in sites of the Middle Missouri Tradition. They occur in considerable numbers in the Post-Contact Coalescent sites which were occupied before the final years of the 18th century. They disappear almost entirely from the artifact assemblages of the very late 18th and of the 19th centuries. They were replaced with metal awls (fig. 101) which were small and light enough to be traded into the area in quantity before the water route up the Missouri was well established.

Bone and horn punches, the blunt-pointed objects presumably used mainly for stone flaking, occur in forms similar to those of the Middle Missouri Tradition. These tools are fairly common in the earlier Post-Contact Coalescent sites, but their numbers decrease in the later ones. This presumably reflects the transition from chipped stone to metal tools in the later sites.

Bone spatulas (fig. 102) are found in the contact period sites, but they are much less common than in the Middle Missouri Tradition villages. An appreciably higher proportion of the ones found in the late sites are decorated with fine lines incised in the smooth surface.

Knife handles of native origin are usually made of bone. The most common form was fashioned from a segment of large rib or vertebral spine, with a slot in the end of one edge to receive the metal blade. The slots were much narrower than those in the older pieces which were cut to hold stone knife blades.

Fleshers (fig. 103) made from bison or elk metatarsals occur in considerable numbers in the Post-Contact Coalescent sites. Most of them have flat diagonal cuts through the shaft of the bone and toothed cutting edges. Many of them are found with the tarsals in articulation. The one apparent difference from the earlier fleshers again appears to relate to the availability of metal tools for manufacturing. The diameters of many of the late fleshers have been reduced appreciably by chipping away most of the surface of the shaft of the metatarsal. This could have been done quite easily with a heavy steel knife or a light ax, but it would have been very difficult with stone tools.

Metal blades used with the fleshers are extremely rare in the 18th-century sites, and

1 CM

1 CM

FIGURE 101

FIGURE 102

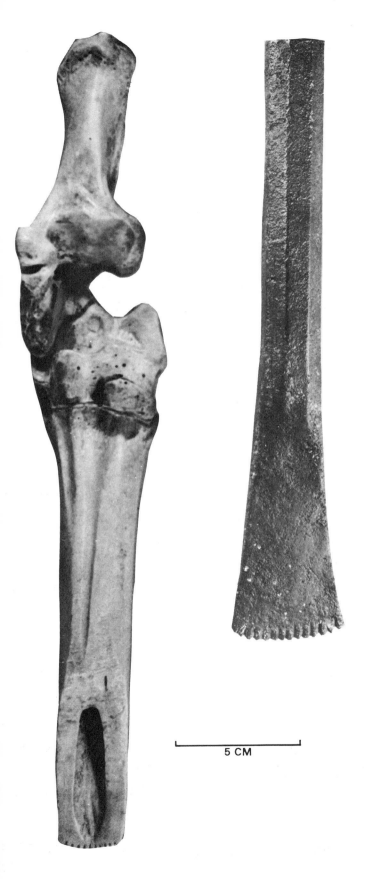

5 CM

few fleshers made from musket barrels or other types of metal have been found.

Elk antler fleshing adzes probably had metal blades attached as a general rule during Post-Contact times, but blade and handle are rarely found together. These L-shaped adzes have been found in greater numbers in the Post-Contact Coalescent villages than in any of the earlier groups of sites in the region. This may be partly due to the fact that elk antler does not survive well in the ground, but it probably also reflects a general increase in the number of hide-dressing tools used during the contact period owing to the demands of the fur trade.

Scapula knives are reasonably common in Post-Contact Coalescent sites and show a close resemblance to those found in Middle Missouri Tradition sites.

Arrow shaft wrenches seem to occur more commonly in the Post-Contact Coalescent villages than in earlier sites. They are usually made from large ribs or vertebral spines. Antler, used with some frequency during earlier times, was hardly ever employed. The shaft wrenches characteristically have two or more holes which show the same wear pattern as the earlier forms.

FIGURE 103

FIGURE 104

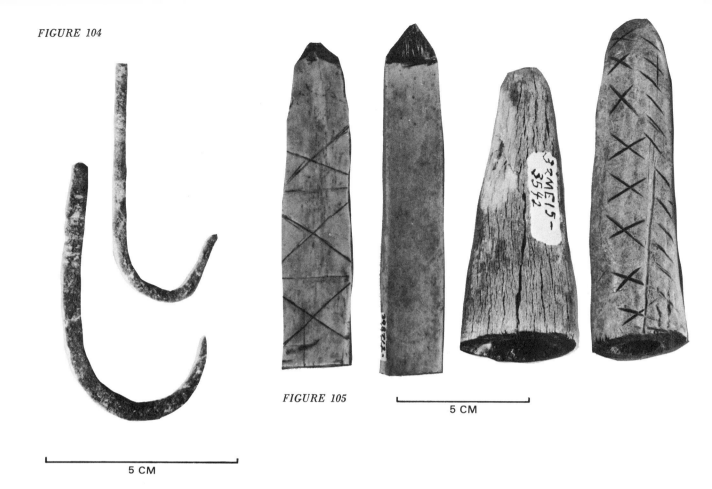

FIGURE 105

5 CM

5 CM

FIGURE 106

10 CM

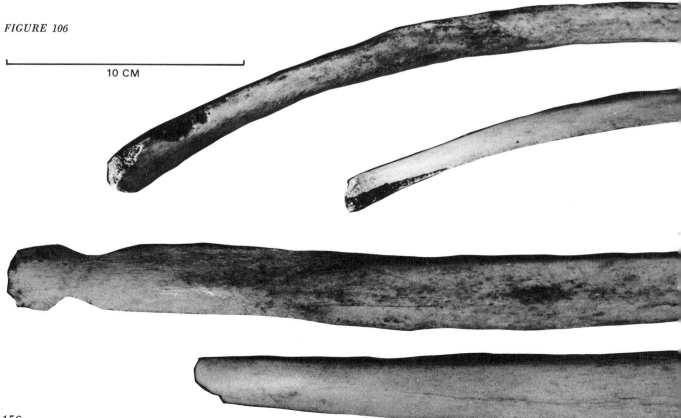

Fishhooks (fig. 104) from the Post-Contact Coalescent sites are almost always J-shaped pieces without barbs or eyes. Many of them are made of bone, like the earlier hooks; others appear to have been made by the Indians from trade iron, brass, or copper in the same style as the bone pieces. There are numerous references, dating from the early part of the 19th century, to machine-made fishhooks being brought into the region, but these are seldom recognizable as such in archeological contexts.

Bone sliders and snow snakes (fig. 105) are game pieces which appear in considerable numbers in many of the Post-Contact Coalescent sites. Bone sliders are like the ones from earlier periods. Most of them were undecorated, but some have patterns of notches and incised lines. The snow snakes are made from tips of antler tines. They are usually more than 10.0 cm. long, and sockets were hollowed out of the square-cut bases, presumably to receive long wooden shafts. In historic examples, the antler tip and a wooden shaft comprised a javelinlike object.

Both the bone sliders and the snow snakes were used in historic times in competitive games in which the players slid their pieces on the ice or crusted snow.

Sled runners (fig. 106) made from bison ribs seem to be largely confined to contact period sites. The ribs which fall into this category have more or less well-developed wear facets on the convex side. In many cases, small transverse holes were drilled through the dorsal ends of the bones. Wear patterns and drilling indicate that these pieces had been parts of the buffalo-rib sleds which were used for coasting by the children of many of the Northern Plains tribes. Ewers (1958, p. 151) has described them well:

Boys used cleverly made sleds with five to ten buffalo rib bone runners. The ribs were separated from the backbone and reassembled in exactly the same order. They were tied together tightly at each end by a rawhide rope that wound around a cross-piece of split willow. The seat was a piece of the leg skin of a buffalo, tied at each end to the willow crossbars. A buffalo-tail ornament was sewed or tied to the rear of the seat. A rawhide rope, tied to the front end, served to pull the sled uphill and to guide it in sliding down. Before riding on the sled, the owner pulled it around in the snow until the runners were coated with ice. In coasting, the boy sat on the hide seat, leaned well back, and balanced his weight by extending his legs forward and upward at an angle. He held the rawhide rope in his hands and jerked it to one side if he wished to turn his sled. The buffalo-tail decoration trailed behind, flopping crazily in the breeze.

5 CM

Miscellaneous artifacts of native manufacture (fig. 107) from the Post-Contact Coalescent sites include a number of forms. Bone tubes, beads, and whistles are similar to those from the Middle Missouri Tradition sites. Antler cylinders are found in the late sites, together with antler hammers. These consist of the base of the beam and the brow tine of an elk antler. The beam was chopped away at about the top of the brow tine, and the tip of the brow tine was also chopped off. The roughly circular base of the beam is the head of a hammer or mallet and the brow tine is the handle.

Grooved or notched ribs have been found. The more common form has grooves across the convex surface of the bone and probably served as a musical rasp. A less common form has notches on the edge and was almost certainly used as a musical rasp. Hide grainers made by cutting through the head of a bison humerus so as to expose a large area of cancellous tissue occur frequently. Paintbrushes consist of thin slabs of cancellate tissue of a large bone, such as the head of a bison humerus. They are porous enough to have held either water-soluble or grease-base paints, and are frequently stained with red or yellow pigment. Fragments of carved birchbark are found occasionally in the contact period villages in North Dakota.

FIGURE 107 Miscellaneous artifacts of native manufacture: carved birchbark, grooved rib, antler hammer, and hide grainers.

158

5 CM

FIGURE 108 Metal
ornaments: bracelets,
buttons, thimble, bell,
tinklers, and pendants.

5 CM

FIGURE 109 Horse
trappings: metal bit, clay
horse, and antler saddle bow.

Ornaments (fig. 108) from the contact
period sites include both pieces of native
manufacture and trade items. Native-made
shell beads, disks, and pendants occur, including ones made from marine species such
as *Olivella*. They are relatively rare. A few
beads and pendants made from bone or
horn, or from limestone, catlinite, and other
stones have also been found. Drilled elk
teeth occur with some regularity, and bear
claws drilled for stringing are fairly common. I know of no archeological evidence
for porcupine quill decoration on leather,
but the trait was almost certainly present.
Small rectangles of bone with open centers,
which may have been used as a sort of
buckle, continued to be made. This form
was sometimes reproduced in metal.

Imported materials were also used extensively in native-made ornaments. Conical metal tinklers which were attached to
the fringe on various garments are quite
common. Most of those found in the early
contact period sites were made of brass or
copper. Iron tinklers seem to have become
increasingly common during the latter part
of the period. Tubular metal beads were

also made, usually of brass or copper, and
a few metal finger rings and bracelets appear to be native products. One ingenious
native modification of a utilitarian item
into an ornament involved drilling a hole
through the top of a thimble so it could be
suspended as a pendant earring. Glass trade
beads were ground up, melted, and recast
into beads or pendants by members of all
three village tribes (cf. Gilmore, 1924; Stirling, 1947; Tabeau in Abel, 1939, p. 149;
Lewis in Thwaites, 1959, vol. 1, pp. 273–
274; Maximilian in Thwaites, 1966, vol. 23,
p. 278).

White-manufactured ornaments became
increasingly common through the contact
period, with a corresponding decrease in
the native-made varieties. Particular types
are itemized in the section dealing with
trade goods.

Horse trappings (fig. 109) and other evidence of the acquisition of the horse by the
Post-Contact Coalescent villagers are surprisingly rare in the archeological collections. Horse bones have been found only
occasionally in the village debris, and
identifiable horse gear has appeared infre-
quently. Wedel (1955, pp. 161–162) reports

a horseshoe from a grave at the Leavenworth Site (39CO9). Two metal bridle bits are included in the Thompson collection from the 19th-century Mandan village, Deapolis (32ME5), together with a small toy horse of fired clay with sockets for stick legs. Rock Village (32ME15), a presumed Hidatsa site in the Garrison region, yielded two antler bows or cantles from what Wilson (1924, p. 191) refers to as the "woman's saddle" or "pack saddle."

Trade goods include both metal and glass used by the Indians as raw materials and machine-made items utilized in their original forms. The latter items amount to a significant addition to the total trait inventory of the native cultures, but they are generally rare in the archeological assemblages which date from the 18th century. Functionally, the trade pieces fall into two categories: utilitarian items such as knives, axes, and firearms, which were related directly to the native economy; and ornaments, mirrors, combs, etc., which had esthetic or cosmetic value but which contributed nothing to the group's struggle for survival. The archeological record of the trade goods is necessarily incomplete. Such perishable items as tobacco, liquor, gunpowder, and textiles are not preserved, and much of the iron is rusted beyond recognition.

NEGATIVE TRAITS

Negative traits—items no longer present or extremely rare—are also important to any conceptualization of Post-Contact Coalescent culture. The long-rectangular house of the Middle Missouri Tradition seems to have been given up except for possible early holdovers at the Ward and Sperry sites, and the trait of arranging houses in rows also disappeared. Rectilinear fortification plans had become obsolete, and bastions are extremely rare in villages occupied after the beginning of the 18th century.

The ceramic technology which was necessary to produce the fine, thin, hard-paste pottery of the Extended Coalescent Variant had been lost before the beginning of the 18th century. Specific ceramic attributes which had dropped out of fashion include cord roughening, which did not survive beyond the end of Initial Middle Missouri and Initial Coalescent times, and flared rims. Rims with thickened collars and the sharply curved S-rims are also rare to non-existent in the late assemblages.

A number of artifact types of the earlier complexes seem to have disappeared almost completely. These include the large percussion-flaked leaf blades, stone celts with pecked bodies and polished blades, stone axes, scapula hoes with sockets, picks made from bison radii with socketed proximal ends, hooked bone knives, scapula sickles, elaborately carved bone knife handles, and the distinctive thunderbird silhouettes of the Middle Missouri Tradition. Fine, narrow, asymmetrical leaf blades and the small grooved stones occur rarely in late sites in South Dakota, but they are fairly common in the 18th-century villages in North Dakota.

In some cases functional reasons for the rejection of pre-existing traits can be postulated. It seems likely that the preference for the circular house reflects a better design for heating. Thanks to the positioning of the firepits of the long-rectangular structures well down toward the entrance end of the floor, the back parts of those houses must have been miserably cold during the long Dakota winters. In contrast, the centrally located firepits of the circular houses would have been much more efficient for heating the whole interior of the structure. The layout of the Post-Contact Coalescent towns, in which the houses were scattered rather than arranged in rows as villages of the Middle Missouri Tradition, may simply reflect the fact that circular structures are more difficult to aline than rectangular ones. David Thompson's narrative suggests, however, that the irregular placement of houses in a village had a tactical advantage in the eyes of the Indians:

They [the Mandan] *enquired how we built our houses, as they saw me attentively examining the structure of theirs; when informed; and drawing a rough plan of our Villages, with Streets parallel to each other, and cross Streets at right angles, after looking at it for some time; they shook their heads, and said, In these straight Streets we see no advantage the inhabitants have over their enemies. The whole of their bodies are exposed, and the houses can be set on fire; which our houses cannot be, for the earth cannot burn; our houses being round shelter us except when we fire down on them, and we are high above them; the enemies have never been able to hurt us when we are in our Villages; and it is only when we are absent on large hunting parties that we have suffered; and which we shall not do again.* (Glover, 1962, p. 173)

CHRONOLOGY

The chronology of the Post-Contact Coalescent Variant is based primarily on historical sources. The occurrence of items of European origin, such as metal and glass, is one of the most important diagnostic traits. The history of the expansion of the fur trade into the regions north and west of the Great Lakes makes it likely that some trade materials were reaching the Missouri Valley through Indian intermediaries by 1675. This is a convenient beginning date. The smallpox epidemic which began in the year 1780 thoroughly disrupted the village tribes. That year marks the end of the Post-Contact Coalescent Variant.

TAXONOMIC SUBDIVISIONS

The subdivisions of the Post-Contact Coalescent Variant can be recognized with greater certainty than in the case of any of the preceding cultural configurations. They include a Heart River Phase, which is approximately equivalent to Will and Hecker's (1944) Later Heart River complex and Bowers' (1965) Painted Woods and Heart River Foci; a Le Beau Phase, which corresponds to the Le Beau and Four Bear Foci (Hurt, 1957; 1962); a Bad River Phase, which includes the former Stanley and Snake Butte Foci (Lehmer, 1954b); a Talking Crow Phase, which is partially equivalent to C. S. Smith's Fort Thompson Focus (C. S. Smith, 1959; Stephenson, 1954); and a Felicia Phase, corresponding to the Felicia Focus (Caldwell, 1966), which includes materials that appear to be transitional between the late Extended Coalescent complexes of the Big Bend region and the Talking Crow Phase. Correspondences between these complexes and the contemporary village pattern in the Central Plains show that the materials of the latter may be recognized as also belonging to the Post-Contact Coalescent Variant, and may be assigned provisionally to a Lower Loup Phase (cf. Strong, 1935; Dunlevy, 1936; Wedel, 1936 and 1959).

The Bad River Phase has been discussed in detail elsewhere (Hoffman and Brown, 1967; Lehmer and Jones, 1968, pp. 95–100), and Smith and Johnson (1968, pp. 45–51) discuss the Felicia Phase at some length. The other phases are not as well known, but it is possible to characterize them with a reasonable degree of assurance. The Post-Contact Coalescent phases hold the majority of their traits in common. They are mainly distinguished by differences in geographic distribution, village plan, ceremonial lodges, pottery, relative amounts of trade items, and estimated ages. The characteristics of the ones in the Missouri Valley are summarized in outline form in appendix 2.

Tribal identifications of the Post-Contact phases can be made with considerable assurance. The Heart River Phase equates with the 18th-century Mandan and Hidatsa, and the Felicia, Talking Crow, and Bad River phases almost certainly relate to the Arikara. There is some question about the tribal identity of the Le Beau Phase, but it too probably relates to the Arikara. The Lower Loup Phase has been identified as protohistoric Pawnee.

ORIGINS

The origins of the Post-Contact Coalescent Variant trace back to both the Coalescent and the Terminal Middle Missouri Variants, with the individual Post-Contact Coalescent subdivisions apparently relating more directly to one or the other of the older complexes. Lower Loup and the Felicia, Talking Crow, Bad River, and Le Beau Phases (Pawnee and Arikara) seem to have been primarily outgrowths of the Coalescent complexes and ultimately the Central Plains Tradition. In contrast, the Heart River Phase (Mandan and Hidatsa) appears to derive directly from the Terminal Middle Missouri Variant.

There is every indication that the late village groups of the Northern Plains reached essentially the same cultural destination from different starting points. Processes of cultural convergence, involving a series of trait selections from known alternatives or equivalents, must have operated on a large scale. In most cases it is possible to suggest the source of the important Post-Contact Coalescent traits. Some of these— characteristic of each of the major cultural variants—were drawn from what might be thought of as the common reservoir of the Plains Village Pattern.

The house is the outstanding item derived from the earlier Coalescent complexes. The irregular arrangement of houses within the villages is also a Coalescent trait. Other Central Plains and early Coalescent traits which carried over into the Post-Contact Coalescent Variant may include the burial pattern of individual primary inhumations which is found occasionally in the Central Plains. The common rim forms of the late pottery of the Middle Missouri—direct, braced, and shallow S—were all present in the Extended Coalescent Variant. Late artifacts which seem to have derived from the Central Plains Tradition by way of the earlier Coalescent variants include tenoned or socketed bone projectile points, diamond-shaped knives with alternating beveled edges, grooved ribs or musical rasps, and stone pipes. The use of catlinite may have come by way of the Coalescent development.

Middle Missouri Tradition traits are also well represented in the Post-Contact Coalescent Variant. The central plazas of the Mandan towns are a feature which had developed at least as early as Terminal Middle Missouri times. Fortification systems consisting of ditches and palisades evidently made their first appearance in the Northern Plains in some of the Middle Missouri Tradition villages. This may have been the initial source for the ditches and palisades of the Post-Contact communities, but their patterns were radically changed during the late period. Post-Contact Coalescent fortifications were curved rather than angular, and bastions disappeared almost completely. Curved fortification lines are found in villages of the Initial Coalescent Variant and in some of the Extended Coalescent communities. The Post-Contact Coalescent scheme may have been a carryover from the earlier Coalescent manifestations.

The fabric of Post-Contact Coalescent pottery is much more like that of the Middle Missouri Tradition than that of the Extended Coalescent Variant. The simple stamped body treatment is an obvious retention of a trait which appeared during Extended Middle Missouri times, and the extensive use of cord-impressed decoration is common to both Middle Missouri Tradition and Post-Contact Coalescent wares.

Late nonpottery artifacts of native origin which are also typical of the Middle Missouri Tradition include chalcedony plate knives, large triangular side-notched knives, and grooved mauls. Bone and antler implements common to the two complexes include horn scoops, spatulas, metatarsal fleshers, and antler fleshing adzes. When these forms are added to those that occur in both Middle Missouri and Central Plains Tradition sites, there is a remarkably close correspondence between the artifact inventories of the Middle Missouri Tradition and the Post-Contact Coalescent Variant.

CULTURAL INTERACTION, A.D. 1675–1780

Cultural interactions among the villages of the Missouri Valley in the 18th century were dominated by a new element in the Northern Plains—the horse tribes. The sudden upsurge of the mounted bison hunters created a second power block in the region, which increased in importance year by year.

The growth of this new complex was a direct consequence of the introduction of the horse and its incorporation into Plains culture. That process was dealt with in detail by the ethnologists and historians of a generation ago, but it is worth reviewing briefly. Horses originally came to the Plains tribes from the Spanish settlers in the Southwest (Haines, 1938a, 1938b), presumably in the early part of the 17th century, and, according to Haines and to Roe (1955), had spread throughout most of the Plains area before the middle of the 18th century. The horse provided a new and efficient means of transportation and was the basis for a considerable elaboration of the native culture.

Wissler (1914) pointed out that many of the elements of post-horse Plains culture had been in existence during pre-horse times. He cited such items as the migratory way of life, primary dependence on hunting, periodic mass hunting expeditions by the Pawnee and other eastern tribes, the custom of war parties setting out on foot, transport by the travois pulled by dogs, and the skin tent. While these traits would not normally be evident in archeological contexts, it is likely that most of them were typical of the Foraging complexes of the Northwestern Plains. The possession of the horse elaborated and intensified the earlier Plains pattern. Kroeber (1939, pp. 76–77) summed the situation up in these words: *Wissler found that when the Plains tribes took up the horse they did not make their culture over. Travois transportation, the tepee, the bison hunt under control, had all been there before. The horse was simply put into the old patterns and made these more productive. It was easier for the tribes to do this than to evolve or adjust to a new set of patterns. As an analysis of cultural dynamics or social psychology, this was a valid demonstration. Too largely, however, it seems to have been tacitly interpreted also as a historical conclusion, that Plains culture after the horse went on much as before. Very little reflection shows that this could not have been so. Could any good-sized group have lived permanently off the bison on the open plains while they and their dogs were dragging their dwellings, furniture, provisions, and children? How large a tepee could have been continuously moved in this way, how much apparatus could it have contained, how close were its inmates huddled, how large the camp circle? How often could several thousand people have congregated in one spot to hold a four or eight days' Sun dance? By the standard of the nineteenth century, the sixteenth-century Plains Indian would have been miserably poor and almost chronically hungry, if he had tried to follow the same life. Showy clothing, embroidered footgear, medicine-bundle purchases, elaborate rituals, gratuitous and time-consuming warfare, all these he could have indulged in but little—not much more than the tribes of the intermountain or southern Texas regions.*

A major influx of population into the western Plains was as important as the introduction of the horse to the development of the late culture climax there. Northern Plains tribes which participated fully or partially in that climax were the Arapaho, Assiniboin, Blackfoot (including the Piegan and Blood), Cheyenne, Crow, Dakota, Gros Ventre, Plains Cree, Plains Ojibwa, Sarsi, and Wind River Shoshone. Only the three Blackfoot groups seem to have been long-time residents of the region. The Wind River Shoshone came only into the western margins of the area. The Sarsi were a Northern Forest tribe which allied itself with the Blackfoot. The Plains Cree and Plains Ojibwa were late comers who moved into the Canadian prairies from the forested regions north of Lake Superior. The Crow were a recent offshoot of the semisedentary Hidatsa. The Assiniboin, Cheyenne, and Dakota are all known to have moved west from the valleys of the Red River of the North and the upper Mississippi. Mooney cites an Arapaho tradition that they and the Gros Ventre also came from that same area (Hodge, 1910, vol. I, p. 72).

While the large migration into the Plains from the east and northeast was partly a response to the newly developed horse culture, another factor must have been just as important. This was the series of intertribal wars around the Mississippi headwaters which were a byproduct of the fur trade. The upper Mississippi was a rich source of beaver and a number of Indian groups fought to control it during the 17th and 18th centuries. Tribes such as the Fox and Ojibwa had a considerable advantage since they were in close contact with Canadian traders who supplied them with guns and ammunition. The pressure they were able to exert must have been a major factor in pushing the emigrant tribes out into the Plains.

The fur trade also laid its stamp on the situation in the Plains during the 1700's through influences which originated from trading centers far to the north and east. The first trading center established in North America consisted of the French settlements at Quebec, Three Rivers, and Montreal in the St. Lawrence Valley. It had its inception with the founding of Quebec in 1608. At first the merchants waited for Indian customers to make their way down to the settlements along the St. Lawrence. Gradually, missionaries and explorers ranged far into the interior. The secular function of these expeditions was to cement alliances with the tribes of the hinterland and to direct their trade toward the settlements.

Another early trading center was Hudson Bay and its southern appendix James Bay. This was the first important area of English operations in the North American fur trade. English commercial penetration began there in 1668, with an expedition promoted by two veterans of the French fur trade in Canada—Medard Chouart Sieur des Groseilliers and his brother-in-law Pierre Esprit Radisson. They sailed from Gravesend in June of that year in two ketches, *Eaglet* and *Nonsuch.* Storms forced *Eaglet,* with Radisson aboard, back to port. Groseilliers, in *Nonsuch,* got as far south as James Bay and returned to England in 1669 with furs which sold for nearly 30 times the value of the trade goods used to obtain them.

In 1670 Charles II signed a charter for "The Governor and Company of Adventurers of England Trading Into Hudson's Bay." During the decade of the 1670's, trading posts or factories were built at strategic locations at the mouths of rivers which drained from the east, south, and west into Hudson and James Bays. Like the French, the Hudson's Bay Company traders made little attempt to penetrate inland. Instead, they waited for canoe-loads of Indian customers to come down to them from the interior. The customers, including Ojibwa, Cree, and a few Assiniboin, came from the country to the north and northeast of the Middle Missouri.

The early fur trade pattern of fixed posts with a minimal penetration of the interior by Europeans meant that the Indians filled a major role in the operation. Members of some of the interior tribes had to make the long and dangerous journey down to the posts, bringing in cargoes of furs which were worth a fortune by European standards. They took back trade stuffs of fabulous value by Indian standards. Some of these goods were kept for their own use; the rest were passed along to tribes which were not in direct contact with the Europeans. In this way the earliest stage of the fur trade saw the development of groups of Indian middlemen who carried the trade far beyond the range of the European traders themselves. The most elaborate structure of this sort seems to have been the Huron trading empire, which grew up in eastern Canada and the Great Lakes region early in the 17th century (Hunt, 1940). But Indian middlemen operated in a less complex fashion all through the fur trade country and were responsible for the initial introduction of European goods into the Middle Missouri Valley.

The operations of the middlemen, the value of the trade goods they carried into the interior, and the profits they reaped are all illustrated by Perrot's account of the contact between the Ottawa and the Dakota in the upper Mississippi region in the mid-17th century:

The Scioux, who had no other acquaintance with the firearms and other implements which they saw among the strangers . . . hoped that these new peoples who had come near them would share with them the commodities which they possessed; and, believing that the latter were spirits, because they were acquainted with the use of iron—an article which was utterly unlike the stone and other things which they used—conducted them, as I have said, to their own villages. . . .

The Outaouas and Hurons gave the Scioux in turn a friendly reception, but did not make them presents of much value. The Scioux returned to their own country, with some small articles which they had received from the Outaouas, and shared these with their allies in other villages, giving to some hatchets, to others knives or awls. All those villages sent deputies to those of the Outaouas; as soon as they arrived there . . . they entreated the strangers to have pity on them, and to share with them the iron, which they regarded as a divinity . . . They gave to the envoys a few trifles, such as knives and awls . . . the Outaouas fired some guns which they had; and the report of these weapons so terrified the Scioux that they imagined it was the thunder or the lightning, of which the Outaouas had made themselves masters in order to exterminate whomsoever they would.   (Blair, 1911, vol. I, pp. 159–163)

In time the Europeans were forced to expand their own operations into the hinterland. In 1642 Iroquois war parties slashed north from New York State in an attempt to capture the Canadian fur trade and divert it to the Dutch in the Hudson Valley. Iroquois wars continued to flare up for over two decades (Hunt, 1940). When they finally ended, the old pattern of the fur trade on the St. Lawrence was completely disrupted.

Long before the close of these wars, the French had begun penetrating far into the interior to trade for furs. Their traders traveled the Illinois country, moved into the region of the western Great Lakes, and crossed southern Manitoba. This began a new trading pattern, one in which the European trader followed the streams and lakes to his Indian customers' homelands instead of waiting for the Indians to come to him.

By 1658 Groseilliers and Radisson had headed west to Lake Superior, established a temporary post at Chequamegon Bay, and traveled inland to visit the Dakota villages in the Mississippi headwaters. Duluth and others continued trading in the Lake Superior region during the latter part of the 17th century. There was a steady trickle of French traders into Green Bay during this period, and the Ottawa and some Huron, displaced from the eastern Great Lakes country by the Iroquois, were an important factor in the western trade during the middle 1600's. Their canoe brigades repeatedly made the long journey to Montreal and Three Rivers, taking down furs they had traded from the tribes west of Lake Michigan and hauling back cargoes of trade goods. In the spring of 1673 Jolliet and Marquette pioneered the route west from Green Bay, which went up the Fox River, crossed an easy portage to the Wisconsin River, and went down the Wisconsin to the Mississippi. From that time on the Fox-Wisconsin passage was followed by numbers of French traders on their way to the tribes in the interior, including the Dakota on the upper Mississippi and beyond (cf. Kellog, 1925; Blair, 1911; Innis, 1962; Phillips, 1961).

After 1720 the French traders, stimulated by English competition from the south and by declining supplies of beaver, moved west from Lake Superior. They worked past Rainy Lake, into the Lake Winnipeg country, and up the lower reaches of the Assiniboin River drainage. This placed them across the Indian line of movement to the British posts to the north, forcing the Hudson's Bay Company to establish competing posts in southern Manitoba and Saskatchewan (Innis, 1962, pp. 84–99 and 151–160).

In 1738 Pierre Gaultier de Varennes, Sieur de la Vérendrye, made the first recorded visit by a white man to the Middle Missouri Village tribes. When La Vérendrye traveled west and south from his fort at the mouth of the Red River of the North, his route intersected a well-established Indian trade route. There is little doubt that it tapped the Hudson's Bay Company posts far to the north, as well as the newer French establishments west of Lake Superior. Its southern section was almost certainly the main avenue by which the trade goods which La Vérendrye found among the Mandan had reached their villages. The Assiniboin who accompanied him on the latter part of his journey were familiar travelers of that route, and they must have been carrying metal and glass to the northern Middle Missouri villages for a considerable time before La Vérendrye made his journey. His account refers to a well-established trade pattern between the two groups (Burpee, 1927, pp. 153, 160, 254, 323, 332, 336–338).

The Assiniboin were closely tied to the Cree in their trading operations. The 17th-century Cree were a Northern Forest tribe of migratory hunters. They moved through the broad arc of country between Lake Superior and Hudson Bay, ranging as far east as James Bay, and as far to the northwest as the Nelson River after the Hudson's Bay Company established a post near that river's mouth in 1682.

Cree trading parties visited the Hudson's Bay Company posts every season, delivering furs and taking cargoes of trade goods back into the hinterland. A substantial part of those goods were kept for their own use, but there seems to have been a healthy surplus which was passed on to other Indian groups. Until trading posts were set up in the Lake Winnipeg area, much of that surplus went to the Cree's traditional allies, the Assiniboin. The Assiniboin themselves seem to have had less direct contact with European traders until the Lake Winnipeg posts were established. Trade goods in the hands of both Cree and Assiniboin were passed on to the Mandan and Hidatsa towns, which were at the other end of the northern tribes' trading cycle.

The Arikara villages along the Missouri River in South Dakota were much farther away from the Canadian trading establishments than the Mandan and Hidatsa. The Arikara may have received some trade goods by way of the Mandan villages, but these were probably of negligible importance. The first appreciable effects of the fur trade on the Arikara most likely came from the Wisconsin-Minnesota region.

The route west from Green Bay along the Fox and Wisconsin Rivers seems to have connected with the eastern terminus of an early 18th-century trade route which reached the southern margins of the Middle Missouri subarea. The Delisle map of 1718 (Tucker, 1942, pl. XV) shows a double dashed line marked *"Chemin des Voyageurs,"* which runs almost due west from the Mississippi opposite the end of the Fox-Wisconsin passage. The line ends at a tributary labeled *"R. du Rocher,"* which flows into the Missouri from the north. Conventionalized houses are shown on both banks of the *Rocher* where the trail ends—those on the east designated *"Aiouez,"* and those on the west *"Maha."* From its relation to the course of the Missouri and to the tributaries downstream, there can be little doubt that the *"R. du Rocher"* is either the Big Sioux or its eastern confluent, the Rock River. This certainly raises the possibility that *voyaguers* were going west over the *"Chemin"* to the settlements of the Iowa and Omaha by the beginning of the 18th century.

The same map shows a group of villages on the next tributary west of the *Rocher,* presumably the James River, which are labeled *"Aricara."* Another group of villages on the Missouri itself between latitude 43°30′ and 44° N., in what appears to be the Big Bend and Lower Bad-Cheyenne regions, is designated *"40 Villages des Panis."* These are, in all probability, the Arikara towns of the early 18th century. If, as seems likely, traders were going west from the upper Mississippi to villages on the Big Sioux, trade goods were almost certainly passed on by Indian middlemen from those villages to the Arikara towns on the Missouri.

The Dakota occupied a position comparable to that of the Cree and Assiniboin in the trade with the village tribes, especially the Arikara. The Dakota had been pushed west from the country of the Mississippi headwaters by the intertribal wars of the 18th century, and the westernmost bands had come to dominate most of eastern North and South Dakota before 1800. During their movement, those western bands had remade their culture in the image of the migratory hunters of the western Plains. Throughout most of the year, the individual bands went their separate ways. But they did follow the custom of an annual rendezvous or trade fair. This institution is well documented for the opening years of the 19th century by Truteau (Nasatir, 1952, vol. II, pp. 301, 311), Lewis and Clark (Thwaites, 1959, vol. 6, pp. 45, 95), Tabeau (Abel, 1939, pp. 121–123), and others.

During the early 1800's the rendezvous was held on the James River in eastern South Dakota. Groups such as the Sisseton and Yankton came from the east bringing trade goods which they had gotten at posts on the Minnesota and Des Moines Rivers and catlinite from the quarries in southwestern Minnesota. The Teton came from the west, bringing the products of their hunts and horses that had been traded up from the Southwest. They carried trade goods back from the rendezvous, and some of these were passed along to the villagers on the Missouri. While good historical evidence for the beginning of this pattern is lacking, there is reason to believe that it was an old one among the Dakota.

The movement of trade goods to the Middle Missouri villages from Canada and the western Great Lakes region was balanced by trade relations with the tribes which ranged over the country to the west and south of the river. Ewers has suggested that the village tribes were involved in a fairly extensive trading network in prehistoric times, and this is supported by the occurrence in precontact archeological sites of Pacific and gulf coast shells and of pieces of obsidian, native copper, and catlinite. In analyzing the early pattern, Ewers points out that it was mainly an exchange of the villagers' crops for products of the hunt, and he concludes:

In aboriginal times there was little incentive for trade between two horticultural tribes or two hunting peoples, as neither possessed an abundance of desirable articles which the other did not have. But barter between hunting and gardening peoples enabled each group to supplement its own economy with the product of the other's labor. It was a mutually profitable exchange. . . .

This aboriginal pattern of trade must have had the effect of intensifying the labors of the nomads and the horticulturalists in their own specialities. In order for the nomadic tribes to enjoy the advantages of a vegetable diet without the necessity for rais-

FIGURE 110 *Patterns of intertribal commodity exchange.*

ing crops themselves, they had to kill more wild game, to dry more meat, and to dress and work more skins than would have been the case had they attempted to supply their needs solely by their own labors. Conversely, in order to decrease their reliance upon the buffalo hunt and to free themselves of the necessity of dressing large numbers of skins and of making dress clothing, the gardening peoples had to plant, cultivate, and harvest much larger crops than were required for themselves alone. (Ewers, 1968, pp. 19–22)

The advent of European settlers in eastern North America and the Southwest stimulated the older trade patterns enormously, and the Middle Missouri villagers were ideally situated to profit from the increased activity. Trade goods from east and north of the Missouri were in great demand by the tribes to the west and south of the river. Horses and mules obtained by the western tribes from the Spanish ranches in the Southwest were in equally great demand by the eastern groups. The villagers along the Middle Missouri became, in effect, brokers who managed the actual exchanges between the eastern and western tribes with a considerable profit for themselves.

Parties from the west arrived at the villages at intervals, bringing horses and mules and their own products including leather goods, dried meat and pemmican, and flour made from the prairie turnip. The western tribes appear to have contributed little in the way of other manufactured items. Lewis and Clark (Thwaites, 1959, vol. 3, p. 19; and vol. 6, p. 103) and others do mention bridle bits, stirrups, and blankets reaching the Plains from the Southwest. The blankets had presumably been made by Southwestern

Indians, and the bits and stirrups were probably rare items. The general lack of trade goods from the Southwest is readily understandable, since the Spanish settlers were themselves at the end of a long and tenuous supply line which wound its way up from the Valley of Mexico across the barren northern plateaus. Also, the Spanish colonial pattern was not oriented toward extensive trade with the Indian populations.

The western tribes exchanged their wares for the villagers' garden crops and for guns and other trade goods. The villagers then used the horses and mules, supplemented by their crops, to renew their supply of trade goods through exchanges with the Dakota, Assiniboin, and possibly some Cree and Ojibwa middlemen (fig. 110).

The intertribal trade was only one expression of the cultural interactions involving the 18th-century Middle Missouri villages. The presence of Europeans themselves in the area was another factor. Some, such as La Vérendrye and his sons and David Thompson, came mainly as explorers. Tabeau speaks of a "Spanish prisoner" who taught the Arikara women how to melt glass trade beads and mold them into other forms (Abel, 1939, p. 149). This might refer to a European, but it seems just as likely that he was an Indian who had been held captive by the Spaniards.

The most important class of Europeans in the area before 1800 were the traders who lived in the Indian villages, rather than in their own forts or trading posts, and may be characterized as *tenant traders*. It is difficult to document their operations, since they left little in the way of diaries and other records. Many of them were illiterate, and a number were probably in some sort of trouble with the colonial authorities and had no desire to call attention to themselves.

The 1718 Delisle map bears a notation just above the 44°30′ north latitude line which reads: "*Les Francois n'ont remonte le Mifsouri que jusquicy.*" This suggests that some trader or explorer had gotten as far up the river as the Bad-Cheyenne region by the early years of the 18th century. There is a definite record of an anonymous Frenchman in the region in 1742. When La Vérendrye's sons reached the Missouri near Pierre in that year, they were told that a Frenchman was living 3 days' journey from

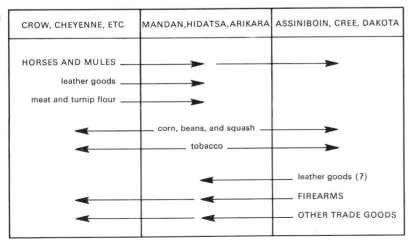

CROW, CHEYENNE, ETC.	MANDAN, HIDATSA, ARIKARA	ASSINIBOIN, CREE, DAKOTA
HORSES AND MULES ————————→	————————→	
leather goods ————————→		
meat and turnip flour ————————→		
←———— corn, beans, and squash ————————→		
←———— tobacco ————————→		
	←———— leather goods (?)	
←———— ←———— FIREARMS		
←———— ←———— OTHER TRADE GOODS		

the village where they were staying (Burpee, 1927, pp. 426–428).

Some of the tenant traders acquired Indian wives and became more or less permanent residents of the villages. Toussaint Charbonneau and René Jessaume, who joined the Lewis and Clark expedition at Fort Mandan, are well-known examples, and they must have had many predecessors. The men of this sort probably had relatively small stocks of trade goods to contribute because of their isolation from sources of supply. They must, on the other hand, have been of considerable use to the villagers because of their knowledge of European technologies such as gun repair.

Other men who went to the Middle Missouri villages during the 18th and early 19th centuries were employees of organized trading concerns, or were independent and often unlicensed traders. Pierre Antoine Tabeau and Hugh McCracken, both in the region during Lewis and Clark's visit, are good examples. Such men moved into the villages temporarily with stocks of goods which were exchanged for furs and sometimes for food and horses. They must have been responsible for the introduction of fair amounts of trade goods.

The tenant trader tapped the same sources of supply as the Indian middlemen, with the exception of the Hudson's Bay Company posts on the bay itself. Trading posts in the Lake Winnipeg area and the trade into the western Great Lakes were the most important sources, with St. Louis running a bad third until near the end of the 18th century. The relatively permanent trading posts or forts which represent the late phase of the fur trade in the Middle Missouri country did not become a significant factor until after the first decade of the 19th century.

Warfare must have been another important factor in the cultural interaction in the Missouri Valley during the 18th century. This too relates to the rise of the horse tribes. Sedentary farmers have been targets for raids by migratory groups since mankind first developed villages. The Middle Missouri towns, with their wealth of stored crops, horses, and trade goods, must have been attractive targets for any mounted bison hunters. The evidence points to the Dakota as the most serious threat.

Dakota groups, presumably still without horses, seem to have pushed into eastern South Dakota during the first decades of the 18th century. There are suggestions that they were exerting considerable pressure on the village tribes before 1750. The presence of strong fortification systems at all but the earliest and northernmost Post-Contact Coalescent villages appears to be concrete evidence of that pressure. There are indications that some sections of the valley were abandoned by the village tribes around the middle of the 18th century, although adequate series of dates from individual sites to support this are not available. It seems likely that most of the Talking Crow Phase sites in the Big Bend region had been abandoned by 1750, although two of the six dates which Weakly reports from the Medicine Crow Site (39BF2) are listed as 1768+ and 1776+, with the others falling between 1705+ and 1717+ (Weakly, MS., p. 105). It seems probable that the mid-18th century saw the villagers driven out of most of the towns on the left bank of the Missouri in the Bad-Cheyenne region, except for a small pocket in the Little Bend opposite the mouth of the Cheyenne River.

This would have left the Arikara occupying fortified villages on the right bank of the Missouri in the Bad-Cheyenne region, and on both banks of the river in the Grand-Moreau region, with an especially heavy concentration across from the mouth of the Grand. The contraction of the Arikara area of occupation might have been caused by any one of several factors. Pressure from the Dakota is the most likely explanation at this point. There seem to be no indications of comparable population movements on the part of the Mandan and Hidatsa during the first three-quarters of the 18th century.

Two native artifact types seem to make their first appearance in the Middle Missouri Valley during Post-Contact Coalescent times. They are carved birchbark and bison rib sled runners. These items probably originated in the forested regions to the northeast of the Middle Missouri country, and suggest borrowing from tribes such as the Cree, Ojibwa, and possibly the Assiniboin and the Dakota.

The addition of the horse to the village cultures was particularly important in connection with the intertribal trade. Horses were actually used far less by the villagers than by the migratory hunting tribes, but they did provide an improved means of transportation. This must have been especially important in connection with the villagers' exploitation of the bison herds.

A pattern of the wholesale abandonment of the villages for seasonal hunting expeditions is well documented for Central Plains tribes such as the Pawnee and Omaha. There are indications that this pattern was also present among the Mandan, Hidatsa, and Arikara after they acquired horses. For example, Chardon's journal (Abel, 1932), written at Fort Clark between 1834 and 1839, contains numerous references to members of all three tribes leaving their settlements on expeditions "to make dried meat." However, there is some question in my mind that this hunting pattern was quite as important to the northern villagers as it was to the Central Plains groups.

The extremely large amounts of bison bone found in many of the villages along the Middle Missouri indicate a significant amount of hunting done close to home. This is presumably a direct consequence of the fact that large numbers of bison moved into the valley itself at different times of the year.

The hostile pressure exerted by the Dakota also served to discourage the villagers from sending out large-scale hunting parties, especially after the late 1830's. This pressure must have been felt as early as the latter half of the 18th century, but does not seem to have become really serious until after the smallpox epidemics had drastically reduced the fighting strength of the village tribes. This was particularly true after the epidemic of 1837–38. The losses at that time left the Dakota with relatively little to fear in the way of reprisals, and ethnohistorical sources for the late 19th century document a constant series of attacks on villagers who were out hunting or even working in their gardens.

Adoption of the horse was certainly accompanied by some technological changes. Saddles and other riding gear were manufactured, along with the travois adapted for use with the horse. Herding, the feeding of cottonwood branches during the winter, and the stabling of prize animals in the owner's earthlodge were all adopted. Toy horses were also added to the list of children's playthings.

Metal and glass traded into the region were often made into artifacts by the Indians themselves. Scraps of iron, brass, or copper were transformed into arrow points, cutting tools, fishhooks, and other items including ornaments. For the most part, the forms tended to resemble older ones made of stone or bone. The important change was in the material. A great deal of scrap metal was used in this way, mostly derived from worn or broken trade items. Sometimes manufactured metal items were deliberately cut up for stock. Alexander Henry, writing of his visit to the Mandan villages in 1806, says:

I saw the remains of an excellent large corn mill [given the Mandan by Lewis and Clark] *which the foolish fellows had demolished to barb their arrows; the largest piece of it, which they could not break or work up into any weapon, was fixed to a wooden handle, and used to pound marrowbones to make grease.*

(Coues, 1965a, vol. 1, p. 329)

There seems to have been almost nothing added to the native technology in the way of special metal-working techniques. Native-made metal artifacts were produced by filing, cutting, and cold-hammering. Mining, smelting, casting, even the use of the bellows and forge, seem to have been completely bypassed as technological innovations, despite the fact that the Indians were aware of metal-working techniques at the level of the blacksmith shop by the opening years of the 19th century. I am not aware of references to the adoption of even such a rudimentary technique as the casting of bullets in a mold until late in the 19th century, although the rare lead-inlaid pipes indicate some use of molten metal. In view of this, it is surprising that the village tribes did learn and use techniques for grinding, melting, and recasting glass trade beads.

The addition of metal tools to the village cultures was itself responsible for some technological changes. Baerreis and Dallman (1961, pp. 181–182) have already pointed out that bone working is far easier with metal than with stone tools, and that more bone was removed during the manufacture of many of the scapula hoes found in contact period sites. This situation can also be noted in the metatarsal fleshers. The shaft diameter of many of the fleshers found in Post-Contact Coalescent villages has been systematically reduced by chipping away small flakes from over the entire surface. This would have been a very difficult process with stone tools. It could have been accomplished quite easily with a heavy steel knife or a light hatchet.

The economic system of the village tribes was profoundly modified by their participation in the trading network. This involvement is evidenced by numerous items in the archeological record. Most obvious are the physical remains of the trade goods themselves—metal, glass, and occasional horse bones found in the village sites. It is my impression that the ratio of scapula hoes to other bone artifacts is generally higher in the Post-Contact Coalescent villages than in the earlier ones. If this is the case, it may well be a reflection of increased agricultural production to meet the demands of the intertribal trade.

It also seems likely that the location of the 18th-century villages was partly a function of the intertribal trade. There is a strong tendency for them to be clustered in the vicinity of the mouths of the major western tributaries of the Missouri, especially the Bad, Cheyenne, Grand, Heart, and Knife Rivers. The valleys of these east-flowing streams would have provided wood and water for groups moving down to the Missouri from the high Plains, and it seems likely that the stream courses would have delineated natural lines of movement for trading parties from the western tribes. If this was the case, there would have been a strong incentive to locate villages near the mouths of the tributaries to intercept the western traders when they arrived in the valley.

Finally, the archeological content of the late sites has a richness which contrasts strikingly with the remains of the earlier manifestations of the Coalescent Tradition. Many of the Middle Missouri Tradition sites contain a wealth of specimens, but it is my impression that the Post-Contact Coalescent villages, especially the ones of the Heart River Phase, have a higher artifact yield per cubic yard of refuse than any others in the region. This appears to be a good indication that the intertribal trade swept the

Post-Contact Coalescent villages into a period of prosperity which lasted until the pattern collapsed under the combined impact of epidemics, Dakota raiders, and the drastically changed trading patterns which followed the opening of the water route up the Missouri from St. Louis.

DISORGANIZED COALESCENT VARIANT

The village tribes of the Middle Missouri subarea rode a wave of prosperity and cultural elaboration through the third quarter of the 18th century. Then another European introduction, epidemic diseases, came close to wiping out the population, and left the survivors with a badly disorganized remnant of their former culture. This is the phase of the village development recorded by almost every early historical account of the region. It deserves recognition as a separate configuration because of a number of significant differences from the preceding stage of the contact period.

Smallpox is a word which recurs again and again in the 19th-century accounts of the region, and it seems to have been the one epidemic disease which was regularly recognized by the contemporary traders and explorers. Measles, chickenpox, and cholera were also present to take their toll of the native populations. Whatever the actual disease or diseases, it is certain that the epidemics lumped under the convenient rubric "smallpox" had disastrous consequences for the native population. The Stearns' study (1945) of smallpox and the American Indian deals with the subject in some detail. These authors catalog four major epidemics among the village tribes of the Middle Missouri up to the mid-19th century. They are listed for the years 1780–81 (or 1781–82), 1801–02, 1837–38, and 1856 (Stearn and Stearn, 1945, pp. 46–48, 75–77, and 130–131). Details of the earlier ones, such as mortality rates, are not well documented. The epidemic of 1837–38 is described in harrowing detail by Chittenden (1954, vol. 2, pp. 620–627), and Chardon's journal gives day by day notes of its effect on the Mandan and Hidatsa (Abel, 1932). According to Stearn and Stearn (1945, table I), mortality rates among the three Middle Mis-

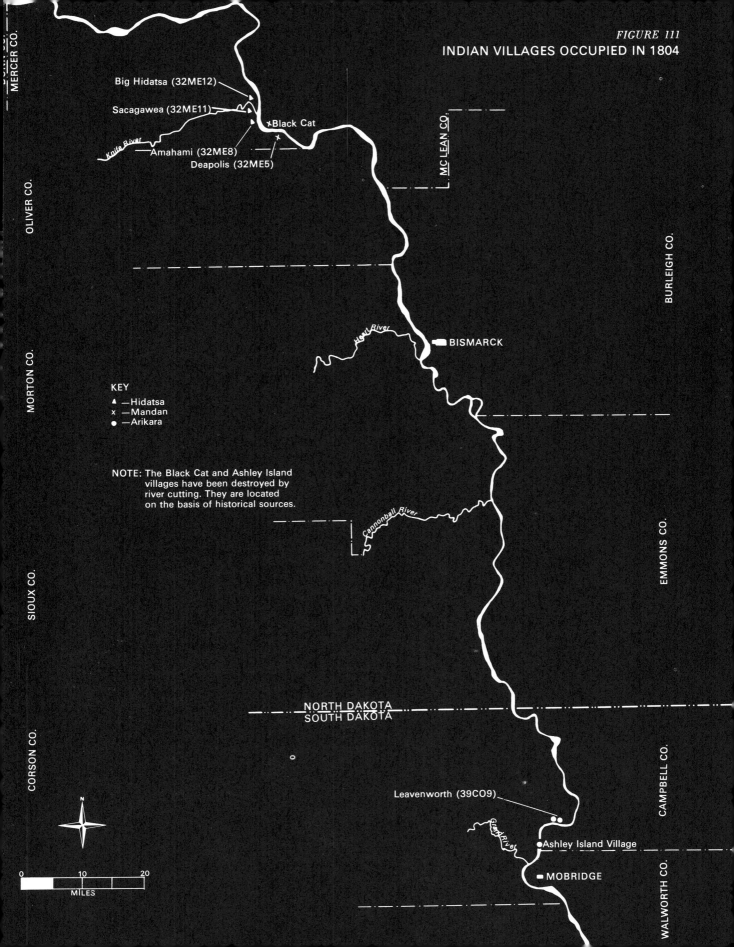

FIGURE 111

INDIAN VILLAGES OCCUPIED IN 1804

souri village tribes from the 1837 epidemic were 33 percent for the Hidatsa, 50 percent for the Arikara, and 98 percent for the Mandan. These figures may be rather high for the Mandan and low for the Hidatsa, but they indicate that average decline in the total population of 1836 was in excess of 60 percent. The epidemic of 1856 was almost as serious for both the Arikara village at Fort Clark and the Hidatsa-Mandan settlement at Fort Berthold. Earlier mortality rates must have been at least as high.

The Stearns' list probably omits some epidemics in the Middle Missouri Valley. The outbreaks of 1780–81 and 1801–02, and of 1837–38 and of 1856, are separated by periods of 20 and 18 years. These periods would have been long enough for new generations without acquired immunity to the disease to grow up. Such nonimmune generations would have been large enough for outbreaks of the disease to reach epidemic proportions.

If 18 years is taken as the approximate generational interval between epidemics, it seems likely that there was an outbreak about the middle of the 35-year period between the epidemics of 1801–2 and 1837–38. Stearn and Stearn note (1945, p. 78) that in 1818–19 "a rather severe localized epidemic occurred among some tribes along the White River of South Dakota." I have not been able to locate a reference in the limited sources available to an outbreak among the village tribes at that time, but I strongly suspect that there was one. If there was, it would leave intervals of 16 years between the epidemics of 1801–02 and 1818–19 and 18 years between 1818–19 and 1837–38.

There is a possibility that the epidemic of 1780–81 was not the first one to strike the Middle Missouri villages. Truteau, writing of the year 1795, said:

In ancient times the Ricara nation was very large; it counted thirty-two populous villages, now depopulated and almost entirely destroyed by the smallpox which broke out among them at three different times. A few families only, from each of the villages, escaped; these united and formed the two villages now here, which are situated about half a mile apart upon the same land occupied by their ancestors.

(Nasatir, 1952, vol.1, p.299; emphasis mine)

The epidemics of 1837–38 and 1856 resulted from white carriers spreading the infection to the village tribes. Some of the earlier outbreaks may have been due to direct contagion from the Whites, but there seems to be a good possibility of transmission to the village tribes by Indians rather than Whites. Stearn and Stearn (1945, pp. 46–49) cite a passage from Warren's *History of the Ojibway* in which there is a description of the spread of smallpox to that tribe by a war party which raided a Hidatsa village during the epidemic of 1780–81, and they report that in the same period smallpox killed over 5,000 of the Indians of the Mission Pueblos in New Mexico. The occurrence of epidemics in the Southwest and the Middle Missouri subarea in the same years raises the possibility of a spread from one area to another. It seems likely that the traffic in horses from the Southwest to the Middle Missouri subarea was the vehicle for transmission.

The pandemic of 1780–81 struck across most of western North America. It had disastrous consequence for the Middle Missouri villagers and seems to have been the main factor contributing to their cultural decline.

GEOGRAPHIC DISTRIBUTION

The distribution of the Disorganized Coalescent tribes showed an enormous reduction from that of the preceding period. There is also ample evidence of a great deal of tribal mobility after 1780. Some of the Arikara survivors of the epidemic occupied two villages (presumably sites 39ST25 and 39ST50) on the right bank of the Missouri just below the mouth of the Cheyenne

* Some secondary sources speak of the Mandan villages near the Heart River as having been abandoned 40 years prior to the arrival of the Lewis and Clark expedition. This is clearly incorrect. The Original Journals refer to those villages as having been inhabited "About 25 years since" (Thwaites, 1959, vol. 6, p. 90), and Clark's field notes say they were "occupied about 25 years ago" (Osgood, 1964, p. 164). This would indicate an abandonment around 1780. The 40-year figure apparently comes from a misreading of the Original Journals and one of Biddle's interpolations (Thwaites, 1959, vol. 5, p. 347), which refer to a statement by the Mandan Chief Big White that he was *born* in one of the Heart River villages about 40 years before.

River until 1795 (Nasatir, op. cit.). Small groups of Arikara moved over a wide area from North Dakota to Nebraska during the next 8 years (Wedel, 1955, pp. 78–81; Lehmer and Jones, 1968, pp. 92–95). The Mandan abandoned their villages in the southern part of the Knife-Heart region after 1780,* moving upstream to settle near the Hidatsa villages at the mouth of the Knife (Thwaites, 1959, vol. 5, pp. 347–348, vol. 6, p. 90; and Thwaites, 1966, vol. 23, pp. 317–318).

When the Lewis and Clark Expedition went up the river in 1804, there were only eight occupied villages in the whole Middle Missouri Valley (fig. 111). These included three recently established Arikara towns a short distance above the Grand River, and the two Mandan and three Hidatsa settlements in the vicinity of the mouth of the Knife River. The Arikara abandoned the last of their towns near the Grand in 1832, and 5 years later they settled in the deserted Mandan village near Fort Clark. In 1845, the Hidatsa and some Mandan survivors of the smallpox epidemic of 1837 established Like-a-Fishhook Village, and they were later joined there by the rest of the Mandan and by the Arikara in 1862. Thus by that year the geographic extent of the village tribes was reduced to a single community in the lower Garrison region. The whole long reach of the river downstream had been abandoned.

HOUSES, CACHE PITS, AND MISCELLANEOUS STRUCTURES

The houses, cache pits, and miscellaneous structures were similar to those of the Post-Contact Coalescent Variant. The traditional earthlodge continued to be used in ceremonial contexts until the early 20th century (Metcalf, 1963a, pp. 12–22). It was gradually replaced by log cabins and frame houses like those of the Whites during the latter part of the 19th century.

VILLAGE SIZE AND PLAN

Village size and plan varied, but many of the late villages had well over 50 houses, which were irregularly placed. Central plazas seem to have been rare (fig. 112).

FORTIFICATIONS

Fortifications continued to be used, but were generally not as strong as those of the Post-Contact Coalescent villages. Palisades were often used without ditches. Some of the fortifications are reported to have been built by Whites rather than Indians (cf. Maximilian in Thwaites, 1966, vol. 23, p. 269).

BURIAL CUSTOMS

Burial customs remain unchanged from the preceding period, with the Arikara practicing inhumation and the Mandan and Hidatsa both scaffold burial and some inhumation.

FIGURE 112 Fort Clark in winter. After painting by Carl Bodmer.

POTTERY

The pottery varies considerably from one context to another. The majority of the rim sherds from the Arikara villages above the Grand, which make up the Leavenworth Site (39CO9), fall within the range of the Stanley types. This pottery does not appear to be inferior to that of the Bad River Phase sites. In contrast, Mandan and Hidatsa pots made after 1780 are vastly inferior to those of the Heart River Phase. They are coarse, thick-walled, and poorly made. The shallow S-rim is almost completely lacking, and braced rims are sloppy and carelessly executed. Decoration is minimal. The late decline of Plains village pottery has commonly been attributed to the fact that it was being displaced by metal trade kettles. While this probably accounts for the situation in the very late sites, it does not explain the sudden and marked deterioration of the Mandan-Hidatsa pottery near the end of the 18th century. It is more likely that the decline is a reflection of the loss of expert potters during the smallpox epidemic.

NON-POTTERY ARTIFACTS

The non-pottery artifacts of native manufacture from Disorganized Coalescent archeological contexts duplicate those from the preceding period. There is, however, a considerable change in the relative quantities due to the substitution of trade pieces. This is particularly true of chipped stone items such as arrow points, knives, drills, and scrapers, which were replaced with metal equivalents of native or European manufacture as rapidly as possible. Ground stone pieces such as mauls and pipes continued to be made in quantity. Metal axes, picks, and hoes were valued highly, although the scapula hoe was still used by many of the women. Bone handles for metal knife blades, metatarsal fleshers, antler fleshing adzes (with metal blades attached), and bone sliders and snow snakes were all common well into the 19th century. Fishhooks and awls of bone are rare, while their metal counterparts are common.

Ethnographic collections made after 1800 greatly enlarge the trait list of the village tribes since they include large numbers of specimens made from leather, wood, and other perishable materials. They give a much more complete picture of the material culture than do the archeological collections. This array of specimens will not be discussed here because data on the prototypes are lacking.

TRADE GOODS

Trade goods were present in increasing amounts, especially after large-scale water transportation up the Missouri from St. Louis replaced the overland routes from Canada and the western Great Lakes. The utilitarian items most commonly found in archeological sites include ax and adz heads, awls, files, hoes, knives, kettles, and strike-a-lights or fire steels. Firearms are represented by gun parts, musket balls, gun worms, gunflints, and, in the later sites, percussion caps. Rarer finds demonstrate the introduction of auger bits, bridle bits, clay pipes, glazed china, hammerheads, horseshoes, patent medicines, razors, saddle tacks, scissors, spikes, and spools of copper or brass wire. Items with an esthetic rather than a utilitarian value include buttons of metal, bone, glass, and mother-of-pearl; bracelets of iron or brass; brass or copper bells; combs; double-barred crosses; glass beads; hair pipes; mirrors; and metal finger rings, often with glass sets.

CHRONOLOGY

The chronology of the Disorganized Coalescent Variant is based on historical sources. The beginning date of 1780 corresponds to the first recorded smallpox epidemic. The year 1862, when the Arikara joined the Mandan and Hidatsa at Like-a-Fishhook Village, has been arbitrarily chosen as the end date.

TAXONOMIC SUBDIVISIONS

The subdivisions include a Knife River Phase, which covers the Mandan and Hidatsa cultures through the abandonment of the Knife River villages. Lack of data makes it difficult to predicate phases for the Arikara. Hoffman and Brown are of the opinion that the Leavenworth Site, known to have been occupied by the Arikara from about 1797 to 1832, "equates with . . . the Bad River Phase in terms of house styles, fortifications, and settlement pattern, as well as general and specific artifact styles. The ceramic similarities are particularly striking" (Hoffman and Brown, 1967, p. 333). This suggests that Leavenworth may be classifiable as a third subphase of Bad

River. Archeological data relating to the Arikara occupations in North Dakota, particularly at Fort Clark Village, are so scarce that it is impossible to suggest phase classifications.

CULTURAL INTERACTION, A.D. 1780–1862

After 1780 the Middle Missouri villagers were subjected to increasing pressures from the horse nomads, especially the Dakota, and to the effects of the first movement of white settlers into the valley. Both factors accelerated the breakdown of the old native way of life.

The 19th-century accounts leave no doubt that the Dakota were a constantly increasing danger. This was due partly to their growing strength as a military force, and partly to the serious decline in the village populations as a result of the epidemics. Each outbreak reduced the number of women available to build fortifications, and drastically cut down the number of warriors available to defend the villages. The Dakota also suffered from the epidemics, but their losses seem to have been proportionately lighter. They had the advantage, as attackers, of being able to concentrate against a single village. This was an important factor, despite the fact that the warriors of neighboring towns frequently went to each others assistance. Maximilian, for example, reports that about 1796 "1300 or 1400 Sioux, united with 700 Arikaras, attacked the foremost Mandan village, and about 1000 Manitaries [Hidatsa] hastened to assist the latter" (Thwaites, 1966, vol. 23, p. 230). Fear of the Dakota was undoubtedly the most important reason the villagers abandoned most of the Missouri Valley and had their remaining towns close together.

The establishment of posts in the Middle Missouri Valley by St. Louis traders also dealt a heavy blow to the village tribes. Men from the precarious French settlements in the Illinois country and from St. Louis, after it was founded in 1764, were slow to make their way up the river. They first operated in the Middle Missouri as tenant traders in the Arikara villages and at a few small posts set up for trading with the Dakota. Lewis and Clark's description of Cedar

Island, 20-odd miles below the mouth of the Bad River, reports that: "on the South side of this Island Mr. Louiselle, a trader from St. Louis, built a fort of Cedar and a good house to trade with the Seaux and Wintered last winter" (Thwaites, 1959, vol. 1, p. 160). The explorers also mention that, a short distance above the Cheyenne, "2 frenchmen were at the house with good[s] to trade with the Seaux" (ibid., p. 175).

After the Lewis and Clark Expedition returned in 1806, organized companies sent a rush of traders up the river into the Middle Missouri Valley. These later traders ignored the Arikara, Mandan, and Hidatsa villages as bases of operations. They built substantial posts of their own, locating them at strategic points along the river as far upstream as the northern parts of the High Plains, and occupied them for years at a time. Posts like Fort Pierre, Fort Clark, and Fort Union were elaborate establishments, usually protected by stockades with two blockhouses at opposite corners (fig. 112). Some of the blockhouses were two stories high, and had light artillery pieces mounted on the first floor. Structures inside the protective works included dwellings, offices, blacksmith and carpenter shops, warehouses, stables, fur presses, and so on. The buildings commonly backed against the palisade, so that defenders could stand on the roofs to fire over the wall. (Cf. Miller's view of the interior of Fort Laramie in DeVoto, 1947, pl. IX, and Bodmer's painting of Fort McKenzie in Thwaites, 1966, vol. 25, pl. 75.)

The size of the contingent varied somewhat throughout the year, but there frequently were as many as 100 people living at one of the larger posts. It was a rigidly stratified society, with the proprietor or bourgeois and his clerk or clerks having complete authority over the hunters, trappers, artisans, and other members of the establishment. The big posts frequently had their own hunters to provide meat for the resident personnel, and they also commonly had their own gardens and dairy cattle. (See Thwaites, 1966, vol. 22, pp. 317–319 and 376–383, vol. 23, pp. 234–236; Chittenden, 1954, vol. 1, pp. 44–58.)

The extension of the trading posts up the Missouri cut across the east-west arteries of the old intertribal trade and effectively disrupted both that trade and the villagers' position as brokers in it. Trade goods no longer dribbled into the Northern Plains through tenant traders and Indian middlemen. Instead, they came up the Missouri by the ton in keelboats and later steamers out of St. Louis. Easy water transportation made the export of buffalo hides and robes economically feasible, providing a demand for a product which the migratory hunting tribes could produce in quantity. As a result, the trade goods of the Dakota, Assiniboin, and Cree lost their old importance, and those tribes turned to producing buffalo robes wherever it was practical. The tribes west of the Middle Missouri were also able to produce a commodity of direct value to the traders, one which richly supplemented the horse in their trading operations.

This effected a major realinement of both the geographic and the economic orientation of the trade in the Northern Plains. There was no longer a two-directional flow between the northeast and southwest through the intermediate point of the Middle Missouri villages. Instead, the trade funneled directly from both northeast and southwest into the posts along the Missouri, and from them down the river itself. There was no longer an important direct exchange of horses and trade goods through Indian hands. The buffalo robes of the migratory hunters were passed directly to the traders, and the trade in horses was reduced to secondary importance.

All of this cost the villagers their old and profitable position as brokers in the pan-Indian trade. There was still a demand for their crops. They could sell whatever hides they themselves had to the traders, and there were vestiges of the old trade in horses and guns. But the rich profits which the villagers had reaped from the 18th-century trade dried up. That economic loss was one more factor contributing to their cultural decline.

The United States Government became an increasingly important factor in the Middle Missouri Valley during the 19th century. The journey of the Lewis and Clark Expedition of 1804–6 was the first appearance of Federal officials in the region. Leavenworth's inept campaign in 1823 against the Arikara villages above the Grand River was another early contact (Chittenden, 1954, vol. 2, pp. 588–606). More sys-

tematic relations developed under the various Indian agencies.

The affairs of the village tribes were dealt with directly by the Upper Missouri Agency after it was established in 1819. The agency had a checkered administrative history. It was under the supervision of the Governor of Missouri Territory until 1822. From 1822 to 1851 it was subordinate to the St. Louis Superintendency, and it came under the jurisdiction of the newly created Central Superintendency in 1851. The organization and operation of the agency itself were the items of immediate concern to the Middle Missouri Valley tribes. Agency headquarters were located at Council Bluffs, Fort Leavenworth, and Bellevue (Nebraska) at various times. In 1824 two subagencies were established—one for the Dakota, and a Mandan subagency responsible for the Mandan, Arikara, Hidatsa, Crow, and Assiniboin. The Mandan subagent was headquartered at the Mandan villages until 1838, when the subagency's functions were absorbed by the Upper Missouri Agency in the wake of the smallpox epidemic of 1837–38. In 1864 an agent, usually headquartered at Fort Berthold, was assigned to the village tribes and to the Assiniboin and Crow. This agent was only responsible for the village tribes after the Fort Berthold Reservation was established for them in 1870.

The considerable amount of culture contact and culture change which went on during the precontact period enriched the village tribes. This was also largely true for the early contact period, from 1675 to 1780. That era apparently saw the abandonment of the Big Bend region as a result of poor geographic location and hostile pressures, but the villages farther upstream were flourishing entities which continued to demonstrate their ability to cope with and absorb external influences.

Three factors contributed directly to the late decline of the villages. These were the rise of the horse nomads, the extension of the fur trade up the Missouri from St. Louis, and new epidemic diseases.

The growing power of the Dakota was certainly a threat to the villages, but it was one with which they were, on the whole, able to deal during most of the 18th century. Enemy strikes against hunting parties and women working away from the villages in the fields were a constant hazard, but it was one the villagers were able to survive until their population was seriously depleted by smallpox epidemics. Without the epidemics, the villagers would probably have been able to adjust successfully to their predatory neighbors.

The invasion of the Middle Missouri Valley by the St. Louis traders unquestionably changed the villagers' economic situation for the worse. But there is reason to wonder if the 19th-century trading pattern would have developed along the same lines if the earlier village population had been strung along the Missouri from the Bad to the Knife Rivers. Even in their debilitated state during the 19th century, the Arikara seriously interfered with movement up and down the Missouri. Given three or four times as many villages distributed along the whole run of the river, it seems likely that the villagers would have been able to maintain a far larger stake in the trade.

The cumulative effects of epidemic diseases, the rising power of the horse tribes, and the economic competition from the trading posts brought an end to the village tribes' dominance of the Middle Missouri as documented by archeological and historical records. Bruner has given a graphic summary of the Mandan's situation during the latter half of the 19th century, and much of what he says applies equally well to the other two village tribes. It is a fitting epitaph for a vanished way of life.

By the middle of the nineteenth century the Sioux were stealing Mandan horses and plundering their crops at will, killing women working in the fields . . . ambushing hunting parties, [and attacking villages]. In some years the Mandan did not produce enough food for their own consumption. To meet these crises the government provided assistance in the form of annuities, not for humanitarian motives alone, but to compensate the Mandan for accepting reservation boundaries.

(Bruner, 1961, p. 229)

BIBLIOGRAPHY

Abel, Annie Heloise, ed.

1932.   Chardon's Journal at Fort Clark, 1834–1839. Department of History, State of South Dakota. Pierre.

1939.   Tabeau's narrative of Louisel's expedition to the Upper Missouri. Trans. by Rose Abel Wright. University of Oklahoma Press. Norman.

Antevs, Ernst

1962.   Late Quaternary climates in Arizona. American Antiquity, vol. 28, no. 2, pp. 193–198. Salt Lake City.

Baerreis, David A., and Reid A. Bryson

1965.   Climate episodes and the dating of Mississippian cultures. The Wisconsin Archeologist, vol. 46, no. 4. Madison.

Baerreis, David A., and John E. Dallman

1961.   Archaeological investigations near Mobridge, South Dakota. Archives of Archaeology, no. 14. Madison.

Barrett, S.A.

1933.   Ancient Aztalan. Bulletin of the Public Museum of the City of Milwaukee, vol. 13, Milwaukee.

Bass, William M., III

1962.   A preliminary analysis of burial data on 255 individuals from the Sully Site, 39SL4, Sully County, South Dakota. Proceedings of the 19th Plains Conference. Plains Anthropologist, vol. 7, no. 16, pp. 77–78. Lincoln.

1964.   The variation in physical types of the prehistoric Plains Indians. Plains Anthropologist, memoir 1, vol. 9, no. 24. Lincoln.

Bass, William M., III, and Richard L. Jantz

1965.   Two human skeletons from 39LM227, a mound near the Stricker Site, Lyman County, South Dakota. Plains Anthropologist, vol. 10, no. 27, pp. 20–30. Lincoln.

Biddle, Nicholas, ed.

1961.   The Lewis and Clark expedition. 3 vols. Philadelphia.

Birkby, Walter H.

1962.   A preliminary report on the dentition of the skeletal population of the Sully Site. Proceedings of the 19th Plains Conference. Plains Anthropologist, vol. 7, no. 16, p. 79. Lincoln.

Blair, Emma H.

1911.   The Indian tribes of the Upper Mississippi valley and region of the Great Lakes. 2 vols. Cleveland.

Blegen, Theodore C.

1963.   Minnesota, a history of the state. University of Minnesota Press. Minneapolis.

Bolton, Herbert E., ed.

1952.   Spanish exploration in the Southwest, 1542–1706. New York.

Bowers, Alfred W.

1950.   Mandan social and ceremonial organization. University of Chicago Press. Chicago.

1963.   Investigations in the Mobridge area, South Dakota. Proceedings of the 20th Plains Conference. Plains Anthropologist, vol. 8, no. 20, p. 118. Lincoln.

1965.   Hidatsa social and ceremonial organization. Bureau of American Ethnology, Bulletin 194. Washington.

MS.   A history of the Mandan and Hidatsa. Unpublished Ph.D. dissertation, 1948. University of Chicago.

Brown, Lionel A.

1966a.   The Gillette Site (39ST23), Oahe Reservoir, South Dakota. Plains Anthropologist, vol. 11, no. 34, pp. 239–289. Lincoln.

1966b.   Temporal and special order in the Central Plains. Plains Anthropologist, vol. 11, no. 34, pp. 294–301. Lincoln.

Bruner, Edward M.

1961.   Mandan. *In* Perspectives in American Indian culture change, ed. by Edward H. Spicer. University of Chicago Press. Chicago.

Bryson, Reid A., and Wayne M. Wendland

1967.   Tentative climatic patterns for some late glacial and post-glacial episodes in central North

America. *In* Life, land, and water. University of Manitoba Press. Winnipeg.

Burpee, Lawrence J.
1927.   Journals and letters of Pierre Gaultier de Varennes de la Vérendrye and his sons. The Champlain Society. Toronto.

Bushnell, David I., Jr.
1922.   Villages of the Algonquian, Siouan, and Caddoan tribes west of the Mississippi. Bureau of American Ethnology, Bulletin 77. Washington.
1927.   Burials of the Algonquian, Siouan, and Caddoan tribes west of the Mississippi. Bureau of American Ethnology, Bulletin 83. Washington.

Caldwell, Warren W.
1961.   Excavations at certain La Roche and Thomas Riggs sites in the Big Bend and Oahe Reservoirs, 1960. Proceedings of the 18th Plains Conference. Plains Anthropologist, vol. 6, no. 12, pt. 1, p. 57. Norman.
1963.   Investigations in the lower Big Bend Reservoir, South Dakota. Proceedings of the 20th Plains Conference. Plains Anthropologist, vol. 8, no. 20, p. 118. Lincoln.
1964.   Fortified villages in the Northern Plains. Plains Anthropologist, vol. 9, no. 23, pp. 1–7. Lincoln.
1966a.   The Middle Missouri Tradition reappraised. Plains Anthropologist, vol. 11, no. 32, pp. 152–157. Lincoln.
1966b.   The Black Partizan Site. Smithsonian Institution River Basin Surveys, Publications in Salvage Archeology, no. 2. Lincoln.
1966c.   Archeological investigations at the McKensey village (39AR201), Oahe Reservoir, central South Dakota. Plains Anthropologist, memoir 3, vol. 11, no. 31, pp. 2–38. Lincoln.

Caldwell, Warren W., and Richard E. Jensen
1969.   The Grand Detour Phase. Smithsonian Institution River Basin Surveys, Publication in Salvage Archeology, no. 13. Lincoln.

Caldwell, Warren W., Lee G. Madison, and Bernard Golden
1964.   Archeological investigations at the Hickey Brothers Site (39LM4), Big Bend Reservoir, Lyman County, South Dakota. River Basin Surveys Papers, no. 36, Bureau of American Ethnology, Bulletin 189. Washington.

Catlin, George
1965.   Letters and notes of the manners, customs, and condition of the North American Indians. Minneapolis.

Champe, John L.
1936.   The Sweetwater culture complex. *In* Chapters in Nebraska Archaeology, ed. by Earl H. Bell. University of Nebraska. Lincoln.
1946.   Ash Hollow Cave. University of Nebraska Studies, new series, no. 1. Lincoln.
1961.   Aksarben. Plains Anthropologist, vol. 6, no. 12, pt. 2, pp. 103–107. Norman.

Chittenden, Hiram M.
1954.   The American fur trade of the Far West. 2 vols. Stanford.

Coogan, Alan H., and William N. Irving
1959.   Late Pleistocene and Recent Missouri River terraces in the Big Bend Reservoir, South Dakota. Abstracts of the Iowa Academy of Science, vol. 66, pp. 317–327. Des Moines.

Cooper, Paul L.
1936.   Archaeology of certain sites in Cedar County, Nebraska. *In* Chapters in Nebraska Archaeology, ed. by Earl H. Bell. University of Nebraska. Lincoln.
1949.   Recent investigations in Fort Randall and Oahe Reservoirs, South Dakota. American Antiquity, vol. 14, no. 4, pt. 1, pp. 300–310. Menasha.
1955.   The archeological and paleontological salvage program in the Missouri Basin, 1950–1951. Smithsonian Miscellaneous Collections, vol. 126, no. 2. Washington.
1958.   Archeological investigations in the Heart Butte Reservoir area, North Dakota. River Basin Surveys Papers, no. 9, Bureau of American Ethnology, Bulletin 169. Washington.

Coues, Elliott, ed.
1965a.   The manuscript journals of Alexander Henry and David Thompson, 1799–1814. 2 vols. Minneapolis.
1965b.   History of the expedition under the command of Lewis and Clark. 3 vols. New York.

Culin, Stewart
1907.   Games of the North American Indians. 24th Annual Report, Bureau of American Ethnology, 1902–03. Washington.

Davis, Leslie B.
1966.   Avonlea point occurrence in northern Montana and Canada. Plains Anthropologist, vol. 11, no. 32, pp. 100–116. Lincoln.

Deetz, James
1965.   The dynamics of stylistic change in Arikara ceramics. Illinois Studies in Anthropology, no. 4. University of Illinois Press. Urbana.

DeLand, Charles E.
1906.   The aborigines of South Dakota. Pt. I, The Arikara. South Dakota Historical Collections, vol. 3. Pierre.

DeVoto, Bernard
1947.   Across the wide Missouri. Boston.

Dunlevy, Marion Lucile
1936.   A comparison of the cultural manifestations of the Burkett and Gray-Wolfe Sites. *In* Chapters in Nebraska Archaeology, ed. by Earl H. Bell. University of Nebraska. Lincoln.

Ewers, John C.
1954.   The Indian trade of the Upper Missouri before Lewis and Clark. Bulletin of the Missouri Historical Society, vol. 10, no. 4, pl. 1, pp. 429–446. St. Louis.
1955.   The horse in Blackfoot Indian culture. Bureau of American Ethnology, Bulletin 159. Washington.
1958.   The Blackfeet, raiders on the Northwestern Plains. University of Oklahoma Press. Norman.
1968.   Indian life on the Upper Missouri. University of Oklahoma Press. Norman.

Fenenga, Franklin
1954.   The interdependence of archeology and ethnology as illustrated by the ice-glider game of the Northern Plains. Plains Anthropologist, no. 1, pp. 31–38. Lincoln.

Fenneman, Nevin
1931.   Physiography of western United States. New York.

Flint, Richard Foster
1955.   Pleistocene geology of eastern South Dakota. Geological Survey, Professional Paper 262. Washington.
1957.   Glacial and Pleistocene geology. New York.

Frantz, Wendell
1962.   Crazy Bull Site (39LM220), Big Bend Reservoir, South Dakota. Plains Anthropologist, vol. 7, no. 15, pp. 36–42. Lincoln.

Gant, Robert D.
1967.   Archeological investigations at the Arp Site, 39BR101, Brule County, South Dakota, 1961. W. H. Over Dakota Museum, University of South Dakota, Archeological Studies, Circular no. 12. Vermillion.

Gass, Patrick
1958.   Journals of the Lewis and Clark expedition. Minneapolis.

George, Edythe L.
1949.   Report of the investigations of the Robinson Site, Hughes County, South Dakota, Peoria Bottom, 1948. State Archaeological Commission, Archaeological Studies, Circular no. 1. Pierre.

Gilmore, Melvin R.
1919.   Uses of plants by the Indians of the Missouri River region. 33rd Annual Report, Bureau of American Ethnology, 1911–12. Washington.
1924.   Glass bead making by the Arikara. Museum of the American Indian, Heye Foundation, Indian Notes and Monographs, vol. 1. New York.

Glover, Richard
1962.   David Thompson's narrative, 1784–1812. The Champlain Society. Toronto.

Goggin, John M.
1949.   Culture traditions in Florida prehistory. *In* the Florida Indian and his neighbors, ed. by John W. Griffin. Winter Park.

Haines, Francis
1938a.   Where did the Plains Indians get their horses? American Anthropologist, vol. 40, no. 1, pp. 112–117. Menasha.
1938b.   The northward spread of horses among the Plains Indians. American Anthropologist, vol. 40, no. 3, pp. 429–437. Menasha.

Hall, Robert L.
1961.   An archaeological investigation in the Gavins Point area, Yankton County, South Dakota. W. H. Over Museum, Museum News, vol. 22, no. 7, pp. 1–3. Vermillion, S. Dak.

Harmon, George Dewey
1941.   Sixty years of Indian affairs. The University of North Carolina Press. Chapel Hill.

Hartle, Donald D.
1963.   The dance hall of the Santee Bottoms on the Fort Berthold Reservation, Garrison Reservoir, North Dakota. River Basin Surveys Papers, no. 28, Bureau of American Ethnology, Bulletin 185. Washington.
MS.   Rock Village: an ethnohistorical approach to Hidatsa archaeology. Unpublished Ph. D. dissertation, 1960. Columbia University.

Henning, Darrell D.
1965.   The Alkire Mound (32SI200). Plains Anthropologist, vol. 10, no. 29, pp. 146–151. Lincoln.

Hewes, Gordon W.
1949a.   The 1947 summer field session in archeology, University of North Dakota. Proceedings of the Fifth Plains Conference for Archeology. University of Nebraska, Laboratory of Anthropology, Note Book, no. 1. Lincoln.
1949b.   Pottery from the sites excavated by the 1947 North Dakota field session. Proceedings of the Fifth Plains Conference for Archeology. University of Nebraska, Laboratory of Anthropology, Note Book, no. 1. Lincoln.

Hill, Walter E., Jr., and Robert W. Neuman
1966.   Copper artifacts from prehistoric archaeological sites in the Dakotas. Science, vol. 154, no. 3753, pp. 1171–1173. Washington.

Hoard, Lyon J.
1949.   Report of the investigation of the Meyer Site, Stanley County, South Dakota. South Dakota State Archaeological Commission, Archaeological Studies, Circular no. 2. Pierre.

Hodge, Frederick W., ed.
1910.   Handbook of American Indians north of Mexico. Bureau of American Ethnology, Bulletin 30. 2 parts. Washington.

Hoffman, J. J.
1963a.   Excavations at Molstad Village in Oahe Reservoir. Proceedings of the 20th Plains Conference. Plains Anthropologist, vol. 8, no. 20, pp. 118–119. Lincoln.
1963b.   Investigation of the Swift Bird House (39DW233) in the Oahe Reservoir, South Dakota. Plains Anthropologist, vol. 8, no. 22, pp. 249–256. Lincoln.
1967.   Molstad Village. Smithsonian Institution River Basin Surveys, Publications in Salvage Archeology, no. 4. Lincoln.
1968.   The La Roche Site. Smithsonian Institution River Basin Surveys, Publications in Salvage Archeology, no. 11. Lincoln.

Hoffman, J. J., and Lionel A. Brown
1967.   The Bad River Phase. Plains Anthropologist, vol. 12, no. 37, pp. 323–339. Lincoln.

Howard, James H.
1959.   Report of the investigation of the Tony Glas Site, 32EM3, Emmons County, North Dakota, 1958. University of North Dakota, Anthropological Papers, no. 1. Grand Forks.
1962.   Report of the investigation of the Huff Site, 32MO11, Morton County, North Dakota, 1959. University of North Dakota, Anthropological Papers, no. 2. Grand Forks.

Howson, Joan
MS.   A protohistoric Arikara village: the Buffalo Pasture Site. Unpublished M. A. thesis, 1941. Columbia University.

Hrdlička, Aleš
1927.   Catalogue of human crania in the United States National Museum collections: the Algonkin, and Related Iroquois; Siouan, Caddoan, Salish and Sahaptin, Shoshonean, and Californian

Indians. Proceedings of the U.S. National Museum, vol. 69. Washington.

Hunt, George T.
1940.   The wars of the Iroquois. University of Wisconsin Press. Madison.

Hurt, Wesley R., Jr.
1951a.   Report of the investigations of the Swanson Site, 39BR16, Brule County, South Dakota, 1950. South Dakota Archaeological Commission, Archaeological Studies, Circular no. 3. Pierre.

1951b.   The Sommers Site. W. H. Over Museum, Museum News, vol. 12, no. 4, pp. 1–8. Vermillion, S. Dak.

1952.   Report of the investigation of the Scalp Creek Site, 39GR1, and the Ellis Creek Site, 39GR2, Gregory County, South Dakota, 1941, 1951. South Dakota Archaeological Commission, Archaeological Studies, Circular no. 6. Pierre.

1953.   Report of the investigation of the Thomas Riggs Site, 39HU1, Hughes County, South Dakota, 1952. South Dakota Archaeological Commission, Archaeological Studies, Circular no. 5. Pierre.

1954.   Report of the investigation of the Spotted Bear Site, 39HU26, and the Cottonwood Site, 39HU43, Hughes County, South Dakota, 1953. South Dakota Archaeological Commission, Archaeological Studies, Circular no. 6. Pierre.

1957.   Report of the investigation of the Swan Creek Site, 39WW7, Walworth County, South Dakota, 1954–1956. South Dakota Archaeological Commission, Archaeological Studies, Circular no. 7. Pierre.

1959.   Report of the investigations of the Rosa Site 39PO3, Potter County, South Dakota, 1957. South Dakota Archaeological Commission, Archaeological Studies, Circular no. 9. Pierre.

1961.   Archaeological Work at the Tabor and Arp Sites. W. H. Over Museum, Museum News, vol. 22, no. 8, pp. 1–6. Vermillion. S. Dak.

Hurt, Wesley R., Jr., William G. Buckles, Eugene Fugle, and George A. Agogino
1962.   Report of the investigations of the Four Bear Site, 39DW2, Dewey County, South Dakota, 1958–1959. W. H. Over Museum, State University of South Dakota, Archaeological Studies, Circular no. 10. Vermillion.

Husted, Wilfred M.
1965a.   The Meander Site (39LM201) in Fort Randall Reservoir, South Dakota. Plains Anthropologist, vol. 10, no. 29, pp. 152–165. Lincoln.

1965b.   Site 39LM219 in the Big Bend Reservoir, South Dakota, Plains Anthropologist, vol. 10, no. 29, pp. 171–180. Lincoln.

Innis, Harold A.
1962.   The fur trade in Canada. Yale University Press. New Haven.

Jablow, Joseph
1951.   The Cheyenne in Plains Indian trade relations, 1795–1840. Monographs of the American Ethnological Society, vol. 19. New York.

Jackson, Donald, ed.
1962.   Letters of the Lewis and Clark expedition, with related documents, 1783–1854. University of Illinois Press. Urbana.

Jennings, Jesse D.
1955.   The archeology of the Plains: an assessment (multilithed). National Park Service and University of Utah, Department of Anthropology. Salt Lake City.

Johnson, Frederick
1966.   Archeology in an emergency. Science, vol. 152, no. 3729, pp. 1592–1597. Washington

Johnston, Richard B.
1966.   An analysis of the survey collections from the Pascal Creek Site (39AR207), Armstrong County, South Dakota. Plains Anthropologist, vol. 11, no. 33, pp. 176–185. Lincoln.

1967a.   The Hitchell Site. Smithsonian Institution River Basin Surveys, Publications in Salvage Archeology, no. 3. Lincoln.

1967b.   The Thomas Riggs Site (39HU1) revisited, Hughes County, South Dakota. American Antiquity, vol. 32, no. 3, pp. 393–395. Salt Lake City.

Johnston, Richard B., and J. J. Hoffman
1966.   An analysis of four survey collections from Armstrong County, South Dakota, 39AR2 (No

Heart Creek Site), 39AR4, 39AR5, and 39AR7. Plains Anthropologist, memoir 3, vol. 11, no. 31, pp. 39–75. Lincoln.

Kehoe, Thomas F., and Bruce A. McCorquodale
1961. The Avonlea point, horizon marker for the Northwestern Plains. Plains Anthropologist, vol. 6, no. 13, pp. 179–188. Norman.

Kellogg, Louise Phelps
1925. The French regime in Wisconsin and the Northwest. State Historical Society of Wisconsin. Madison.

Kivett, Marvin F.
1950. Archaeology and climatic implications in the Central Plains. Proceedings of the Sixth Plains Conference for Archeology. University of Utah, Anthropological Papers, no. 11. Salt Lake City.
MS. The Oacoma Site. Lyman County, South Dakota. Unpublished manuscript, 1958. National Park Service, Omaha.

Krieger, Alex D.
1964. Early man in the New World. *In* Prehistoric man in the New World, Jesse D. Jennings and Edward Norbeck, eds. University of Chicago Press. Chicago.

Kroeber, A. L.
1939. Cultural and natural areas of native North America. University of California Publications in American Archaeology and Ethnology, vol. 38. Berkeley.

Lehmer, Donald J.
1951. Pottery types from the Dodd Site, Oahe Reservoir, South Dakota. Plains Archeological Conference News Letter, vol. 4, no. 2, pp. 3–15. Lincoln.
1952a. The Fort Pierre Branch, central South Dakota. American Antiquity, vol. 17, no. 4, pp. 329–336. Salt Lake City.
1952b. Animal bone and Plains archeology. Plains Archeological Conference News Letter, vol. 4, no. 4, pp. 53–55. Lincoln.
1954a. The Sedentary Horizon of the Northern Plains. Southwestern Journal of Anthropology, vol. 10, no. 2, pp. 139–159. Albuquerque.
1954b. Archeological investigations in the Oahe Dan area, South Dakota, 1950–51. River Basin Surveys Papers, no. 7, Bureau of American Ethnology, Bulletin 158. Washington.
1965. Salvage archeology in the Middle Missouri. Administrative Report, National Park Service (multilithed). Washington.
1966. The Fire Heart Creek Site. Smithsonian Institution River Basin Surveys, Publications in Salvage Archeology, no. 1. Lincoln.

Lehmer, Donald J., and Warren W. Caldwell
1966. Horizon and Tradition in the Northern Plains. American Antiquity vol. 31, No. 4, pp. 511–516. Salt Lake City.

Lehmer, Donald J., and David T. Jones
1968. Arikara archeology: the Bad River Phase. Smithsonian Institution River Basin Surveys, Publications in Salvage Archeology, no. 7. Lincoln.

Lewis, Meriwether, and William Clark (see Thwaites, 1959)

Lewis, Oscar
1942. The effects of white contact upon Blackfoot culture. Monographs of the American Ethnological Society, no. 6. Seattle.

Libby, O. G.
1908. Typical villages of the Mandans. Collections, State Historical Society of North Dakota, vol. 2. Bismarck.

Lowie, Robert H.
1954. Indians of the Plains. American Museum of Natural History, Anthropological Handbook, no. 1. New York.

Mallory, Oscar L.
1965. Report of field activities for 1964. Proceedings of the 22nd Plains Conference, Plains Anthropologist, vol. 10, no. 27, pp. 47–48. Lincoln.

Malouf, Carling
1951. Archaeological studies of aboriginal occupation sites in northwestern North Dakota. Mon-

tana State University, Anthropology and Sociology Papers, no. 7. Missoula.

1963. Crow-Flies-High (32MZ1), a historic Hidatsa village in the Garrison Reservoir area, North Dakota. River Basin Surveys Papers, no. 29, Bureau of American Ethnology, Bulletin 185. Washington.

Mandelbaum, David G.

1940. The Plains Cree. American Museum of Natural History. Anthropological Papers, vol. 37, no. 2. New York.

Margry, Pierre

1875–86. Découvertes et établissements des Francais dans l'ouest et dans le sud de l'Amerique Septentrionale (1614–1754). Memoires et documents originaux. Pts. 1–6. Paris.

Martin, Paul S., George I. Quimby, and Donald Collier

1947. Indians before Columbus. Chicago.

Martin Paul S., James Schoenwetter, and B. C. Arms

1961. Southwestern palynology and prehistory: the last 10,000 years. Geochronology Laboratories, University of Arizona. Tucson.

Masson, L. R.

1960. Les bourgeois de la Compagnie du Nord-Quest. New York.

Mattes, Merrill J.

1947. Historic sites in Missouri Valley reservoir areas. Nebraska History, vol. 28, no. 3, pp. 1–15. Lincoln.

1960. Historic sites archeology on the Upper Missouri. River Basin Surveys Papers, no. 15, Bureau of American Ethnology, Bulletin 176. Washington.

Mattison, Ray H.

1951. Report on the historical aspects of the Garrison Reservoir area, Missouri River (mimeographed). National Park Service. Omaha.

1953. Report on historic sites in the Oahe Reservoir area, Missouri River (mimeographed). National Park Service. Omaha.

1955. Preliminary report on historic sites in South Dakota (mimeographed). National Park Service. Omaha.

1962. Report on historic sites in the Big Bend Reservoir area, Missouri River, Stanley, Hughes, Buffalo, and Lyman Counties, South Dakota (mimeographed). National Park Service. Omaha.

Meleen, Elmer E.

1938. A preliminary report of the Mitchell Indian village and burial mounds on Firesteel Creek, Mitchell, Davison County, South Dakota. University of South Dakota, Archaeological Studies, no. 2, pt. 1. Vermillion.

1948. A report on an investigation of the La Roche Site, Stanley County, South Dakota. University of South Dakota Museum, Archaeological Studies, Circular no. 5. Vermillion.

1949a. Summary report of field work in South Dakota, 1940–1947. Proceedings of the Fifth Plains Conference for Archeology. University of Nebraska, Laboratory of Anthropology, Note Book, no. 1. Lincoln.

1949b. A preliminary report on the Thomas Riggs Village Site. American Antiquity, vol. 14, no. 4, pt. 1, pp. 310–321. Menasha.

Metcalf, George

1963a. Small sites on and about Fort Berthold Indian Reservation, Garrison Reservoir, North Dakota. River Basin Surveys Papers, no. 26. Bureau of American Ethnology, Bulletin 185. Washington.

1963b. Star Village: A fortified historic Arikara site in Mercer County, North Dakota. River Basin Surveys Papers, no. 27, Bureau of American Ethnology, Bulletin 185. Washington.

Miller, Carl F.

1960. The excavation and investigation of Fort Lookout Trading Post II (39LM57) in the Fort Randall Reservoir, South Dakota. River Basin Surveys Papers, no. 17, Bureau of American Ethnology, Bulletin 176. Washington.

1964. Archeological investigations at the Hosterman Site (39PO7), Oahe Reservoir area, Potter County, South Dakota, 1956. River Basin Surveys Papers, no. 35, Bureau of American Ethnology, Bulletin 189. Washington.

Mills, John E.

1960. Historic sites archeology in the Fort Randall Reservoir, South Dakota. River Basin Surveys Papers, no. 16, Bureau of American Ethnology, Bulletin 176. Washington.

Mishkin, Bernard

1940. Rank and warfare among the Plains Indians. Monographs of the American Ethnological Society, no. 3. Seattle.

Missouri Basin Chronology Program, Missouri Basin Project, Smithsonian Institution, Lincoln.

1958. Statement no. 1.

1959. Statement no. 2.

1962. Statement no. 3.

1962. Statement no. 4.

1964. Statement no. 5.

Montgomery, Henry

1906. Remains of prehistoric man in the Dakotas. American Anthropologist, n.s., vol. 8, no. 4, pp. 640–51. Lancaster.

Mulloy, William

1958. A preliminary historical outline for the Northwestern Plains. University of Wyoming Publications, vol. 22, no. 1. Laramie.

Nasatir, A. P.

1952. Before Lewis and Clark. 2 vols. St. Louis Historical Documents Foundation. St. Louis.

Neuman, Robert W.

1960a. The Truman Mound Site, Big Bend Reservoir area, South Dakota. American Antiquity, vol. 26, no. 1, pp. 78–92. Salt Lake City.

1960b. Indian burial mounds in the Missouri River Basin. Progress, Interior Basin Field Committee, pp. 35–45. Billings.

1961a. Excavations at four mound sites in the Oahe Reservoir. Proceedings of the 18th Plains Conference. Plains Anthropologist, vol. 6, no. 12, pt. 1, pp. 57–58. Norman.

1961b. The Olson Mound (39BF223) in Buffalo County, South Dakota. Plains Anthropologist, vol. 6, no. 13, pp. 164–170. Norman.

1961c. Salvage archaeology at a site near Fort Thompson, South Dakota. Plains Anthropologist, vol. 6, no. 13, pp. 189–200. Norman.

1962. A green pigment from North Dakota burial mounds. Plains Anthropologist, vol. 7, no. 18, pp. 266–267. Lincoln.

1963. Field work in Dewey County, South Dakota, Oahe Reservoir area. Proceedings of the 20th Plains Conference. Plains Anthropologist, vol. 8, no. 20, pp. 121–122. Lincoln.

1964a. Projectile points from preceramic occupations near Fort Thompson, South Dakota. A preliminary report. Plains Anthropologist, vol. 9, no. 25, pp. 173–189. Lincoln.

1964b. The Good Soldier Site (39LM238), Big Bend Reservoir, Lyman County, South Dakota. River Basin Surveys Papers, no. 37, Bureau of American Ethnology, Bulletin 189.

1967. Radiocarbon-dated archaeological remains on the northern and central Great Plains. American Antiquity, vol. 32, no. 4, pp. 471–486. Salt Lake City.

Orr, Kenneth Gordon

1946. The archaeological situation at Spiro, Oklahoma; A preliminary report. American Antiquity, vol. 11, no. 4 pp. 228–256. Manasha.

Osgood, Ernest Staples, ed.

1964. The field notes of Captain William Clark, 1803–1805. Yale University Press. New Haven.

Over, W. H., and Elmer E. Meleen

1941. A report on an investigation of the Brandon Village Site and the Split Rock Creek Mounds. University of South Dakota Museum, Archeological Studies, Circular no. 3. Vermillion.

Petsche, Jerome E., compiler

1968. Bibliography of salvage archeology in the United States. Smithsonian Institution Publications in Salvage Archeology, no. 10. Lincoln.

Phillips, Paul Chrisler

1961. The fur trade. 2 vols. University of Oklahoma Press. Norman.

Reid, Russell

1930. The earth lodge. North Dakota Historical Quarterly, vol. 4, no. 3. Bismarck.

Roberts, Frank H. H., Jr.
1961.   Status of the salvage program in the Missouri Basin. *In* Symposium on salvage archaeology, ed. by John M. Corbett. National Park Service. Washington.

Roe, Frank Gilbert
1955.   The Indian and the horse. University of Oklahoma Press. Norman.

Secoy, Frank Raymond
1953.   Changing military patterns on the Great Plains. Monographs of the American Ethnological Society, no. 21. New York.

Smith, Carlyle S.
1951.   Pottery types from the Talking Crow Site, Fort Randall Reservoir, South Dakota. Plains Archaeological Conference News Letter, vol. 4, no. 3, pp. 32–41. Lincoln.

1960.   The temporal relationships of Coalescent village sites in Fort Randall Reservoir, South Dakota. *Actas del XXXIII Congreso Internacional de Americanistas*, Tomo II, pp. 111–123. San Jose de Costa Rica.

1963.   Time perspective within the Coalescent Tradition in South Dakota. American Antiquity, vol. 28, no. 4, pp. 489–495. Salt Lake City.

Smith, Carlyle S., and Roger T. Grange, Jr.
1958.   The Spain Site (39LM301), a winter village in Fort Randall Reservoir, South Dakota. River Basin Surveys Papers, no. 11, Bureau of American Ethnology, Bulletin 169. Washington.

Smith, Carlyle S., and Alfred E. Johnson
1968.   The Two Teeth Site. Smithsonian Institution River Basin Surveys, Publications in Salvage Archeology, no. 8. Lincoln.

Smith, G. Hubert
1954.   Archeological work at 32ML2 (Like-a-Fishhook Village and Fort Berthold), Garrison Reservoir area, North Dakota, 1950–1954. Plains Anthropologist, no. 2, pp. 27–32. Lincoln.

1960a.   Fort Pierre II (39ST217), a historic trading post in the Oahe Dam area, South Dakota. River Basin Surveys Papers, no. 18, Bureau of American Ethnology, Bulletin 176. Washington.

1960b.   Archeological investigations at the site of Fort Stevenson (32ML1), Garrison Reservoir, North Dakota. River Basin Surveys Papers, no. 19, Bureau of American Ethnology, Bulletin 176. Washington.

1968.   Big Bend historic sites. Smithsonian Institution River Basin Surveys, Publications in Salvage Archeology, no. 9. Lincoln.

MS.   Like-a-Fishhook Village and Fort Berthold, Garrison Reservior, North Dakota. *In press.*

Spaulding, Albert C.
1956.   The Arzberger Site, Hughes County, South Dakota. Occasional Contributions from the Museum of Anthropology of the University of Michigan, no. 16. Ann Arbor.

Sperry, James E.
1968.   The Shermer Site (32EM10). Plains Anthropologist, memoir 5, vol. 13, no. 42, pt. 2. Lawrence.

Sperry, James E., and Richard A. Krause
1962.   1961 summer excavations at the Leavenworth Site, 39CO9. Proceedings of the 19th Plains Conference. Plains Anthropologist, vol. 7, no. 16, p. 80. Lincoln.

Stearn, E. Wagner and Allen E.
1945.   The effect of smallpox on the destiny of the Amerindian. Boston.

Stephenson, Robert L.
1954.   Taxonomy and chronology in the Central Plains–Middle Missouri River area. Plains Anthropologist, no. 1, pp. 15–21. Lincoln.

1962.   Three Smithsonian salvage sites. Proceedings of the 19th Plains Conference. Plains Anthropologist, vol. 7, no. 16, pp. 80–81. Lincoln.

1967.   Reflections on the River Basin Surveys' Program. Desert Research Institute, Reprint Series no. 48, University of Nevada. Reno.

1969.   Blue Blanket Island (39WW9), an historic contact site in the Oahe Reservoir, near Mobridge, South Dakota. Plains Anthropologist, vol. 14, no. 43, pp. 1–31. Lawrence.

Stirling, Matthew W.
1924.   Archeological investigations in South Dakota. Explorations and Field-work of the Smithsonian Institution in 1923. Washington.
1947.   Arikara glassworking. Journal of the Washington Academy of Sciences, vol. 37, no. 8, pp. 257–263. Washington.

Strong, William Duncan
1933.   Studying the Arikara and their neighbors on the Upper Missouri. Explorations and Field-work of the Smithsonian Institution in 1932. Washington.
1935.   An introduction to Nebraska archeology. Smithsonian Miscellaneous Collections, vol. 93, no. 10. Washington.
1940.   From history to prehistory in the northern Great Plains. Smithsonian Miscellaneous Collections, vol. 100. Washington.

Stuiver, Minze, and Hans E. Suess
1966.   On the relationship between radiocarbon dates and true sample ages. Radiocarbon, vol. 8. New Haven.

Suhm, Dee Ann, Alex D. Krieger, and Edward B. Jelks
1954.   An introductory handbook of Texas archeology. Bulletin of the Texas Archeological Society, vol. 25. Austin.

Thompson, David (see Glover, 1962)

Thwaites, Reuben G., ed.
1959.   Original journals of the Lewis and Clark expedition, 1804–06. 8 vols. New York.
1966.   Early Western Travels, 1748–1846. 33 vols. New York.

Tucker, Sara Jones
1942.   Indian villages of the Illinois Country, vol. II, Scientific Papers, Illinois State Museum. pt. I, Altas. Springfield.

Turner, Frederick J.
1920.   The frontier in American history. New York.

Wallace, Ernest, and E. Adamson Hoebel
1952.   The Comanches, Lords of the South Plains. University of Oklahoma Press. Norman.

Weakly, Harry E.
1946.   A preliminary report on the Ash Hollow charcoal. *In* Ash Hollow Cave, by John L. Champe, pp. 105–110 (Appendix I). University of Nebraska Studies, new series, no. 1. Lincoln.
1949.   Dendrochronology in Nebraska. Proceedings of the Fifth Plains Conference for Archeology. University of Nebraska, Laboratory of Anthropology, Note Book, no. 1. Lincoln.
1950.   Dendrochronology and its climatic implications in the Central Plains. Proceedings of the Sixth Plains Conference for Archeology. University of Utah, Anthropological Papers, no. 11. Salt Lake City.

Weakly, Ward F.
1961.   A site in the Fort Randall Reservoir, Brule County, South Dakota. Plains Anthropologist, vol. 6, no. 14, pp. 230–241. Norman.
MS.   Tree-ring dating and archaeology in South Dakota. Unpublished manuscript, 1967. National Park Service. Omaha.

Webb, Walter Prescott
1931.   The Great Plains. Boston.

Wedel, Waldo R.
1936.   An introduction to Pawnee archeology. Bureau of American Ethnology, Bulletin 112. Washington.
1940.   Culture sequence in the central Great Plains. Smithsonian Miscellaneous Collectors, vol. 100. Washington.
1941.   Environment and native subsistence economies in the central Great Plains. Smithsonian Miscellaneous Collections, vol. 101, no. 3. Washington.
1943.   Archeological investigations in Platte and Clay Counties, Missouri. U.S. National Museum, Bulletin 183. Washington.
1947.   Prehistory and the Missouri Valley Development Program: Summary report on the Missouri River Basin Archeological Survey in 1946. Smithsonian Miscellaneous Collections, vol. 107, no. 6. Washington.

1948.	Prehistory and the Missouri Valley Development Program: Summary report on the Missouri River Basin Archeological Survey in 1947. Smithsonian Miscellaneous Collections, vol. 111, no. 2. Washington.
1949.	Some provisional correlations in Missouri Basin Archaeology. American Antiquity, vol. 14, no. 4, pt. 1, pp. 328–339. Menasha.
1951.	The use of earth-moving machinery in archeological excavations. *In* Essays on Archeological Methods. Museum of Anthropology, University of Michigan, Anthropological Papers, no. 8. Ann Arbor.
1953a.	Prehistory and the Missouri Valley Development Program: Summary report on the Missouri River Basin Archeological Survey in 1948. River Basin Surveys Papers, no. 1, Bureau of American Ethnology, Bulletin 154. Washington.
1953b.	Prehistory and the Missouri Valley Development Program: Summary report on the Missouri River Basin Archeological Survey in 1949. River Basin Surveys Papers, no. 2, Bureau of American Ethnology, Bulletin 154. Washington.
1955.	Archeological materials from the vicinity of Mobridge, South Dakota. Anthropological Papers, no. 45, Bureau of American Ethnology, Bulletin 157. Washington.
1959.	An introduction to Kansas archeology. Bureau of American Ethnology, Bulletin 174. Washington.
1961.	Prehistoric man on the Great Plains. University of Oklahoma Press. Norman.
1967.	Salvage archeology in the Missouri River Basin. Science, vol. 156, no. 3775, pp. 589–597. Washington.

Wendorf, Fred
| 1962. | A guide for salvage archaeology. Museum of New Mexico Press. Santa Fe. |

Wheeler, Richard P.
| 1956. | 'Quill flatteners' or pottery modeling tools? Plains Anthropologist, no. 6, pp. 17–20. Lincoln. |
| 1963. | The Stutsman Focus: an aboriginal culture complex in the Jamestown Reservoir area, North Dakota. River Basin Surveys Papers, no. 30, Bureau of American Ethnology, Bulletin 185. Washington. |

White, Theodore E.
1952a.	Observations on the butchering technique of some aboriginal peoples: I. American Antiquity, vol. 17, no. 4, pp. 337–338. Salt Lake City.
1952b.	Suggestions on the butchering technique of the inhabitants at the Dodd and Phillips Ranch Sites in the Oahe Reservoir area. Plains Archeological Conference News Letter, vol. 5, no. 2, pp. 22–28. Lincoln.
1953a.	A method of calculating the dietary percentage of various food animals utilized by aboriginal peoples. American Antiquity, vol. 18, no. 4, pp. 396–398. Salt Lake City.
1953b.	Observations on the butchering technique of some aboriginal peoples: no. 2. American Antiquity, vol. 19, no. 2, pp. 160–164. Salt Lake City.
1954.	Observations on the butchering techniques of some aboriginal peoples, nos. 3, 4, 5, and 6. American Antiquity, vol. 19, no. 3, pp. 254–264, Salt Lake City.
1955.	Observations on the butchering technics of some aboriginal peoples, nos. 7, 8, and 9. American Antiquity, vol. 21, no. 2, pp. 170–178. Salt Lake City.

Wilford, Lloyd A.
| 1945. | Three village sites of the Mississippi Pattern in Minnesota. American Antiquity, vol. 11, no. 1, pp. 32–40. Menasha. |
| 1955. | A revised classification of the prehistoric cultures of Minnesota. American Antiquity, vol. 21, no. 2, pp. 130–142. Salt Lake City. |

Will, George F.
1924.	Archaeology of the Missouri Valley. American Museum of Natural History, Anthropological Papers, vol. 22, pt. 6. New York.
1930.	The Mandan lodge at Bismarck. North Dakota Historical Quarterly, vol. 5, no. 1. Bismarck.
1946.	Tree ring studies in North Dakota. Agricultural Experiment Station, North Dakota Agricultural College, Bulletin 338. Fargo.
1948.	Additional notes on dendro-chronology in the Dakotas. Plains Archeological Conference News Letter, vol. 1, no. 4, pp. 68–70. Lincoln.

Will, George F., and Thad C. Hecker
1944.   The Upper Missouri River Valley aboriginal culture in North Dakota. North Dakota Historical Quarterly, vol. 11, nos. 1 and 2. Bismarck.

Will, George F., and George E. Hyde
1917.   Corn among the Indians of the Upper Missouri. Cedar Rapids.

Will, George F., and H. J. Spinden
1906.   The Mandans. A study of their culture, archaeology and language. Peabody Museum of American Archaeology and Ethnology, vol. 3, no. 4. Harvard University. Cambridge.

Willey, Gordon R.
1966.   An introduction to American archaeology; vol. 1, North and Middle America. Englewood Cliffs, New Jersey.

Willey, Gordon R., and Philip Phillips
1962.   Method and theory in American archaeology. University of Chicago Press (Phoenix Edition). Chicago.

Wilmeth Roscoe
1958.   Report of the investigation of the Payne Site, 39WW302, Walworth County, South Dakota, 1956. University of South Dakota, South Dakota Archaeological Commission, Archaeological Studies, Circular no. 8. Pierre.

Wilson, Gilbert L.
1917.   Agriculture of the Hidatsa Indians: an Indian interpretation. University of Minnesota Studies in the Social Sciences, no. 9. Minneapolis.
1924.   The horse and the dog in Hidatsa culture. American Museum of Natural History, Anthropological Papers, vol. 15, pt. 2. New York.
1934.   The Hidatsa earthlodge. American Museum of Natural History, Anthropological Papers, vol. 33, pt. 5. New York.

Wissler, Clark
1914.   The influence of the horse in the development of Plains culture. American Anthropologist, vol. 16, pp. 1–25. Menasha.

Witty, Thomas A.
MS.   The Anoka Focus. Unpublished M.A. thesis, 1962. University of Nebraska. Lincoln.

Wood, W. Raymond
1960.   The Boundary Mound Group (32SI1): An eastern Woodland complex in North Dakota. Plains Anthropologist, vol. 5, no. 10, pp. 71–78. Lincoln.
1962a.   A stylistic and historical analysis of shoulder patterns on Plains Indian pottery. American Antiquity, vol. 28, no. 1, pp. 25–40. Salt Lake City.
1962b.   Notes on the bison bone from the Paul Brave, Huff, and Demery Sites (Oahe Reservoir). Plains Anthropologist, vol. 7, no. 17, pp. 201–204. Lincoln.
1965.   The Redbird Focus and the problem of Ponca prehistory. Plains Anthropologist, memoir 2, vol. 10, no. 28. Lincoln.
1967.   An interpretation of Mandan culture history. River Basin Surveys Papers, no. 39, Bureau of American Ethnology, Bulletin 198. Washington.

Wood, W. Raymond, ed.
1969.   Two house sites in the central Plains: an experiment in archaeology. Plains Anthropologist. memoir 6, vol. 14, no. 44, pt. 2. Lincoln.

Wood, W. Raymond, and Alan R. Woolworth
1964.   The Paul Brave Site (32SI4), Oahe Reservoir area, North Dakota. River Basin Surveys Papers, no. 33, Bureau of American Ethnology, Bulletin 189. Washington.

Woolworth, Alan R.
1956.   Archeological investigations at Site 32ME59 (Grandmother's Lodge). North Dakota History, vol. 23, no. 2. Bismarck.

Woolworth, Alan R., and W. Raymond Wood
1960.   The archeology of a small trading post (Kipp's Post, 32MN1) in the Garrison Reservoir, North Dakota. River Basin Surveys Papers, no. 20, Bureau of American Ethnology, Bulletin 176. Washington.
1964.   The Demery Site (39C01), Oahe Reservoir area, South Dakota. River Basin Surveys Papers, no. 34, Bureau of American Ethnology, Bulletin 189. Washington.

Appendix 1
MAJOR SALVAGE EXCAVATIONS IN THE MIDDLE MISSOURI VALLEY

Following is a summary, in tabular form, of the major site excavations made under the salvage program in the Middle Missouri subarea, extending from about the mouth of the White River in South Dakota to the mouth of the Yellowstone in North Dakota. This is not a complete list of all the sites worked, but an inventory of those sites at which the fieldwork cost at least $2,500. Site locations are shown in figure 113. Cultural classifications of sites for which final reports are not available are tentative. Abbreviations used are:

INSTITUTIONS

KU	University of Kansas
MAC	Midwest Archeological Center
MSU	Montana State University
NSHS	Nebraska State Historical Society
NU	University of Nebraska
RBS	River Basin Surveys
SHSND	State Historical Society of North Dakota
UI	University of Idaho
UM	University of Missouri
UND	University of North Dakota
USD	University of South Dakota
UW	University of Wisconsin

CULTURAL CLASSIFICATIONS

DC	Disorganized Coalescent
EC	Extended Coalescent
EMM	Extended Middle Missouri
IC	Initial Coalescent
IMM	Initial Middle Missouri
MIMM	Modified Initial Middle Missouri
P-CC	Post-Contact Coalescent
TMM	Terminal Middle Missouri

SITE NO.	SITE NAME	INST.	EXCAVATOR	YEARS WORKED	CULTURAL CLASSI-FICATION	FINAL REPORT
32EM1	Havens	SHSND	Sperry	1967, '68	EMM	
32EM3	Tony Glas	SHSND	Howard	1958	TMM	Howard, 1959
32EM10	Shermer	SHSND	Sperry	1965, '66	TMM	Sperry, 1968
32ME15	Rock Village	RBS	Burcaw	1950	DC	
			Hartle	1951, '52	Foraging	
32ME16	Star Village	RBS	Hartle	1951	DC	Metcalf, 1963b
32ME59	Grandmother's Lodge	RBS	Hartle	1952	EMM	Woolworth, 1956
		SHSND	Woolworth and Wood	1953, '54		
32ML1	Ft. Stevenson	RBS	G. H. Smith	1951	Historic	G. H. Smith, 1960b
32ML2	Like-a-Fishhook V.	SHSND	Kleinsasser	1950	DC	
			Howard	1951, '52		
			Woolworth	1954		
	Ft. Berthold I & II	RBS	G. H. Smith	1952, '54	Historic	
		SHSND	Woolworth	1954		
32ML39	Night Walker's Butte	RBS	Hartle	1952	DC	
32MN1	Kipp's Post	SHSND	Woolworth and Wood	1954	Historic	Woolworth and Wood, 1960
32MO2		MAC	Johnson	1969	EMM	
32MO11	Huff	SHSND	Howard	1959	TMM	Howard, 1962
			Wood	1960		Wood, 1967
32MZ1	Crow-Flies-High	MSU	Malouf	1952	Historic	Malouf, 1963
32SI1	Boundary Mound	SHSND	Wood	1956	Woodland	Wood, 1960
		RBS	Neuman	1960		Neuman, 1961a
32SI2	Fire Heart Creek	SHSND	Lehmer	1964	DC	Lehmer, 1966
					EMM	
32SI4	Paul Brave	UND	Hewes	1947 1947	EMM	Hewes, 1949a and b
		SHSND	Wood and Woolworth	1955		Wood and Woolworth, 1964
32SI7	Ben Standing Soldier	RBS	Hoffman	1965	EMM	
32SI19	South Cannonball	RBS	Hoffman	1966, '67	EMM	
			Johnston	1968		
39AR2	No Heart Creek	USD	Hurt	1959	EC	
39BF2	Medicine Crow	RBS	Irving	1957, '58	P-CC	
			Deetz	1958	Foraging	
39BF3	Talking Crow	KU	C. S. Smith	1950, '51, '52	P-CC	
					IC	
					Woodland	
39BF4 & 11	Crow Creek	NSHS	Kivett	1954, '55	IC	
					IMM	
39BF12	Pretty Bull	RBS	Neuman	1957	P-CC	
					IMM	
39BF204	Two Teeth	KU	C. S. Smith	1955	P-CC	Smith and Johnson, 1968
39BF224	Truman Mound	RBS	Neuman	1957, '58	Woodland	Neuman, 1960a
					Foraging	
39BF225	Sitting Crow	RBS	Neuman	1961	Woodland	
					Foraging	
39BF233	Side Hill	RBS	Neuman	1961	Woodland	
					Foraging	
39BR16	Swanson	USD	Hurt S.D.	1950	IMM	Hurt, 1951a
39CA4	Anton Rygh	UI	Bowers	1957, '58	P-CC	
		RBS	Bowers	1959, '63	EC	
39CA6	Bamble	UW	Baerreis	1956	P-CC	Baerreis and Dallman, 1961
39CO1	Demery	SHSND	Woolworth and Wood	1956	EC	Woolworth and Wood, 1964
39CO5	Ft. Manuel	RBS	G. H. Smith	1965, '66	Historic	
					EC	
39CO9	Leavenworth	NU	Holder	1960, '61	DC	
					EC	
39CO14	Davis	RBS	Bowers	1962, '63	EC	
		UM	Wood and Falk	1969		

SITE NO.	SITE NAME	INST.	EXCAVATOR	YEARS WORKED	CULTURAL CLASSIFICATION	FINAL REPORT
39CO19	Potts	RBS	Stephenson	1961	EC	
39CO34	Red Horse Hawk	RBS	Bowers	1962 '63	P-CC	
39DW2	Four Bear	USD	Hurt	1958 '59	P-CC	Hurt, 1962
39DW231	Calamity Village	RBS	Mallory	1963, '64	EMM	
39DW233	Swift Bird	RBS	Neuman	1960, '62	EC	Hoffman, 1963b
					Woodland	Neuman, 1963
39DW234	Molstad	RBS	Hoffman	1962	EC	Hoffman, 1967
39DW240	Grover Hand	RBS	Neuman	1962, '63	Woodland	
39DW242	Stelzer	RBS	Neuman	1962, '63, '65	Woodland	
			Mallory	1963, '64		
39DW252	Arpan Mound	RBS	Neuman	1965	Woodland	
39HU1	Thomas Riggs	USD	Hurt	1952	EMM	Meleen, 1949b
		RBS	Johnston	1965		Hurt, 1953
						Johnston, 1967b
						Hurt, 1954
39HU26	Spotted Bear	USD	Hurt	1953	P-CC	
39HU60	Chapelle Creek	RBS	Folan	1963	P-CC	
			Brown	1964	IMM	
39LM1	Stricker	KU	C. S. Smith	1959	EC	
					IMM	
39LM2	Medicine Creek V.	RBS	Caldwell	1962	EC	
			Jensen	1967	IC	
					IMM	
39LM4	Hickey Brothers	RBS	Golden	1958	EMM	Caldwell et al, 1964
					IMM(?)	
39LM26 & 27	Oacoma	NSHS	Kivett	1951, '52	P-CC	
39LM33	Dinehart	KU	C. S. Smith	1953	IMM	
		RBS	Cooper	1954		
39LM47	Clarkstown	RBS	Cooper	1954	EC	
39LM55	King	RBS	Garth	1950	MIMM	
		KU	C. S. Smith	1953		
39LM57	Fort Lookout	RBS	Garth	1950	Historic	Miller, 1960
			Miller	1951		
39LM208	Jiggs Thompson	RBS	Caldwell and Jensen	1962	IMM	
39LM209	Langdeau	RBS	Caldwell and Jensen	1962	IMM	
39LM218	Black Partizan	RBS	Caldwell	1957, '58	EC	Caldwell, 1966b
					IC	
39LM225	Jandreau	RBS	Caldwell and Carter	1962	IMM	
39LM232	Pretty Head	RBS	Caldwell	1961	IMM	
39LM241		RBS	G. H. Smith	1957	Historic	G. H. Smith, 1968
39LM247	Red Cloud Agency III	RBS	G. H. Smith	1963	Historic	G. H. Smith, 1968
					IMM	
39LM301	Spain	KU	C. S. Smith	1953	EC	Smith and Grange, 1958
39PO3	Rosa	USD	Hurt	1957	P-CC	Hurt , 1959
39PO7	Hosterman	RBS	Miller	1956	EC	Miller, 1964
39SL4	Sully	RBS	Stephenson	1956, '57, '58	P-CC	
			Bass	1957, '58, '61, and 1962	EC	
39SL45	Ft. Sully II	RBS	G. H. Smith	1960	Historic	
39ST1	Cheyenne River	RBS	Wedel	1951, '55, '56	P-CC	
					EC	
					EMM	
39ST3	Black Widow	RBS	Cooper	1952	EC	
39ST6	Buffalo Pasture	RBS	Fenenga	1952	P-CC	Lehmer and Jones, 1968
			Wheeler and Miller	1955		
39ST9	Over's La Roche	RBS	Hoffman	1963	EC	Hoffman, 1968
					IMM	
					Woodland	
39ST11	Fay Tolton	RBS	Hartle	1957	IMM	

FIGURE 113

MAJOR SALVAGE EXCAVATIONS
IN THE MIDDLE MISSOURI VALLEY

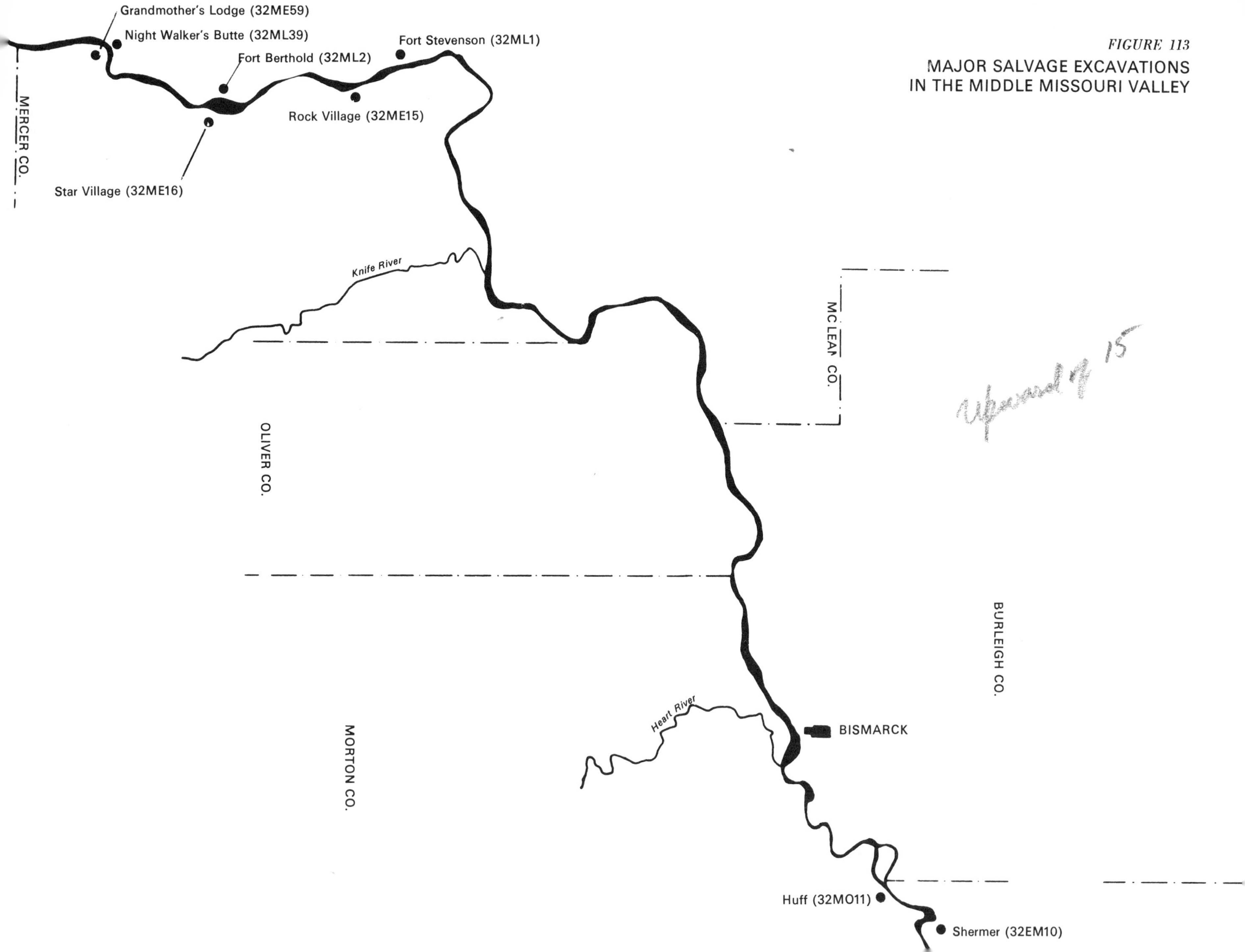

BURLEIGH CO.

MC LEAN CO.

BISMARCK

Heart River

Shermer (32EM10)

Huff (32MO11)

MORTON CO.

OLIVER CO.

Knife River

Fort Stevenson (32ML1)

Rock Village (32ME15)

Fort Berthold (32ML2)

Grandmother's Lodge (32ME59)

Night Walker's Butte (32ML39)

Star Village (32ME16)

MERCER CO.

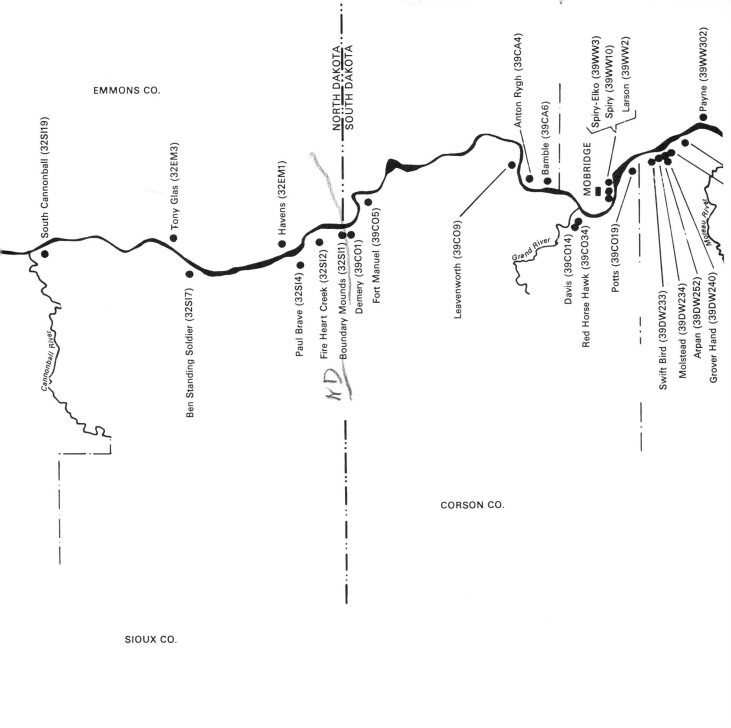

EMMONS CO.

South Cannonball (32SI19)

Tony Glas (32EM3)

Havens (32EM1)

NORTH DAKOTA
SOUTH DAKOTA

Anton Rygh (39CA4)

Bamble (39CA6)

Spiry-Elko (39WW3)
Spiry (39WW10)
Larson (39WW2)

Payne (39WW302)

MOBRIDGE

Ben Standing Soldier (32SI7)

Paul Brave (32SI4)

Fire Heart Creek (32SI2)
Boundary Mounds (32SI1)
Demery (39CO1)

Fort Manuel (39CO5)

Leavenworth (39CO9)

Grand River

Davis (39CO14)

Red Horse Hawk (39CO34)

Potts (39CO19)

Moreau River

Swift Bird (39DW233)
Molstead (39DW234)
Arpan (39DW252)
Grover Hand (39DW240)

Cannonball River

ND

CORSON CO.

SIOUX CO.

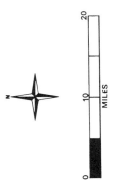

N

20

10

MILES

0

FIGURE 113

MAJOR SALVAGE EXCAVATIONS
IN THE MIDDLE MISSOURI VALLEY

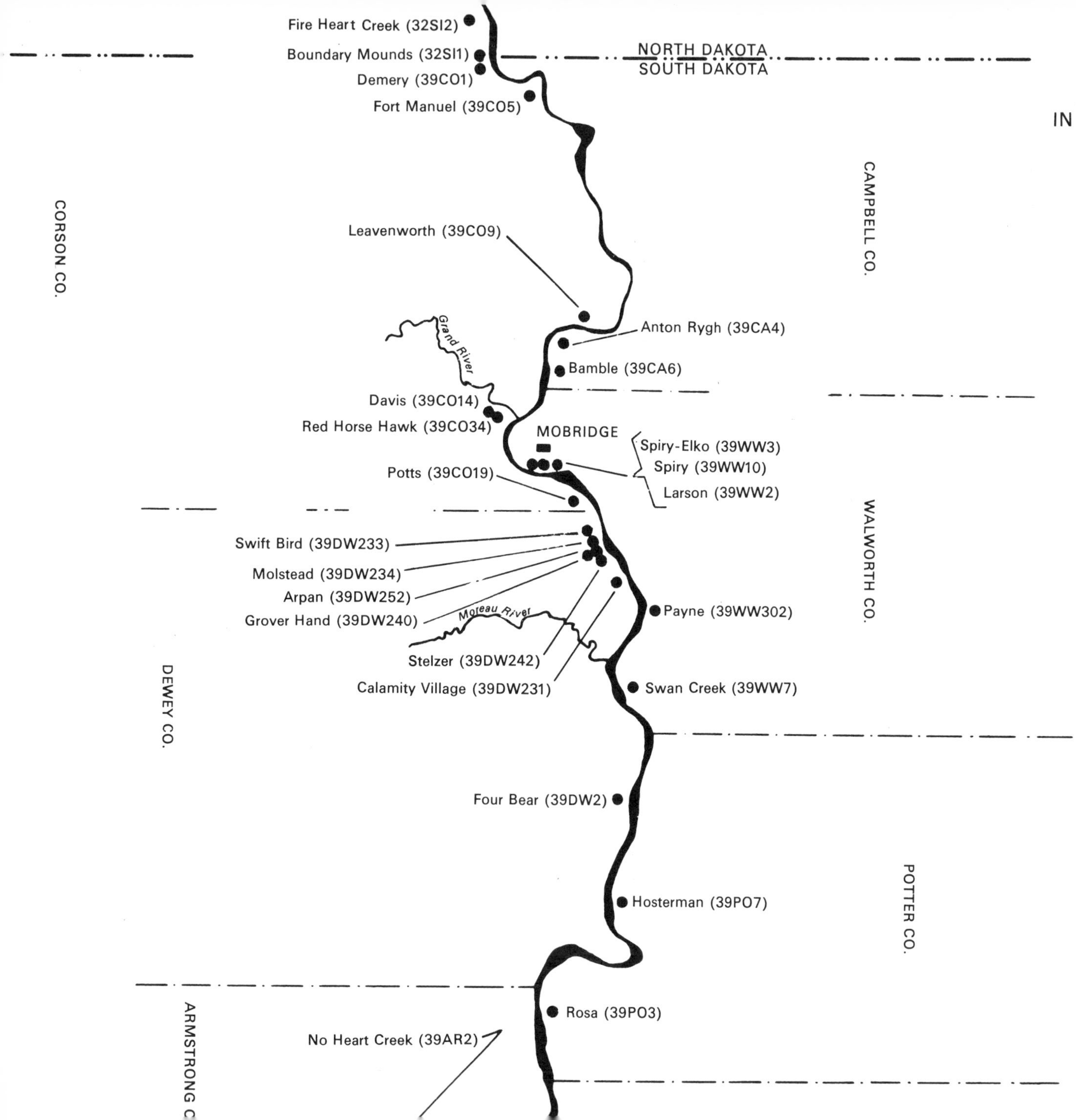

NORTH DAKOTA
SOUTH DAKOTA

POTTER CO.

CAMPBELL CO.

WALWORTH CO.

Anton Rygh (39CA4)

Bamble (39CA6)

Spiry-Elko (39WW3)

Spiry (39WW10)

Larson (39WW2)

Payne (39WW302)

Swan Creek (39WW7)

Hosterman (39PO7)

Fort Manuel (39CO5)

Fire Heart Creek (32SI2)

Boundary Mounds (32SI1)

Demery (39CO1)

MOBRIDGE

Leavenworth (39CO9)

Grand River

Davis (39CO14)

Red Horse Hawk (39CO34)

Potts (39CO19)

Moreau River

Stelzer (39DW242)

Calamity Village (39DW231)

Four Bear (39DW2)

Rosa (39PO3)

Swift Bird (39DW233)

Molstead (39DW234)

Arpan (39DW252)

Grover Hand (39DW240)

No Heart Creek (39AR2)

DEWEY CO.

ARMSTRONG C

CORSON CO.

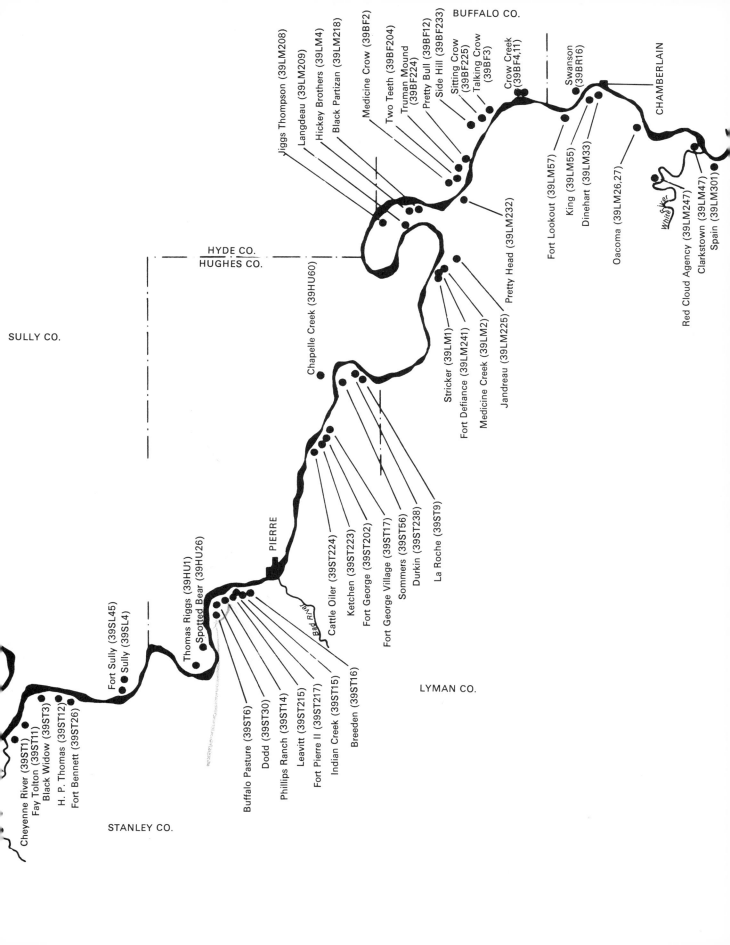

BUFFALO CO.

CHAMBERLAIN

Jiggs Thompson (39LM208)
Langdeau (39LM209)
Hickey Brothers (39LM4)
Black Partizan (39LM218)
Medicine Crow (39BF2)
Two Teeth (39BF204)
Truman Mound (39BF224)
Pretty Bull (39BF12)
Side Hill (39BF233)
Sitting Crow (39BF225)
Talking Crow (39BF3)
Crow Creek (39BF4,11)
Swanson (39BR16)

Fort Lookout (39LM57)
King (39LM55)
Dinehart (39LM33)
Oacoma (39LM26,27)
Red Cloud Agency (39LM247)
Clarkstown (39LM47)
Spain (39LM301)

HYDE CO.
HUGHES CO.

Chapelle Creek (39HU60)

SULLY CO.

Stricker (39LM1)
Fort Defiance (39LM241)
Medicine Creek (39LM2)
Jandreau (39LM225)
Pretty Head (39LM232)

PIERRE

White River

Cattle Oiler (39ST224)
Ketchen (39ST223)
Fort George (39ST202)
Fort George Village (39ST17)
Sommers (39ST56)
Durkin (39ST238)
La Roche (39ST9)

Thomas Riggs (39HU1)
Spotted Bear (39HU26)

Bad River

Buffalo Pasture (39ST6)
Dodd (39ST30)
Phillips Ranch (39ST14)
Leavitt (39ST215)
Fort Pierre II (39ST217)
Indian Creek (39ST15)
Breeden (39ST16)

LYMAN CO.

Fort Sully (39SL45)
Sully (39SL4)

STANLEY CO.

Cheyenne River (39ST1)
Fay Tolton (39ST11)
Black Widow (39ST3)
H. P. Thomas (39ST12)
Fort Bennett (39ST26)

SITE NO.	SITE NAME	INST.	EXCAVATOR	YEARS WORKED	CULTURAL CLASSIFICATION	FINAL REPORT
39ST12	H. P. Thomas	RBS	Wheeler	1958	P-CC EC IMM	
39ST14	Phillips Ranch	RBS	Lehmer	1950, '51	P-CC	Lehmer, 1954b
39ST15	Indian Creek	RBS	Fenenga	1952	P-CC EMM	Lehmer and Jones, 1968
39ST16	Breeden (ex Mathison)	RBS	Fenenga	1952	EC	
			Wheeler	1955	IMM	
39ST17	Ft. George V.	RBS	Hoffman	1964	P-CC	
39ST26	Ft. Bennett Agency	RBS	G. H. Smith	1960	Historic EC	
39ST30	Dodd	RBS	Lehmer	1950	P-CC IMM	Lehmer 1954b.
39ST56	Sommers	RBS	Jensen	1964, '65	MIMM	
39ST202	Ft. George	RBS	G. H. Smith	1962	Historic	G. H. Smith 1968
39ST203	Black Widow Ridge	RBS	Wedel	1957	P-CC EMM	
39ST215	Leavitt	RBS	Wheeler	1955	P-CC EC	Lehmer and Jones, 1968
39ST217	Ft. Pierre II	RBS	G. H. Smith	1956	Historic	G. H. Smith, 1960a
39ST223	Ketchen	RBS	Jones	1965, '66	MIMM	
39ST224	Cattle Oiler	RBS	Moerman	1965	EC	
			Jones	1965, '66	MIMM IMM	
39ST232	Bowers' La Roche	RBS	Hoffman	1963	EC	Hoffman, 1968
39ST238	Durkin	RBS	Jensen	1966	MIMM	
39WW2	Larson	RBS	Bowers	1963, '64	P-CC	
			Hoffman	1966		
39WW3	Spiry-Eklo	UW	Baerries	1956	P-CC	Baerreis and Dallman, 1961
39WW7	Swan Creek	USD	Hurt	1954, '55	P-CC	Hurt, 1957
			Wilmeth	1956	EC	
39WW10	Spiry	UW	Baerreis	1956	EC	Baerreis and Dallman, 1961
39WW302	Payne	USD	Wilmeth	1956	EC	Wilmeth, 1958

FIGURE 114 Burial mound excavation.

Appendix 2
POST-CONTACT COALESCENT AND DISORGANIZED COALESCENT PHASES

The phases provisionally recognized within the Post-Contact Coalescent and Disorganized Coalescent Variants are characterized as fully as possible in the following summaries. The data from many excavated sites assigned to these phases have still to be analyzed and published, and so far excavations in sites of the Heart River Phase, which lie outside the reservoir areas, have been very limited indeed.

Because of the lack of detail regarding the nonpottery artifacts from most of the phases, no attempt has been made to distinguish them on this basis. It is my impression that the Heart River Phase will prove to share more traits of this sort with the Middle Missouri Tradition than the other phases, which appear to have developed out of the Extended Coalescent Variant.

POST-CONTACT COALESCENT PHASES

FELICIA PHASE

SUBPHASES   None recognized.

TYPE SITES   Two Teeth (39BF204), Cadotte (39HE202).

GEOGRAPHIC DISTRIBUTION   Both sides of the Missouri in and just downstream from the Big Bend.

ESTIMATED AGE   A.D. 1675–1700.

VILLAGE SIZE AND VILLAGE PLAN   Felicia villages seem to be small, with the houses grouped in irregular clusters.

FORTIFICATIONS   Apparently absent.

HOUSE TYPE   Circular structure with central firepit, four primary superstructure supports, and entrance passage. The two houses excavated at the Two Teeth Site had diameters in excess of 41 and 52 feet (Smith and Johnson, 1968, pp. 10–12).

BURIALS   Unknown.

POTTERY   Includes Iona Ware, which is also found in Extended Coalescent sites, together with Post-Contact Coalescent varieties. There is a preponderance of Talking Crow types, and a few Stanley sherds.

TRIBAL IDENTIFICATION   Probably ancestral Arikara.

REMARKS   The Felicia Phase, evidently a short-lived configuration with a limited geographic extent, appears to have been transitional between the Extended Coalescent complexes of the Big Bend region and the later Talking Crow Phase.

TALKING CROW PHASE

SUBPHASES   None established to date, but apparent differences between the pottery from Talking Crow Site (39FB3) and Medicine Crow Site (39BF2), on the left bank, and the Oacoma sites (39LM26 and 39LM 27), on the right bank, suggest differences at the subphase level.

TYPE SITES   Medicine Crow (39BF2), Talking Crow (39BF3), Oacoma (39LM26 and 39LM27).

GEOGRAPHIC DISTRIBUTION   The majority of the sites which presently seem to be assignable to this phase are located on both banks of the Missouri in the Big Bend region. A few sites scattered upstream in the Bad-Cheyenne region appear also to be assignable to this unit. Nearly all of the upstream sites are located on the left bank; all of them are represented by small sherd samples. There may also be Talking Crow Phase sites downstream from the White River in the area not covered by this study.

ESTIMATED AGE   1700–50.

VILLAGE SIZE AND VILLAGE PLAN   The Talking Crow villages apparently range in size from about 15 to as many as 50 houses. Houses are clustered in moderately compact groups, with rather thin sheet refuse between the houses.

FORTIFICATIONS   Apparently not usually present.

HOUSE TYPE   Circular structure with entrance passage, central firepit, and four primary superstructure supports. Unusually large structures may have been ceremonial lodges; so far as I know, earthen altars have not been found in any of those associated with this phase.

BURIALS   Primary and possibly secondary inhumations occur rarely in the village areas. No other data.

POTTERY   The pottery assemblage is dominated by types assigned to the Talking Crow Ware (C. S. Smith, 1951). Stanley sherds and pieces resembling Lower Loup types from central Nebraska occur as minority elements.

TRIBAL IDENTIFICATION   The Talking Crow Phase presents some difficulties in terms of a specific tribal identification. It seems probable that the people of the Talking Crow Phase were the ancestors of some of the historic Arikara. However, similarities in the pottery of the Lower Loup Phase of central Nebraska and the Talking Crow Phase, especially as it is represented at the Oacoma Site, indicate close relationships with the historic Pawnee.

REMARKS   To date, no complete report on a large-scale excavation of a Talking Crow Phase site has been published.

BAD RIVER PHASE

SUBPHASES   Bad River 1 and 2.

TYPE SITES   Bad River 1—Dodd A (39ST 30), Indian Creek A (39ST15). Bad River 2—Phillips Ranch (39ST14), Buffalo Pasture (39ST6).

GEOGRAPHIC DISTRIBUTION   Bad-Cheyenne region, almost entirely on the right bank.

ESTIMATED AGE   Bad River 1—1675–1740. Bad River 2—1740–95.

VILLAGE SIZE AND VILLAGE PLAN   Bad River 1 villages seem to average between 15 and 30 houses which are set fairly well apart. Bad River 2 villages are about the same size, although the houses are set much closer together. Areas between the houses are blanketed with sheet refuse of varying depths.

FORTIFICATIONS   Bad River 1—none. Bad River 2—villages enclosed by curvilinear ditches without bastions. There was usually a palisade inside the ditch.

HOUSE TYPE   Circular structure with entrance passage, central firepit, and four primary superstructure supports. There is commonly a large structure, located near the center of the village, which usually has an earth altar opposite the entryway.

BURIALS   Bad River 1—not known. Bad River 2—primary inhumations, flexed or semiflexed on the back or side, in individual graves. Logs or planks were frequently placed over the bodies, many of which were wrapped in buffalo robes. Graves were grouped in cemeteries near the village. Occasional multiple burials are also found.

POTTERY   The pottery assemblage of both subphases is dominated by Stanley Ware. There is considerable variation in the proportions of the individual types from one village to another within the same subphase. Minority elements in the pottery assemblage are Colombe Collared and Talking Crow types.

TRIBAL IDENTIFICATION   The Bad River Phase is clearly identifiable with the Arikara. The geographic distributions of Bad River 1 and 2 correspond closely with the documented Arikara homeland of the 18th century.

REMARKS   Bad River 1 is distinguished by its lack of fortifications and earlier chronological position. Bad River 2 is distinguished by the presence of fortifications and a later position in time, indicated by the occurrence of horse bones and rather plentiful trade goods, including gun parts.

LE BEAU PHASE

SUBPHASES   None recognized to date.

TYPE SITES   Four Bear (39DW2), Larson (39WW2), Spiry-Eklo (39WW3), Swan Creek (39WW7).

GEOGRAPHIC DISTRIBUTION   The Bad-Cheyenne region, almost exclusively on the left bank of the Missouri, and on both banks in the Grand-Moreau region. There is a heavy concentration of Le Beau Phase sites opposite the mouth of the Grand River.

ESTIMATED AGE   1675–1780.

VILLAGE SIZE AND VILLAGE PLAN   Many Le Beau Phase sites are extremely large, although some of the smaller ones have only about 15 houses. Houses tend to be grouped close together, and there is commonly no clear indication of a central plaza. The southern sites of the phase have only sheet refuse between the houses; many of the northern ones have sizable refuse heaps in these areas.

FORTIFICATIONS   Commonly, a curvilinear ditch without bastions encloses all or nearly all of the houses in the village. In some sites there are two ditches around part of the village, indicating an expansion or contraction of the fortified enclosure. Palisades are typically associated with the ditches.

The Le Beau Phase sites in the Bad-Cheyenne region do not appear to have been fortified as regularly as those farther to the north.

HOUSE TYPE   Domiciliary structures conform to the standard circular plan of the other Post-Contact Coalescent phases. Larger, presumably ceremonial, structures have been reported from the Swan Creek and Rosa (39PO3) sites (Hurt, 1957; 1959). Neither structure was excavated completely, but no evidence of an earth altar was found in either one.

BURIALS   Primary single or multiple inhumations, with bodies usually flexed on the back or side. Hurt (1957, pp. 20–22) reports that secondary burials were also found at Swan Creek.

POTTERY   The bulk of the pottery from the Le Beau Phase sites seems to be a sort of hybrid of the Stanley and Talking Crow traditions. Part of the rim sherds found are good Talking Crow types, part of them are good Stanley types; the remainder fall into an "Intermediate" group. A minority representation of the Le Beau S-Rim in assemblages from the northern sites decreases sharply downstream in the Bad-Cheyenne region.

TRIBAL IDENTIFICATION   The Le Beau Phase can most probably be identified with the Arikara, although there have been suggestions that it equates with the Mandan.

Bowers (1950, fn. pp. 116–117) cites traditional evidence that the Awigaxa Mandan lived in the vicinity of the Grand River until fairly late times. In a later publication Bowers (1965, p. 484) says that the Awigaxa "remained near the Grand River until after A.D. 1700." Hurt (1957, p. 29) sug-

gested on the basis of burial patterns at the Swan Creek Site that his Le Beau Focus might be Mandan, but there is little archeological support for such an identification.

There can be little doubt that historic Mandan culture represents a direct continuation of the older Middle Missouri Tradition. There seems to be a complete absence of Middle Missouri Tradition sites in the locality immediately around the mouth of the Grand River. Instead, the early sites there are Extended Coalescent, and apparently a direct local transition from late Extended Coalescent manifestations such as the Davis Site (39CO14) into the Le Beau Phase occurred there.

The absence of Middle Missouri Tradition sites near the Grand River and the geographic extension of Le Beau Phase sites as far south as the lower Bad-Cheyenne region argue against the identification of the Le Beau Phase as Mandan. Moreover, Le Beau Phase pottery shows much closer similarities to that of the Stanley and Talking Crow Phases than to that of any of the manifestations which can be equated with the Mandan. Thus it seems reasonable to identify the Le Beau Phase with the historic Arikara.

REMARKS   Sites of the Le Beau Phase are much more widely distributed along the river than are sites of any of the other Post-Contact Coalescent phases. It seems likely that a comparison of the northern and southern sites assigned to the phase will reveal differences which will justify the recognition of two or more subphases.

HEART RIVER PHASE

SUBPHASES   (tentative) Heart River 1 and 2.

TYPE SITES   Heart River 1—Double Ditch (32BL8), Slant (32MO26), Boley (32MO 37). Heart River 2—Mandan Lake (32OL 21), Smith Farm (32OL9).

GEOGRAPHIC DISTRIBUTION   Heart River 1—on both banks of the Missouri from just below Heart River upstream to about the line between Morton and Oliver Counties. Heart River 2—mainly on the right bank of the Missouri from central Oliver County upstream to Knife River.

ESTIMATED AGE   Heart River 1 and 2—1675–1780.

VILLAGE SIZE AND VILLAGE PLAN   Many of the sites, especially the southern ones, are extremely large. Houses are generally set quite close together. Sites in the southern area commonly have enormous trash mounds between the houses. Those in the north usually have sheet refuse. Some of these middens have depths of well over 3 feet to sterile soil; all of them appear to have a very rich artifact content.

The Heart River Phase sites which appear to equate with the Mandan commonly have an open central area or plaza. This feature is not evident in the towns which can be equated with the Hidatsa (Libby, 1908).

FORTIFICATIONS Nearly all of the Heart River 1 villages show definite indications of an enclosing curvilinear fortification ditch without bastions. Ditches are often double for part of their length, indicating either a reduction or an increase in the fortified area.

Fortifications appear to have been rare at the Heart River 2 sites.

HOUSE TYPE This is not well known because few Heart River Phase houses have as yet been excavated by competent archeologists. Indications point to the use of circular earthlodges with a central firepit, four primary superstructure supports, and probably an entrance passage. Remodeling and/or rebuilding seems to have been much more common than in the southern Post-Contact Coalescent villages.

Bowers (1950, fig. 14) reports that the Mandan had a ceremonial structure which incorporated some of the features of the older long-rectangular houses of the region.

BURIALS Strong (1940, pp. 362–363) reports flexed inhumations, some of which were covered with wooden slabs, at Slant Village. A single infant burial was found in a shallow pit in the floor of the house excavated by the writer at the Boley Site (32 MO37). It is likely that most graves were dug outside of the villages. It also seems probable that platform burials, like those of the 19th-century Mandan and Hidatsa, were common.

POTTERY Heart River Phase pottery ranks technologically and esthetically as some of the best made by any of the villagers of the Middle Missouri Valley. Le Beau S-Rim usually constitutes about two-thirds of the sample from a Heart River Phase site. The paste was hard and compact, vessel walls were thin, and the elaborate decoration (al-most always cord impressed) was meticulously applied. The other major element in the Heart River Phase assemblage has a well-made braced rim which bears a close resemblance to some of the Stanley rims. There are, however, significant differences in vessel form, surface finish, color, and decorative elements which justify assigning this material to a separate category.

TRIBAL IDENTIFICATION The Heart River Phase, as it has been defined here, can be identified, with strong assurance, with the Mandan and the Hidatsa. Documentary sources dating from the first third of the 19th century (especially Lewis and Clark, and Maximilian) specifically identify the Heart River 1 sites as Mandan. Documentary evidence also seems to leave little doubt that the Heart River 2 sites on the Knife River were Hidatsa. There is less evidence for tribal identification of the other sites assigned to the Heart River 2 subphase, and their status should probably be left open pending excavation.

REMARKS There has been much less excavation in Heart River Phase sites than in the ones representing the other Post-Contact Coalescent phases. Because of this, the characterization given here must be considered a provisional one.

Bowers classified the northern and southern Heart River Phase sites as Painted Woods Focus and Heart River Focus sites, respectively. In distinguishing these two foci, he wrote:

A significant group of sites on the Missouri River, between Square Buttes and the Knife River, traditionally occupied by the various Hidatsa groups, are found, from an analysis of lodge forms, village organization of lodges, and pottery types and frequencies, to be essentially alike and to differ in several respects from the contemporaneous Mandan living near the mouth of the Heart River. The diagnostic traits of this Painted Woods Focus are: Circular earth lodges with a well-defined atutish area or section; absence of specialized ceremonial lodges, open circles, or ceremonial areas; indiscriminate arrangement of lodges; absence of fortifications; distinctive pottery types and ranges not characteristic of the contemporary Mandan sites nearby. Type "S" rims fall well below the range for the Mandan while thickened rims, formed by the addition of a narrow band, are common. The incidence of check-stamped rims runs as high as 18 percent of the collection at the Fort Clark Station site a few miles downstream from the mouth of the Knife River. Check-stamped pottery bodies comprise 40 percent of the collection at the Upper Sanger site, and cord-roughened bodies comprise 6.6 percent at the Fort Clark Station site.

(Bowers, 1965, pp. 482–483)

DISORGANIZED COALESCENT PHASES

Only one phase can now be recognized with a reasonable degree of confidence for the materials postdating 1780. Other phase classifications will undoubtedly develop for the Arikara villages of the 19th century.

KNIFE RIVER PHASE

SUBPHASES   Knife River 1 and 2.

TYPE SITES   Knife River 1—Deapolis (32ME5). Knife River 2—Rock Village (32ME15), Night Walker's Butte (32ML 39).

GEOGRAPHIC DISTRIBUTION   In the upper Knife-Heart region, mostly on the right bank of the Missouri, and extending into the lower Garrison region.

Knife River 1—The sites from Boller (32ME6) downstream.

Knife River 2—The sites from Amahami (32ME8) upstream.

ESTIMATED AGE   1780–1845.

VILLAGE SIZE AND VILLAGE PLAN   There is a considerable variation in the size of the Knife River Phase villages. Some appear to have had only a dozen or so houses, while others had well over 30. It seems likely that the Mandan towns had central plazas while those occupied by the Hidatsa did not. Sheet refuse between the houses seems to be the rule. Varying considerably in thickness, it reaches depths of as much as 4 feet in the more stable Knife River 2 communities, but is much thinner in the Knife River 1 sites, which were occupied for shorter periods.

FORTIFICATIONS   The great majority of Knife River Phase villages had encircling curvilinear ditches which generally seem to have lacked bastions. Historic descriptions indicate the common use of palisades.

HOUSE TYPE   The circular Post-Contact Coalescent earthlodge lasted into this period, and is evidenced both by archeological excavation and a number of historical accounts.

BURIALS   There are indications of cemeteries, presumably containing at least some primary inhumations, associated with some of the Knife River Phase villages. Historical sources also document the practice of platform burial.

POTTERY   There is a marked deterioration in the quality of the Knife River Phase pottery from Heart River Phase standards. The Le Beau S-Rim disappears almost completely. Most of the Knife River pottery appears to be a decadent variety of the Heart River braced rim ware. There is considerable variation in the rim bracing. Pronounced braces appear on some sherds, there are vestigal braces on others, and still others show no rim brace at all. This material has been provisionally classified as Knife River Ware.

TRIBAL IDENTIFICATION   Knife River 1— The documented Mandan villages near the Knife River. These are the sites known to have been occupied by the Mandan after they abandoned the Heart River 1 villages.

Knife River 2—The documented and presumed Hidatsa villages of the period 1780–1845. I am not aware of any documentation of a Hidatsa occupation of the late villages in the Garrison region assigned to this phase, but this seems to be the most likely tribal identification of them.

REMARKS   There appears to have been a direct continuity of population from the Heart River to the Knife River Phase. The dividing line between the two was the smallpox epidemic of 1780, which drastically reduced the population and disrupted the existing culture. Changes in material culture of the Knife River Phase are particularly evident in the inferior pottery compared to that of the Heart River Phase. It seems likely that this decline mirrors the death of many of the skilled craftsmen of the earlier period. Other differences between the two phases reflect changing patterns of the fur trade during the early 19th century.

One of the main distinctions between the Mandan and Hidatsa communities of the late period involves the stability of the villages themselves. The principal historic Hidatsa towns were located on the Knife

River. Big Hidatsa (32ME12) appears to have a Heart River 2 and a Knife River 2 component, and to have been continuously occupied from Heart River times until after the smallpox epidemic of 1837. Stratigraphic tests made at the Lower Hidatsa Site (32ME10) demonstrated the superposition of a Knife River 2 component on a Heart River 2 component. The village seems to have been abandoned, probably during the very late 1700's, when the Knife River changed its course and left the community stranded inland. There is reason to assume that the inhabitants moved a few hundred yards to the east and established themselves at the Sacagawea Site (32ME11). A very considerable accumulation of refuse during Knife River times has been demonstrated at Lower Hidatsa and Sacagawea, and this is presumably also the case at Big Hidatsa. There also seems to be a respectable refuse mantle at the Amahami Site (32ME8). Refuse accumulation and documentary sources indicate long and stable occupations of the historic Hidatsa towns on the Knife River, but Hidatsa sites in the Garrison region do not appear to have been occupied as long.

In contrast, Mandan occupation during Knife River 2 was far less stable. Refuse accumulations are generally much thinner than in the Hidatsa towns, and contemporary accounts speak of the considerable movement and resettlement of Mandan villages within a limited area just below the mouth of the Knife River.

U.S. GOVERNMENT PRINTING OFFICE: 1971   O—377-884